THE
GOLDEN MOMENT
Recording Secrets from the Pros

Keith Hatschek

Backbeat
Books

San Francisco

Published by Backbeat Books
600 Harrison Street, San Francisco, CA 94107
www.backbeatbooks.com
email: books@musicplayer.com

An imprint of the Music Player Network
Publishers of *Guitar Player, Bass Player, Keyboard, EQ,* and other magazines
United Entertainment Media. Inc.
A CMP Information company

CMP
United Business Media

Distributed to the book trade in the US and Canada by
Publishers Group West, 1700 Fourth Street, Berkeley, CA 94710

Distributed to the music trade in the US and Canada by
Hal Leonard Publishing, P.O. Box 13819, Milwaukee, WI 53213

Cover design by Doug Gordon
Composition by Maureen Forys, Happenstance Type-O-Rama
Front cover photo by David Goggin

Photos of interview subjects provided courtesy of interviewees, unless otherwise noted. Photos of Paul Klingberg, Richard Dodd, Anthony Cole, and Steve Genewick by author.

All photos of microphones provided through the courtesy of their respective manufacturers, unless otherwise noted.

Photos of vintage mic preamps courtesy of John La Grou, unless otherwise noted.

All photos of CD-R duplicating and printing equipment courtesy of Discmakers.

Special thanks to Karen Dunn of the TEC Awards for the photo of Al Schmitt with Messrs. Dowd, Wonder, and Paul.

Library of Congress Cataloging-in-Publication Data

Hatschek, Keith.
The golden moment : recording secrets from the pros / by Keith Hatschek.
    p. cm.
  Includes index.
ISBN-13: 978-0-87930-866-7
ISBN-10: 0-87930-866-4 (pbk. : alk. paper)
1. Sound recordings—Production and direction. 2. Sound—Recording and reproducing. 3. Sound recording executives and producers—Interviews. I. Title.

  ML3790.H378 2005
  781.49—dc22

                        2005028535

Printed in the United States of America

05 06 07 08 09   5 4 3 2 1

Contents

Foreword

by Al Schmitt

If you ask ten producers to pick their top three engineers, the name Al Schmitt is likely to pop up on many of the lists. And it's no wonder, as Al has racked up an amazing 17 Grammy awards in his more than 40 years as a top recording engineer. There aren't many engineers still charting No. 1 hits today who can claim to have also recorded Elvis Presley in his glory days. In short, he's been on the front lines of the past half-century of the modern recording revolution.

I asked Al to contribute a foreword to this collection because he is a prime example of how engineering techniques have been passed on from generation to generation—from engineer to engineer. In fact, rather than hoarding any of his trade secrets, Al openly shares his wisdom with any and all engineers with whom he comes into contact. He is a truly gracious and superbly talented music engineer. He invited me to meet him at Capitol Studios in Hollywood, where he was putting the finishing touches on Till Then, *out on Verve by keyboardist Danilo Perez.*

If any up-and-coming sound engineer or producer asks, "Who should I emulate?" my one-word answer would be simple: Al.

—KH

I started going to the recording studio at the age of seven. I'd ride the subway over on the weekends and watch sessions. My uncle, Harry Smith, operated Harry Smith Recording Studios, the first independent commercial studio in New York City at 2 W. 46th St. He was pretty well known and had recorded the Andrews Sisters, Guy Lombardo, and many other top artists of that era. At that early age, I didn't learn much about specific techniques, other than to see that they recorded with one microphone and everyone took their shoes off in the studio. But my uncle did teach me how delicate the equipment was, how a good microphone must be handled like a Swiss watch, and that has always stuck with me.

A dapper Al Schmitt in his "office" in the 1960s.

I got my first job in the studio as a teenager at Apex Recording in New York City. My mentor there was Tom Dowd, who had incredible work habits. He was always on time. He was always prepared. He always knew beforehand what microphones he was going to use and how each would be placed. He instilled in me the importance of prepa-

> I have the greatest job in the world.

ration from Day 1. I would keep a little notebook, in which I would draw diagrams of every session and note what microphones were in use and their placement, etc. In those days we didn't have any equalizers or compressors, so it was all microphone technique. Tom also taught me another very important skill: how to set the musicians up in the studio.

We had a board with six inputs and often recorded 20 or more musicians, so we'd often be sharing one mic between an upright bass and a guitar, or the bass and the piano. We'd move the mic until we got the correct balance and that was it! Solving a particular problem by adjusting a mic's placement is another skill I use almost every session.

I learned there is a partnership between the engineer, the musician, and the producer, and all of you are there for only one purpose—to make a great record.

Tom taught me that the best friend an engineer has is the musician. It's important to get comfortable with the players and really communicate. They know more about their instrument than you'll ever know. If you're having a problem, you can talk with them, and they'll offer a suggestion or two on what has worked well to record their instrument in the past. If you try it, you're likely to find out that their suggestion will work fine.

I also found out what it takes to be the engineer who always stays booked. It's the guy who is easiest to get along with. You have to come in with a smile on your face and be known as a person that is easy to talk to, no matter what is going on in the studio.

When I first came to California from New York, I was used to wearing a sport coat and tie to each session, and the guys here would ask me if I had just come from a wedding. Although I stopped wearing the jacket and the tie, I always make it a habit to look neat and professional.

As far as how one would learn to be an engineer today, the many schools and programs are great to teach the basics. But when you get out and get into your first job, as a gofer or an assistant, you pretty much have to forget a lot of what you learned in school and learn the day-to-day work habits of what it takes to be successful in this business.

The best way to do this is attach yourself to a mentor who has good work habits, and emulate them. If you are fortunate enough to work at a studio where a lot of engineers come through, try to work with as many of them as possible so you can learn the best from each one. You may even learn what *not* to do from a few who are having difficulties.

Three recording giants honor Al as he is inducted into the TEC Awards Hall of Fame in 1997. From left to right, Tom Dowd, Al, Stevie Wonder, and Les Paul. Photo courtesy of Mix Foundation/TEC Awards. Photographer: Alan Perlman.

Over time, you'll add this knowledge, the things that work for you, to your arsenal. Eventually, your personality will come through, and you'll begin to build your own following. But I can't overemphasize the importance of learning from a number of talented engineers.

It's a given that anyone coming up today will have strong computer skills. But it's also important to know how to mic every instrument you may encounter. If a guy walks in with a tuba, bassoon, or French horn, you have to know how to mic it. That's why having good communication with the musicians is so important. Don't be afraid to ask the musician; chances are they know what will work, and you all want the same thing. Or ask another engineer because you may find that the proper place is not where you might think!

Another one of my mentors was Bob Doherty. Bob taught me how to record orchestras. My work at Apex was mostly with smaller ensembles, so I was petrified of recording my first orchestral date, which was at Fulton Recording Studio in New York. Bob showed me exactly how he recorded an orchestra, and I wrote down every detail. He told me to just set it up the way he did, and the orchestra would sound fine. And it did. Bob shared his technique, which I knew sounded good. This gave me the confidence to do well. In turn, I try to share what I've learned with every young engineer that I work with.

That passion for learning is something an engineer has to maintain. Today, I am learning all about hard-disk digital recording. I'm working at the higher resolutions, 192 and 96kHz, and it sounds fabulous. I've even convinced my good friend, producer Tommy LiPuma, to use a hard-disk system. Things that used to take us an hour or two to edit—say, a piano solo—we can now do in a few minutes using Pro Tools.

I'm constantly trying out new gear. For instance, I just got a TubeTech three-band tube compressor, and it sounds fantastic. I've been learning how to finesse that, and it has come in handy on quite a number of projects. But keep learning and keep experimenting. That's how you'll continue to grow.

For the future, I think we are seeing a resurgence in acoustic music and ensemble recording, which for me, is nice. So many young engineers are used to recording everything direct or from electronic sources. Instead, I believe that if everyone would learn how to record live orchestras, big bands, and large ensembles, they would learn so much that they could use in any recording situation. You never know when you are going to be called to record or assist on a big date. Every young engineer should also learn how to artfully create a mix in 5.1 that envelops the listener. I'm very excited by the creative possibilities offered by surround music.

Even after my many years as an engineer, when I hear something special, I am still amazed. If a recording really impresses me, the hair on my arms starts to stand up—it's a physical reaction. For me, getting a natural sound on the instruments, proper balances between the musicians, correct use of reverb and effects—all those go into a great recording. But there's also something else, something intangible, that is the result of the engineer capturing a great performance. I'm pleased that this book of recording tips will help pass on a great deal of recording wisdom from friends of mine such as Bruce Swedien, Ed Cherney, Elliot Scheiner, and many others who have developed their own styles and techniques.

I have the greatest job in the world. I'm surrounded by superb musicians every day. I get to work with many of the world's most talented artists. Every morning I sorta feel that I'm fibbing when I tell my wife I'm going to "work." If this is work, I don't ever want it to stop. I'm the luckiest guy alive.

—*Al Schmitt, Summer 2005*

Preface

This practical guide to recording studio techniques is a compilation of interviews and articles that were originally distributed over the last ten years under the banner of the quarterly *Pro Studio Edition* newsletter published by Discmakers of Pennsauken, New Jersey. It struck me that this collection's wide range of topics, and the straightforward, no-nonsense advice it includes from leading engineers and producers, would be helpful to the growing number of musicians and music lovers learning about the art and science of recording. With the power, speed, flexibility, and widespread availability of high-quality recording technology attracting thousands of new recording practitioners annually, this book seemed like an idea whose time had come.

Although there is a number of outstanding textbooks that cover the art and science of recording, it has always seemed to me, as a former professional recording engineer, that the most valuable technique lessons were learned from other engineers, either by observation or in bull sessions at trade shows, at equipment dealers, or while visiting other studios. These gems of anecdotal wisdom seldom find their way into textbooks.

The common thread that leading engineers and producers espouse is this: *Always be willing to experiment, trusting your ears to lead you to the best combination of technology and acoustics, in service of fulfilling the artist's vision for his or her song.* That philosophy underlies all of the interviews, tips, and techniques provided in this collection of artices.

Recording technology has evolved at lightning speed over the ten years in which these interviews were compiled, but the underlying techniques and philosophies have remained constant and will serve you well, no matter what computer, software, or hardware you choose to work with. However, wherever possible, interviewees have shared last-minute updates or have refreshed their articles for inclusion in this book. I have endeavored to update engineers' credits throughout, and have added appropriate Web links to a number of online resources. I found two resources particularly helpful: the All Music Guide (www.allmusic.com) and Paul Verna, Eric Olsen, and Carlo Wolff's excellent volume, *The Encyclopedia of Record Producers*, sadly now out of print. Other worthwhile book and magazine resources are listed in the back of the book. However, in addition to reading about the work of the engineers profiled here, I strongly encourage you to locate and purchase some of the releases that have been completed by these talented individuals. Truly, focused listening is the best way to fully appreciate their techniques and methods.

—*Keith Hatschek*

Chapter 1
In Session with the Pros

Richard Dodd: In Search of the Holy Grail

Richard Dodd is a transplanted English-man who marches to the beat of a different drummer. Known and respected for his work with artists such as Tom Petty and the Heartbreakers, Green Day, Jeff Lynne, Clannad, George Harrison, Chef-Aid (of *South Park* fame), and legendary supergroup the Traveling Wilburys, he spends most of his time at his studio in the Berry Hill suburb of Nashville, mixing and mastering a wide variety of artists. His work on Petty's 1995 album *Wildflowers* earned the Best Engineered Recording Grammy award, and 2001's *Nothing Personal* by Delbert McClinton earned the Best Contemporary Blues Recording Grammy award.

In this wide-ranging interview, the outspoken Dodd talks about guitar tones, mixing, mastering, and an afternoon to remember, working with Eric Clapton and the late George Harrison.

Richard Dodd pictured with one of his favorite mix tools, a vintage Studer C37 two-track recorder.

One of the interesting things about your work with Tom Petty and the Heartbreakers is the diversity of sounds achieved with basically a rock quintet. Although the guitar tracks are sometimes quite sonically dense—for instance, on Echo *and* The Last DJ—*it seems that each part stands out on its own clearly. How does that come about?*

There is no stock answer to that. If you're asking about the guitar playing with Tom's band, then you are primarily referring to the two guitar players, Tom Petty and Mike Campbell. They both know what a good guitar sound is, so the guitar sound they end up with is the one they wanted. They know what works to achieve a particular sound, and there's a little bit of room to see what else might be interesting. Sometimes, they've done a particular part or a sound so many times that they just try a different guitar or a different pick, or play the part standing on their head, just to mix things up. But basically, they are creating *exactly* the sound they want in the studio.

Well, oftentimes, an engineer may be working with a younger artist, who is still defining their sound....

In that case, you have to encourage them to determine what [sound] is you, what the collective of you is, and what [sound] has nothing to do with you. The musician has to define his or her own sound.

On the other hand, when you are working with a really good player with a good instrument, then it's up to the engineer to adapt to what they are playing and to be careful to do no harm to their sound. The best thing to do is...do nothing. Be ready to offer a suggestion or experiment, but be prepared to "boringly" sling a Shure SM 57 in front of the amp and have it sound great. It's fine to do nothing and let the player shine.

The best thing to do is...do nothing.

Do you find the new generation of amp modelers sounding the same or close to the original amps?

There's no end to the electronic devices available to emulate sounds of, say, a vintage Telecaster or Gold Top Les Paul through a Marshall. But if you compare it side by side to the original guitar and amp in good condition, these devices are nonstarters. I've heard the original instruments played well...and on other projects, played poorly. In fact, if you have the Les Paul and Marshall played well, it can be recorded poorly, or the signal path watered down in such a way that the essence of what made it so different-sounding from an emulation in the first place is left behind.

And if we are discussing modern recording techniques, that is, digital recording, and if we compare it to what I would term "perfect analog," then digital recording is still lacking when it comes to vocals, for instance, and mid-range. Analog by itself is not perfect, and just as there is what I might term "bad digital," there is also "bad analog." But with an analog recording properly done, you will hear the difference.

It's that magic four-letter word, the holy grail of recording: tone.

It takes a long while to recognize tone. Players can hear it first, and then they're on an uphill struggle to find the crew that won't strip them of their tone. Not intentionally, but not everyone hears it.

Can you share an example?

Well, I was privileged to be working with George Harrison at his home on a project. He was playing a Strat into a direct box with a little bit of compression and EQ. During the process of working up a guitar part and getting comfortable with the track, the door-bell rang and it was his friend, Eric Clapton. After talking for a while, George turned to Eric and asked, "Do you fancy having a go at this?"

I was sitting in the center, and I handed the guitar from George Harrison, on my right, to Eric Clapton, on my left, and I thought to myself, "Same song, same sound. This is like a laboratory experiment to see what difference, if any, there might be…"

> "How do you get a good guitar sound?"
> It's simple. Get a good player.

He started to play. As we recorded, I was staring hard down at my shoes, hoping that nobody would say anything to me. When we finished up, George punched my arm and said to me, "How come it don't sound like that when I play it?"

"Well," I thought, "what's the diplomatic answer to that?"

I didn't have one. So George let me squirm a while—he loved to wind people up a bit—then after what seemed an eternity, he laughed and said, "He's good, isn't he?"

You see, he knew it. In fact, he'd known it for a much longer time than I had. For years. Eric Clapton's tone came from the way he played the guitar—his fingertips and the information going to those fingertips. With his technique, there was a different tone when he played the exact same setup.

That said, George himself would produce amazing sounds by various styles and methods that wouldn't be at all like Eric Clapton. And Eric would produce something you'd recognize, and it would be very unique sounding, also. And that's the wonder.

So that is the long answer to a very simple question, "How do you get a good guitar sound?" It's simple. Get a good player. And along with a good player usually come all the necessary trappings. It might be a vintage guitar and amp, or it might be a rectifier or an emulator of some sort, and you know what? That might be right for that project or song.

I could play that Gold Top through a Marshall, and Mike Campbell could play a ukulele, and I'm going to be far more interested in Mike Campbell than I am in me! It's the player that makes all the difference.

To return to our first question, if you get an album to mix and it has a lot of guitars, resulting in a loss of clarity among the various parts, what can you do to fix it in the mix, besides muting some of the parts?

It's too bad that mono is a thing of the past, since it's one of our best assets. If you monitor in mono, you can't escape it and you can't deceive yourself. You can find out exactly what is obscuring and blurring the track. So Mono is a good button to use. When you've decided, from a musical standpoint, which elements are carrying parts, but sonically they're interrupting the mix, then you go back to stereo and start to see if you can move things around.

Then it's a matter of balancing the parts, and of course, back to the tone—because if a particular part sounds great, it's very hard to turn it off. It's really all about the tune and the tone. If you have two [guitar] parts and the good one has tone and sounds alright thin or thick, and the second part is a bit weaker and only sounds good thick, then you go back and thin out the good sound so they can mesh. Because the good part is going to survive. Sometimes, rather than tone, the part is what it's all about, the sequence of notes, so you can mess about with the sound something horrible and still have it make sense, because somewhere else in the track you have great tone.

We've talked a lot about electric guitar sounds, but what about a rock track that also needs to have an acoustic guitar added?

Well, most great rock records have an acoustic guitar even though you may not notice it. In my experience, string choice and pick choice affect an acoustic guitar more than an electric. With a 12-string acoustic guitar, I've found that when you're changing the strings, it's best to leave one each of the old strings on the top three strings so you can use the guitar straight away on a track and not wait for it to settle in.

And mic choice and placement?

Refer to the previous question! It's no different, because everything starts with the player, the song's requirement, the right part, the instrument, and the politics.

The politics?

Right. A number of times, I've had the wrong person playing the right guitar. You spend three hours trying to get the part down, when the person who conceived the part and taught it to the person playing is in the next room and they can play it perfectly in one take. You know, someone asks, "Why is he the drummer?" and you answer, "Because he's my brother."

But for the mic, I would favor a condenser mic, a nontube model, such as a Neumann KM 140 or 84 or 85. Or an AKG 451, because I know the sound of those microphones, so therefore I'll use them to investigate. But the best mic, for almost anything, is a KM 56!

[*Note:* This is a rare Neumann vintage, small, fixed diaphragm, dual-capsule tube condenser with three pickup patterns.]

The first thing to do is to listen—but do so carefully, and don't put your ear 2 inches away from a snare drum. For instance, on an acoustic guitar, you can use one ear and block the other, to quickly hear what is happening 2, 3, or 12 inches away from the guitar. Find a spot that sounds good and start there. Choose a mic you've used successfully before. Because if that's working, why waste time experimenting?

A pair of Newmann's vintage KM 56 multipattern condensers. Photo courtesy of Blue Lake Studios (www.bluelake.ch).

You're recording this interview with a cassette. If Roy Orbison decided to make a return performance to this Earth for one song right now, guess what would be the best thing to record him with? That cassette, because it's already in "Record!" I could hand-deliver the best equipment in the world 30 seconds after he's gone, but at that point, it's not relevant. Being ready to capture that golden moment is paramount.

So even if I don't have the perfect mic or compressor setup on a part, if the artist is really nailing it, you keep it and work with it, because that performance is what will make the best recording?

That's right. If I'm working with a band in the studio and I've decided which song I'd like to record first, I'll actually have them warm up and get my sounds on another song, so that when we start the song we're going to record, I'm ready. The same with a vocalist. The only time you've got to experiment is while they warm up. The moment they're ready, you've got to be ready. Your first choice has got to be a good choice, because everything should be usable.

And sometimes, even though your first choice was the right choice, a vocalist may not be making the grade. So you might go out and switch mics to another that you know will also work, and say, "You know, it really wasn't sounding quite right, let's try this other mic," and often that change will help the vocalist to get the part right, because they think that now there's been an improvement.

From politics to psychology, we're covering a lot of ground. I understand that your focus has shifted now so that you mostly are doing mixing and mastering. How did you get into mastering?

Well, a few years back, I had mixed an album for an artist, and before we sent it out to mastering, I had purchased a new device called the TC Finalizer, and I thought, "Let's just run the mix through this thing as a sort of experiment." We did, and then we set out for a major mastering studio, where the album was booked in to be mastered.

After the mastering engineer had mastered it, the tracks didn't seem to sound as good as what we had done in our experiment. I asked the mastering engineer to play the CD we had made via the Finalizer and he was impressed; he had yet to hear it. He ripped my Finalizer version into his system, resequenced it, topped and tailed it, tweaked it a bit, and six hours later, we had a very expensive version of what we had done on our own back home. So, over time, I felt that we could do a good job with the tools at hand, and I eased into mastering projects here in Nashville. I don't own any of the gear you'd find in a traditional mastering house. Instead, I approach it the same way I mix: using what I like the sound of, rather than what traditional mastering rules dictate. Over time, word of mouth has built up the mastering client base. I've mastered quite a few albums in the Contemporary Christian world—Jars of Clay, Petra, Phil Keaggy, to name a few—and of course I also mastered Tom Petty's *The Last DJ* (2003).

How did that come about?

Well, we had just finished mixing the album, and at that moment, Tom said something to the effect of, "Wouldn't it be great if we could just keep that sound and feel, and didn't have to get it mastered?" So I asked George Drakoulias, who was coproducing the album with Tom and Mike, if I could show what I thought might be done to master the album. He told me to go for it. Tom said, "Where do we have to go?" and I said we could do it right at the mix room, since I had my laptop with me.

Since I knew the album inside and out, having recorded some of it and mixed it all, I felt it didn't need too much. About two hours later, I called them in and said, "Listen to this."

I had set it up so we could A/B the mix track with the mastered track in the final sequence. I knew what Tom liked and had worked to achieve that. We listened back for about an hour and a half, and everyone seemed pleased, so I made a CD reference and gave it to him to check.

The next day we came back to the studio, and I asked what we were going to change. They said, "Nothing."

There was still the question of were we *really* done. I said to Tom, "That's it, we're done," and Tom got exactly what he heard that day and what he wanted on that record. He commented that sometimes he hated being told that the tracks didn't sound right by a mastering engineer, so I felt pretty good about helping him to retain exactly the sound he wanted.

For a complete discography of Richard's work, visit www.RichardDodd.com.

Steve Genewick: When It Comes to Jazz, the Invisible Man Delivers

Capitol Studios is one of the busiest studios in Los Angeles. After 13 years on staff at Capitol, engineer Steve Genewick has learned that being ready to record or mix an album for Capitol's top-flight clientele is all in the preparation. Genewick's credits include engineering work with a veritable Who's Who of contemporary artists, including Larry Carlton, the Goo Goo Dolls, Natalie Cole, John Fogerty, En Vogue, as well as soundtrack work on films such as *Cold Mountain*, *Hope Floats*, *Brother Bear*, and others.

He was attracted to engineering because, as a kid, he knew he wasn't going to earn his livelihood as a professional guitarist. Instead, he began asking his musician friends, "What does the guy with all the knobs do?" The rest is history, as he began by learning how to mix on the fly doing live sound. He eventually graduated to a coveted staff position with Capitol, one of the few major labels that still maintains its own world-class studios.

In this interview, he discusses his recent experiences recording and mixing the much-anticipated album *Translinear Light* by jazz luminary Alice Coltrane—her first new jazz recording in 24 years. He shares a few tips on how to remain transparent in the recording process.

Tell us a bit about the lineup for the new Alice Coltrane album.

It was a very creative set of musicians. Alice performed on piano, synthesizer, and her unique-sounding Wurlitzer organ. Her son Ravi played saxes and percussion, and produced the dates. Jack DeJohnette or Jeff "Tain" Watts handled drums, and bass duties were split between Charlie Haden and James Genus. Another of Alice's sons, Oran, also played alto on one track.

That's quite a talented lineup!

Yes, and the interesting thing about it that was so unlike most of the rock or pop dates that I do, is that much of the music was literally created spontaneously by the musicians' live interactions. Every note was recorded live. There were no overdubs at all. They would start by talking through the musical blueprint, the song's structure, and then just play. So I had to basically be ready to get every nuance down on each take. I captured every take, each of which was unique. Some of the takes ran 20 minutes! It was real jazz, in the Coltrane tradition. Then when Ravi and I came back together to mix, we were able to pick and choose exactly which takes or passages he and Alice wanted to use.

Did you go digital or analog?

You could say the best of both worlds. We worked mainly at two studios. I used Studio B's Neve 8068 for the tracking done at Capitol. For the tracking at O'Henry Studios (in Burbank), they have an equally gorgeous-sounding, custom-built board based on the API 550 A & B EQs. Then I pushed everything out of the boards directly in Pro Tools HD. The musicians themselves wanted to achieve sort of an old-school sound. Let me clarify that: they didn't want the record to sound old, but they were looking for the relaxed, flowing vibe that so many of the great classic jazz records have.

Of course, without great musicians and great-sounding instruments, you probably won't make a great record. But with these players, and great-sounding rooms at O'Henry and Capitol, top mics, and smooth sounding vintage analog boards, the sounds were amazing. And of course, with Pro Tools, having every take, we had the flexibility to go back later, make a tweak here or there to fine-tune the sound. But really, when you hear Charlie Haden play his bass…well, you just know it's Charlie!

> …too much technology may actually impede the creative process.

So preparation is key?

Definitely. Pretty much for many of the jazz records I work on, I like to say that all my work is done before the musicians even show up. If I've done my job right, the mics are already placed behind the drums; I'll use an assistant to tap around a bit to set basic levels.

Then when the musicians arrive, all I need is a quick run-through, maybe 10–15 minutes at most, and then I sit back and listen to amazing music all day!

Another point is that some artists really aren't impressed by the myriad of options offered by new technology. They want to make and share good music, explore where that music will take them, and then they are done. So, too much technology may actually impede the creative process.

That's an interesting premise! Would you say that your job on a record like Translinear Light *is to stay out of the way, but to capture the essence of the performances?*

Right. I owe a lot of my ability to do that to one of my mentors, Al Schmitt. He taught me, "Don't become part of the project. Instead, let it go through you." And I couldn't agree more. Nobody really needs to know that I'm there, so long as I do my job. When I came up doing live sound [which Genewick archly describes as "fun-house mixing"], nobody would acknowledge me unless I screwed up. So actually, I don't mind being "the guy who's not there," so long as the artist gets what she or he is looking for.

Steve Genewick (right) and Al Schmitt pictured in Studio C at Capitol Studios in Hollywood.

We do a lot of live radio at Capitol, as well, and my live chops definitely help me out on those. The weekly radio series called *Modern Rock Live* would often book time at the studio, bringing in an artist and a studio audience, mix the show live, and feed it across the country. We also have done many of the Sessions@aol and live showcases for artists. For these gigs, you only have one shot to get it.

When I do a jazz date like this record with Alice, I go with what I know. It's not the time or the place to fool around. If you don't know what a particular mic pre sounds like on soprano sax, don't use it. If I want to experiment with a new piece of gear, I'll do it on my time with an existing track.

Working with musicians of this caliber, were there any unique challenges?

First, Jack DeJohnette has the largest drum set I've ever seen—and he uses all of it. He had cymbals like you wouldn't believe. Also, there were six toms, and a set of handmade tuned bells that sat up over his cymbals. I used my overheads (AKG C 12As) to get a lot of his sound. The bells were like big finger cymbals in shape, but they were finely tuned, so he would actually play melodies on them. Recording his kit was pretty intense.

Besides piano, Alice plays a unique Wurlitzer keyboard that has a double manual and a built-in synthesizer. And rather than a direct out, we captured the sound coming out of three different speakers built into the cabinet, each of which reproduced a different part of the instrument. That was a first for me. It was very interesting, capturing the sound right next to her feet. I ended up using AKG 414s, which are basically flat, and they worked out perfectly. It's one of those great mics that I instinctively go to when I'm faced with something new. Another "go-to" mic is the U 67. It's my starting place for just about anything new, because I've never heard it sound bad on anything! There may be a better mic, but the 67 works on everything.

And on a session like this record, you gotta keep going, so either of those mics will work on just about anything.

On Alice's piano, I used [Neumann] M 149s on our 9-foot Yamaha here at Capitol. At O'Henry, they have a Steinway, so I preferred the sound of C 12s on that instrument. The only instrument I remember using a separate mic pre on is the sax, which I ran through a Millenia Media M-2 preamp. Otherwise the pre's in the Neve and the custom API just sound great, so why mess with anything else?

Of course, most of our readers don't have the luxury of having a wealth of rare and wonderful sounding vintage tube mics such as those in the Capitol collection. What mics would you recommend for a home studio today?

Well, there are tons of good affordable mics. Try a [Neumann] TLM 170. It's extremely versatile and doesn't have a tube to worry about. I like a lot of the Audio-Technica mics, especially the 4050 and 4060, two mics that I really like. And with the Audio-Technicas, I know they're going to work every time, so if I'm going out to a rehearsal hall, they are actually better than a rare tube mic. I also like the A-T small diaphragm condenser, the 4051. When you feel you really need a rare tube mic, just rent one for that session.

Back to the Alice Coltrane album, any recollection that sums up your experience on the date?

Yes, there is a duet titled "Triloka" between Alice and Charlie that was done over at O'Henry that summed up the artistry on this record beautifully. We didn't know it at the time, but we had one take to get it. Here's how it happened.

Charlie moved over next to Alice right at the piano, and honestly, the other musicians were still standing around next to the piano, because we all thought this was a run-down. But in fact, the minute they started playing, all of us knew that this was something special. Magic was in the air and you could hear a pin drop. So unless I was totally ready to capture that performance, I would have blown one amazing piece of jazz playing.

So really, for recording jazz, my advice is to have all your work done up front, including a basic headphone mix that usually all the players will use. Then, I'm just there to be "Mr. Invisible" and capture some incredible music.

Visit Capitol Studios online at www.capitolmastering.com and O'Henry Studios at www.ohenrystudios.com.

Jimmy Douglass: Surround Music Mixing

Jimmy Douglass is one of a handful of engineers pioneering new horizons mixing surround music. He's a big believer in the creative potential that emerging surround formats such as DVD-Audio and SACD (Super Audio CD) offer artists, engineers, and producers. In this interview with Jimmy at Magic Mix Studios, his private Manhattan project studio, he discusses mixing new albums in surround for top artists such as Missy Elliot, Ginuwine, and Mary, Mary, as well as the challenge of remixing Marvin Gaye's classic 1982 *Midnight Love* album in multichannel.

You mentioned there being five distinct types of surround projects. How do you differentiate them?

For the Missy Elliot album *Missy E…So Addictive,* I mixed the CD release so that when I was called back in to create a surround-sound version, I could pick things up right where I left off. Since I can recall the stereo mix and am familiar with everything in the tracks, I start experimenting to find the right perspective for placing instruments, vocals, and effects. For this type of project, I have the luxury of being able to spend plenty of time on the effects.

The second type is a current album that I didn't mix. For instance, I recently did the 5.1 channel mix for Ginuwine's *Differences* album. For this type of surround project, I don't start by studying the earlier CD mix. I just put up the tracks and begin creating a mix for each song as I hear it in surround. As I complete each song, I check it against the CD, just to be certain that I haven't gone too far from the original idea.

Type 3 is remixing a catalog album. So far, a lot of the early 5.1-channel titles released have been catalog albums from the 1970s, 1980s, and 1990s. I was approached by Sony's Legacy label to do a multichannel remix of Marvin Gaye's classic album, *Midnight Love.* The album was done in 1982 and featured the No. 1 hit, "Sexual Healing." Marvin played most of the instruments himself. It also turned out to be his last album before his tragic death.

I start by laying the entire CD down in Pro Tools as my reference point. Then, with the original multitrack masters (two sync-ed, 24-track analog tapes) cued up, I start listening to what is on the masters, researching what I have to work from. And let me tell you, listening to these tracks was a revelation. Frankly, the level of engineering and production was so much better than most of the tracks I receive today. [*Note:* The original engineers for *Midnight Love* are listed as Dan Bates and Mike Butcher.]

I cue up each tune on the original multitracks using the 2-channel as a reference, piecing together the tracks in Pro Tools. It's a lot like working on a jigsaw puzzle. The CD reference is like the corners and outside border, then I fit in all the rest of the image from the multitrack elements. On some tracks, everything is laid out smoothly. But there's usually a surprise or two on every 5.1 remix project.

For instance, on one project, it turned out that a solo vocal part was not on any reel of the masters, so I cued up the stereo mix and pulled it off of there to complete the song. On the *Midnight Love* album, I found that the song "Rockin' After Midnight" ran about 3:30 on the reissue CD, but all that existed on the multitrack was a six-minute master take! So obviously, the final version had been edited down somewhere along the line.

About ten years ago, I had this gig recording top-quality sound-alikes for a Japanese karaoke company. Engineering those cover songs to sound *exactly* like the originals really taught me how to listen critically. That skill helped me faithfully recreate "Rockin' After Midnight," which by the way, features 16 different horn parts. I ended up using the entire 5.1 channel sound field to surround the listener with those horns.

The fourth type would be a live concert recording that is remixed to give the listener the impression of being in the house the night of the concert. I worked on a classic recording of the Allman Brothers Band for Epic/Legacy that utilizes this technique.

The fifth type of surround project is where you are creating the music from scratch, composing, recording, and monitoring in multichannel. Right now, I'm working with some friends on new material here at Magic Mix. As we work, we bust out the parts to front L-R and the surrounds. We're monitoring with a 4-channel (4.0) setup. The music is hip-hop–oriented with lots of vocals, so we spread them around. For the instruments, we're writing parts that ping-pong around the listener without sounding too gimmicky. Four speakers create a really big sound field. Working this way takes more time than monitoring in stereo, but we're loving it!

What kind of gear do you use at Magic Mix, to create surround music?

The heart of the studio is a Pro Tools Mix Plus system with 32 outs. I also use Digital Performer and Logic. I've got a 2-inch machine to get analog tape compression when I need that sound, as well as four DA-88s and an Akai MP-3000 sequencer. I use a 56-input Mackie board for monitoring, although I've been looking at the new Sony board, the DMX-R100. I use a lot of preamps, including everything made by Focusrite and the API lunchbox EQs.

How about monitoring?

I like Yamaha NS10s, so I have five of them with an SLS subwoofer. I also have a high-end active 5.1 system from NHT that I use as a second reference. I have a Coleman MS8 switcher so I can choose what system we're hearing. When I'm working in stereo, I also have a pair of the big KRK V8 speakers that I like in addition to the NS10s.

Surround music hasn't really caught on with the masses yet. Do you think it will?

There's no doubt in my mind that it's gonna fly. For every project I've done, the artists have totally flipped when they heard their music in surround. But I think it's going to be a slow build, because there's a lot involved for a listener. They have to hear something well mixed, and then they have to invest in the gear and space in their home.

One place where it may catch fire faster is in the car. I was out in Los Angeles at the Surround Expo last December [2001] and a bunch of us were sitting inside this Jeep with an awesome 5.1 sound system. We listened to some remixes of the Police and they sounded great. Everything was placed very tastefully. Then we popped in the Missy Elliot album, and the subwoofer kicked in big time—the Jeep almost came alive with all the energy in that record. Surround music playback can be so much more efficient in cars, so that may be how it gets some momentum. I just heard that Trent Reznor from NIN is doing some new studio tracks in surround. Now that may get more people's attention.

> ...the artists have totally flipped when they heard their music in surround.

Note: Just prior to publication, I spoke with Jimmy, who has been hopping between New York, Miami, and a new studio he has built with producer and frequent collaborator Timbaland outside of Virginia Beach, Virginia. It's located adjacent to the Neptunes production facility, allowing for an easy interchange of ideas and talent.

Although still very enthusiastic on the creative possibilities for mixing and creating music in the surround format, he cautioned that some record labels don't think it worthwhile to invest in properly remixing an existing master in surround. Or worse, he said, "They may hire the lowest bidder to do a surround mix using stems (stereo submixes of vocals, drums, instruments, and so on), rather than going back to the well—the basic tracks—to craft something that really works in surround. The results just aren't as good as going back to the original tracks and mixing from there."

In Session with Al Schmitt

Part 1: Recording Piano

Noted for the range and depth of his experience, his easygoing manner, and an unprecedented 17 Grammy awards for his engineering artistry, Al Schmitt shares a number of engineering tips he's learned over the years.

Credits include Diana Krall's *Live in Paris* CD and DVD set on Verve, and Natalie Cole's *Ask a Woman Who Knows*, on which he shared engineering duties with Elliot Scheiner. A complete discography can be found on www.allmusic.com.

Al, how do you capture the nuances of the piano?

Well, next to the human voice, the piano is the most difficult instrument to record. My approach depends on the circumstances of the session. If I can isolate the piano, like I do when I work with Danilo Perez and Joe Sample, I will put a couple of mics inside the piano and then a stereo mic, or a pair of mics outside the piano to get the ambience of the room.

I always use [Neumann] M 149s inside the piano, which I switch to omni pattern. The reflections inside the piano enhance the overall sound.

Outside the piano, I may use a C 24 (an AKG large diaphragm stereo condenser) or a couple of B&Ks [Bruel & Kjaer model 4011] to pick up the sound of the piano in the room—the ambience.

Now, if the piano is in the room with a band, and you need a little separation, then I'll use the same mics—the two 149s inside the piano— but I'll use them in a cardioid pattern to minimize leakage into the piano tracks.

What kind of a room do you look for to do a piano recording?

The room itself plays a big part in a piano recording. My rule of thumb is that the better the piano sounds by itself in the room, the easier it will be to capture that sound. This may sound obvious, but you've got to be in the studio with the musician playing to hear what the piano sounds like. Get a mental image of that sound and then go into the booth and try to capture that using some of these tips. If you've got a good player, a good instrument, and a good-sounding room, you really shouldn't have to do too much at the board.

> My rule of thumb is that the better the piano sounds by itself in the room, the easier it will be to capture that sound.

There are three studios, in particular, that I've had a lot of success with for piano. Studio A at Avatar [in New York City] is where I recorded Joe Sample, and I record Diana Krall there all the time. The other is Capitol [in Los Angeles], both A and B. Those rooms are so nice because you can adjust the wall surfaces in A to more wood facing the musicians, which gives you a nice warm, woody sound. The third room that I like to record piano in is Bill Schnee's studio in North Hollywood. He's got this great old custom board, a wonderful sounding room, and one of the most incredible collections of microphones.

Where do you place the room mics that are outside the piano?

If you open the piano wide with the full stick, I put the room mics at the curve of the piano casing. Although they are next to the piano, since they are set in omni pattern, they pick up the whole room. This results in a full, lush sound.

How about the "inside mics?"

I'll aim those toward the hammers to capture the attack sound, and I've got them as high as I can get them before I hit the lid. It's probably about 18 inches away from the hammers. There's one on the low end and one on the high end of the piano's register. You've got to make sure it's an even sound across the entire range of the instrument. If someone plays every note from top to bottom, each note should have equal value in the control room.

How many tracks will you use to record the piano?

If it's featured or solo piano, I'll use four tracks to record it. Otherwise, if it's part of a rhythm section, I'll use two tracks. I always pan the low register to the left and the upper register to the right. Then I'll blend in a bit of the ambience tracks to add the depth and richness that the room provides.

Can you give us an example of this four-mic technique?

I've done three albums recently with Danilo Perez where I've used this technique. [Check out *Till Then, Motherland,* or *Central Avenue* by Perez, released respectively in 2003, 2000, and 1998.] I used the M 149s and the room mics on each of those releases.

I also used that setup on two wonderful albums I did a while back with Joe Sample, *Spellbound* (1989) and *Ashes to Ashes* (1990). In both cases, the piano was in a booth, and we used the four mics to get a nice, rich ambient sound.

When I did those albums with Joe Sample, I was using the C 12 mics inside the piano, but now I would definitely use the M 149s. They have a smooth, balanced sound that works perfectly on piano. I have five of them and use them all the time.

What about compression on the piano tracks?

Well, if I were going to consider any compression on acoustic piano, I'd want to use a tube compressor, and only use a touch, unless you're looking for some kind of an effect.

Part 2: Acoustic Guitar Tracks

What are your microphone preferences on acoustic guitar?

I'm using the Royer SF 1 ribbon mics on acoustic guitars, and I couldn't be happier with the sound. I'll use the Royer on a lot of things, including a guitar amp.

Sometimes a player will insist on an SM 57 for a guitar amp, and there's nothing wrong with that. The most important thing an engineer has to remember is that he's got to keep the musicians happy.

Most of the time, musicians will go with the engineer's choice of mic, but sometimes, especially if they've had good success with a particular mic on their amp, they'll be adamant. Of course, if their choice is going to affect the sound of the record, you can sit down and talk with them, and explain why you think another mic would be much better.

> The most important thing an engineer has to remember is that he's got to keep the musicians happy.

Where do you place the Royer on the guitar?

If I have the tracks available, I'll put two up in stereo configuration. One mic will be about a foot off the guitar and a little to the left of the sound hole (looking toward the guitarist from the front), and the second will be about 18 inches to the right of the first mic, oriented toward the fretboard. Then I can pan these mics in the stereo field. If I'm using one mic, I position it about a foot away from the picking hand, and aimed toward the instrument's sound hole.

I've also used a couple of [Neumann] M 149s or a single M 149 on the acoustic guitar and that gives an incredibly big sound. Your mic selection depends a lot on the part that's being played and the situation in the studio. If it's a strong rhythmic part—sort of a Freddie Green sound—I will go with the Royer. But if it's somebody that's doing a lot of intricate picking, I'll go with the M 149. It gives me a little crisper top end and definition. [*Note:* Freddie Green recorded 32 albums with Count Basie, as well as countless dates with other groups. He's remembered today for his thick, full sound as the quintessential jazz rhythm guitarist.]

What about on ensemble dates?

If the acoustic guitar is going to be the lead solo instrument, I'll put them in a booth to get the necessary isolation. However, if he's part of the rhythm section, I'll keep him in the room with the other guys, but I'll isolate him a bit with some baffles or gobos.

How do you handle acoustic guitars with built-in pickups?

In a lot of cases, I'll use both. In other words, I will use a mic and take a feed from the instrument's pickup. I'll put them on separate tracks. Sometimes it works to blend them together, or I may end up using just the mic or just the pickup. I try to find what fits in the track best and that's what I'll use.

Do you ever use any EQ or signal processing on acoustic guitar tracks?

I rarely use any EQ. If anything, I may add a little top way up there, around 17kHz, to give it some air. Using good microphones, then running them in a good tube preamp gives me my sound. [Al favors the Mastering Lab tube preamp on acoustic guitar.]

Depending on the instrument, I may use a touch of compression. If I do, it'll normally be a Summit TLA-100 or dbx 160SL. I'll pull about 1dB [of compression]; just a little bit. I also have a couple of Neve 33609 outboard compressors that I have been using a lot, and they work very nicely.

Any examples readers can check out of your acoustic guitar sounds?

Yes, I did an album with acoustic guitarist Marc Antoine [2001's *Cruisin'*, available on GRP], and he played beautifully. We got a nice sound that I was very happy with, using two M 149s for his instrument.

Also, readers can check John Pisano's tracks on *Live in Paris* by Diana Krall. His nylon string guitar really came out nicely. It's a live recording, and again, I believe we were either using the Royer or a Neumann 184 [a small diaphragm, cardioid condenser.]

Orchestra and String Secrets of Al Schmitt

Is there a secret to the rich sound you get on string and orchestral dates?

If I'm overdubbing strings or horns, or any orchestral tracks, I always put all my mics in omni pattern. I get the leakage I want, which makes the instruments sound even bigger and more lush.

Of course, it helps if you use really outstanding microphones. Then, this leakage gives you real warmth—a bigger sound. Unfortunately, if you're using cheap omni mics, then the leakage will sound really tinny.

Is this just a technique for overdubs?

I do it on all dates. Even if I'm tracking with the big band, I always put the trumpets, trombones, and saxes on omni mics. I do the same thing if I'm overdubbing strings. With great mics and a good sounding room, you'll be surprised at the richness you capture.

There's a warmth and an ambience that you only get in omni patterns. That's because you pick up the whole room—reflections from the walls and ceilings that give you a much richer sound.

What mics do you like for this application?

For these types of sessions, I like the M 149s from Neumann, but sometimes I'll use [AKG] C 12s or C 24s.

Part 3: Vocal Recording Tips

What microphones do you use to get your signature transparent, present vocal sound, Al?

Lately, there are three mics that I favor, depending on which one fits the voice the best. I have the new Brauner VMA that sounds fantastic. I have my trusty [Neumann] U 67 that I use on Diana Krall and many other vocalists. The other mic I have used on occasion is the Didrik custom-made mic; there are only 24 of them in the world and they are amazing. They are quite expensive, but they are available for rental, so when I need one, that's what I do. [See note at the end of this section for more information on this exotic mic.]

I also have a few mic preamps that I'll mix and match with those mics to get the right sound for a vocalist. I switch between an old Neve 1081 preamp, the Oram Pro Channel preamp that John Oram developed for me, and other times I use the Martech MSS-10. Once I determine the quality of a voice, I can usually preselect which combination of mic and preamp will deliver the best sound.

For a compressor, I use the Summit TLA-100, which I've been using forever. If I go with the Oram, I use its built-in optical compressor that I love, too. On vocals, I rarely pull more than 2dB of compression. I use it instead for the sound of the tube in the unit.

My other little secret is that I don't put it in the cardioid position. Instead, I keep the vocal mic in omnidirectional. I find the sound richer and more pleasing if I can use the omni pattern. In fact, I like to do this on strings, horns, violins, and big bands, whenever I can.

What about the distance of the vocalist to the mic?

About 6–12 inches is optimal. You can put your thumb on your nose and extend your hand (in the universal sign telling someone to screw off), and that distance is about right to start with. Again, it depends on the voice. I remember doing a record with Levi Stubbs, lead singer of the Four Tops, a number of years ago, and we had to back him 2 feet off the mic, and he still almost knocked us out of the control room!

Use your ears to make sure you're not overloading the microphone or the preamp. By experimenting and listening, you'll find a combination [of mic and preamp] that gives you a good sound for each vocalist.

What about an instrumentalist who plays and sings at the same time?

With Diana Krall, everything we record is live. She's always playing and singing simultaneously, even in the recording studio. We may do a small fix here or there, but her records are all live performances. This is a perfect example of a situation where I can't keep the vocal mic in omni; I have to put it in cardioid. I'll place it down a bit in front of her, since she has a tendency to look down a bit while she's performing. The mic is about 6 inches away from her. You have to observe any movements that the vocalist makes while playing and take that into account with your mic placement.

In order to reduce the leakage from her piano, I'll use one of those specially made blankets that isolate the piano pretty well, so I can adequately maintain separation between the vocal and piano. If we have to punch a piano fix, we can do that and still keep the vocal. If it's a little vocal fix, we might have to punch the vocal and the piano, just to keep the ambience the same throughout the whole song.

If the singer is playing an acoustic guitar, the same rules apply. You have to work with the leakage and be careful. You can't totally isolate one from the other. Remember to use good microphones on both, so the leakage is "good." Then be sure that the guitar is not overpowering the vocal, so you maintain some control over each track.

What are your favorite studios for vocals?

I can record a good vocal pretty much anywhere. I've recorded vocals all over the world. You need to get a room where the ambience is pretty good and if the singer is a softer singer, you can record them anywhere. The ones with the bigger voices—you want an open room that can handle their sound level. For instance, Avatar in New York is great, and Capitol, The Village, and Schnee Studios in Los Angeles are all tops for vocals.

What do you find vocalists wanting in their headphone mix?

Nine times out of ten, if you're working with a rhythm section and a vocalist, the vocalist will want lots of themselves, whereas the musicians want very little vocal and mostly their own playing in the cue mix. So I'll have my assistant work to make sure that each performer is hearing exactly what they need in the phones. It keeps the assistant involved in the session and builds a rapport between them and the artists. Years ago, you used to see assistants sitting in the back of the room reading a magazine and that always bothered me. I make it a point to totally involve my assistants in each project so they can learn and build a relationship with the artists.

Usually we'll put some echo into the cue mix for the vocalist. I will often use two chambers. For instance, when I'm at Capitol, I'll use one of their fabulous live chambers

The EMT 250
Electronic Reverberator

a dream becomes reality

The EMT 250 was one of the first, and arguably one of the finest digital reverbs ever devised.

along with an EMT 250 reverb unit. Basically, on every vocal I've recorded in the last 20 years, there has been a blend of two reverb units (or chambers) to get that sound. I also have my own TC Electronics M6000 processor, which I take with me whenever I need it. It's loaded with all of the programs available—even one that I helped TC design to simulate the sound of the 250, because you can't always get a 250 for every mix session. Even when you can, no two units ever sound alike!

Note: The Didrick microphone mentioned in this article is a rare, handcrafted unit made in Sweden by microphone master, Didrick DeGeer. Each is made to order, and there are only six of the mics in the United States at this time. When available, they can be rented from Stephen Jarvis Rentals. For more information on renting these or other exotic microphones, contact Stephen at s.g.jarvis@worldnet.att.net.

For more on the EMT 250's history visit http://www.uaudio.com/webzine/may/ content/content4.html.

Part 4: Mixing

How do you normally start building a mix?

I start with a mix as if I was putting up a building: with the foundation. The first thing I listen to is the bass, then the drums. I'll get those set, first. I also have six or seven echoes or chambers preset and ready to use. Then I'll add piano and guitar and get the whole rhythm section sounding the way I like it.

Then I'll add the voice and fit it in there so it's in the right place. Then I'll take it out and add whatever else is on the track, whether it's strings, brass, or orchestra. Once that's set, I'll bring the voice back in. From there, it's a matter of tweaking, adjusting the echoes, and learning whatever moves have to be made.

What's the advantage of using so many echoes and chambers?

It gives the mix a little more transparency when something is dedicated to each chamber or echo. You don't have a range of signals going into that same chamber. When I first started out, all we ever had was one chamber, and we had to make that work. But when I got to RCA, we had so many great live chambers. On every session I'd have five live chambers. I'd use one for the left, one for the right, one for the center, one for mid-left, and one for mid-right—and you can make adjustments to any one without affecting the sound of the other chambers.

How do you adjust the mix when there are a number of instruments in the same frequency range—for example: guitar, keyboard, and synthesizer?

I normally use very little EQ, but there are times when you may want to EQ a track. I'll tell you what really helps in those situations. When parts do seem to be getting in one another's way in the mix, placement in the mix is extremely important. Sometimes just moving the guitar from mid-left to mid-right opens up the whole mix. We're constantly amazed, when I'm mixing with my assistants. We'll move the location of just one instrument, and we find ourselves saying, "Jesus, what happened?" The impact of simply moving one part in the stereo field can be tremendous.

The other thing is dedicating the right echo on each instrument. You don't want them blending into one another, which will tend to make them sound the same. For instance, on drums or percussion, the echo device I choose will depend on the song. I may try one echo on the overheads and another on the snare, or I may try a different echo on the toms than on the overheads and snare. I hate when someone says, "You can't do that." I think if you have an idea, you should use your gut and your ears to see what it will sound like. Then, while listening to it, decide if it enhances the song or not. Having a choice of good-sounding echo and reverb devices like the TC 6000 and EMT 250, as well as live chambers whenever possible, provides me with lots of choices and combinations.

> I hate when someone says, "You can't do that." I think if you have an idea, you should use your gut and your ears to see what it will sound like.

Back to EQ, I've found that sometimes it's what you take out, not what you add, that makes the difference. For instance on a particular instrument, I might take something out at 300 or 350Hz, or some other frequency, to clear up a track.

What about monitoring your mix? What do you use?

I have the Mastering Lab custom speakers with 10-inch dual-concentric Tannoy drivers. They are custom built for me, with both the cabinets and crossovers designed by the Mastering Lab. We hardly ever use the big studio monitors. My mastering engineer Doug Sax says, "Al, don't ever get rid of your speakers." Because whenever I bring a project to Doug, he cuts 90 percent of my albums flat. He jokes that if he were getting paid by the EQ he applied, he wouldn't make any money on my mixes! Almost everything I've done with Diana Krall, he has cut absolutely flat.

The other thing that I've come to rely on is that Doug will always tell me when something is missing or not right in a mix. It's almost like he's another part of me, and he'll look me right in the eye and tell me, "You know Al…I think you could remix this." That stops me dead in my tracks, but I'll go back and do it, on my own time, and find out he's right.

What time of day do you mix?

I like to start mixing early. The assistants will get to the studio around 8:30 A.M., and I'll get there by 9:30 or so. We'll get to work right away, and I normally don't have the client show up until around 1 P.M. They come in and listen to what we've got, we make our tweaks, and then we print it and move on.

Are you mixing to digital or analog?

For mixdown, I still prefer analog, usually ½-inch, 2-track at 30 IPS, +6dB over 185 nWb/m. I do back it up with a 2-track digital mix at either 96 or 192k sampling rate in Pro Tools. It's convenient to be able to do that right in the computer. Most of the time, we'll master from the analog mix. I'm also doing that now on all my surround records. I'll mix to 2-inch 8-track using a special head stack on a 24-track transport. On some upcoming SACD projects, we'll be using the Sonoma system.

When we get to mastering, we'll normally A/B the digital and analog mix. We'll usually pick the analog, although I have to say, it's getting very close. Working with multitrack in digital, there's now so much we can do that we couldn't do in analog. For instance, moving a bass note on the downbeat if it was just a fraction off. It took forever to do it in analog. With digital, it takes a few seconds. And the sounds are getting so much better; I'm really won over by digital today.

If I'm doing an instrumental jazz record, I still choose 24-track analog tape. But more and more, I'm going digital. For instance, Diana's last record, 2003's *The Girl in the Other Room*, we recorded strictly to Pro Tools.

Is there a particular album that highlights your use of multiple live chambers and echoes?

On Diana's last record I used a lot of echoes, even though it's a small ensemble. For instance, the drums had a separate chamber and the guitar had a separate chamber. Diana had two chambers for her vocal and one more for her piano. Again, since it's a small group, you can hear the depth that having a dedicated chamber (or two) for each part brings to the mix.

I just finished the mix for the Ray Charles *Genius Loves Company* album [released August 31, 2004 on Concord Records], which showcases the multiple echo approach. This record has it all. There were rhythm sections, cuts with horns, large orchestras, and everything in between. The recordings were done by various engineers all over the world. I was called in to mix it and give it a homogenous sound. It was a privilege getting to mix it and work closely with Ray and coproducers Phil Ramone and John Burk.

Ray and I talked a lot about our earlier work together for ABC/Paramount, including the album *Ray Charles & Betty Carter* that we did together in 1961 [available as a 1993 CD reissue on Castle Records/CLA 340]. In addition to that record, I did half of the second country-western album, *Modern Sounds in Country & Western, Volume II,* in 1962. [*Note:* This LP featured one side of big band arrangements of country classics and the other with strings and choir support. It spawned two Top-10 hits, "You Are My Sunshine" and "Take These Chains from My Heart."]

Ray and I shared a lot of good laughs and many fond memories. I worked with him on the *Genius Loves Company* duets project at his personal studio in Los Angeles. The final mixes were all done at Capitol, which has some of the best live chambers anywhere. It's a great record that is also a wonderful tribute to a supremely talented man.

Note: At the 2005 Grammy awards, Al Schmitt was honored with an amazing five Grammy awards in one evening for his stellar achievements mixing the stereo and surround sound version of Genius Loves Company. *That brings his current total to 17 of the coveted awards given by his peers. It couldn't have happened to a more deserving man!*

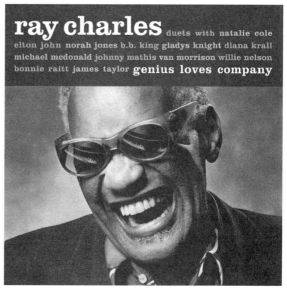

Chuck Ainlay: Mixing Is about More Than Technique

Chuck Ainlay has mixed projects for such country artists as Trisha Yearwood, Vince Gill, Wynonna Judd, and Reba McEntire, among others. His location in Nashville makes him central to the country music scene, but Ainlay has seen his share of rock projects, as well, including work with Mark Knopfler on his solo albums and movie soundtracks, and the Dire Straits reunion album *On Every Street*.

At the time of this interview, Ainlay had recently moved into a studio ownership venture with Soundstage Studios, renovating one of the existing rooms into the new and aptly named Back Stage Studio. An SSL Axiom MT digital console allows him to mix multichannel, high-resolution audio to a Genex magneto optical, while at the same time mixing stereo to his 1-inch ATR 100. Ainlay uses ATC 300s for main monitors and KRK E8s for midfields in a 5.1 arrangement. A large complement of digital and analog outboard gear rounds out his studio.

In this article, Ainlay talks about his mixing style and what guides him in his work.

What's your mixing approach when you first have a song in front of you?

First, I casually push up all the faders and simply sit and listen. I try to find out what the song is about lyrically and form an impression of the song from a genre standpoint. From there, I decide where I need to take the mix.

I always mix for the song, even within an album. I try not to be bound or limited by any rigid concept of how the album should sound. When I listen to a song, it conjures up an image that I suppose comes from years of listening to other people's recordings, what others have done in the past. Once I've created a picture in my mind or feel what the song is trying to express, I start working towards that. I look at the mix from an overview standpoint rather than as individual tracks. I work across the console rather than getting stuck on a particular instrument or sound.

You work with both country and rock artists. Does your approach vary depending on the genre of the song?

I've found that there's a very fine line between the two. With country, you're more concerned with the lyric of the song. The artist is the focal point; you need to make that person sound larger than life. When working with artists who lean more towards pop, the focus is the music bed. In terms of the way I approach reverbs and the aggressiveness of the mix, there really is little difference between the two. In general, though, country music is a bit more acoustic and dynamic. It's more about maintaining the natural sound of the instruments. You're not quite as concerned with pushing the amount of level you can get on the record as you are in some other formats. But today you can put any country record up against a pop record and it's nearly as loud.

How do you get a vocal to sit in the mix?

Again, after pushing up the faders and getting a general overview of the song, I do a little bit of refining as I listen to the song a few times. I'll find a pocket where the vocal is going to sit. From there, it all depends on the kind of song it is. I'll try and find out where the bass is muddy or the acoustics are dull or if I need to roll out some subsonic information here and there to clean it up.

Once I've made each track more pristine, then I can start enhancing the instruments and vocals with either EQ or compression and spatial information with reverbs and delays. Throughout this process, I keep in mind the whole mix, rather than working solely on, say, the bass drum or snare drum for too long. I try to stay away from that approach. I've learned over the years that you can make the greatest-sounding bass drum, for instance, but once you put the whole mix together, it may not even be heard. You have to make each element cut through so that one instrument doesn't mask the sound of another.

For lead vocal, I almost always use a GML 8900 compressor in the mix. The equalizer that I use depends on the recording of the vocal. If it needs softening, I use my Manley Massive Passive. I also may choose the Avalon or Millenia equalizer to EQ the vocals. Lately, though, I've been using the digital EQ and dynamics that the SSL MT has to offer. Each piece of gear offers a different coloration, and it's imperative to know what they can do to the sound so that you can make those choices.

What tracks would you refer people to as examples of your mixing style? Any that you're particularly happy with?

It's always changing. I always think the latest thing I've done is the best. One album I keep going back to, though, is *Lyle Lovett & His Large Band.* I use it a lot when I'm evaluating speakers or when I start work in a new room. I don't know why that record seems to work so well, except that when I recorded it, we maintained a very simple signal path and mastered it flat.

I think what I did with Mark Knopfler on the *Wag the Dog* soundtrack sounds great. The other projects I have done with Knopfler, like the English film *Metroland* and his solo album *Golden Heart,* really sound good to me, too. True to form, though, I'd say his new solo album due for release in the spring probably sounds best. [This was Knopfler's acclaimed *Sailing to Philadelphia* release.]

Some of the 5.1 mixing I've done turns me on more than anything, especially Vince Gill's *High Lonesome Sound* album and Trisha Yearwood's *Where Your Road Leads* album. I really love to mix in 5.1. It's so cool for a mixer not to be restrained by all those preconceived ideas about how you're supposed to do it. You can be more creative, and there is so much space to take advantage of.

What advice would you offer to aspiring mixers?

Basically, always keep seeking to find the next new thing. Allow what you've gained from your years of listening to music to influence you. You can't just be a technical mixer. You have to listen to and appreciate all kinds of music, because you never know when you'll be asked to do something that you've never done before. If you have experience listening, at least you'll know where to draw from.

Mixing is not about technique. Technique comes from years of experience. There's no other way to do it besides getting in there and making mistakes. I don't know that I've ever done anything that I was totally happy with.

Do you have an overriding principle for mixing—something that directs you?

I'm not one to totally sacrifice sonic integrity for level. I want to love the record when I'm done with it. I'm always bugged when I hear something on the radio that sounds so good that I go out and buy it, but when I get it home and listen to it in that environment, many times I'm just let down. I may listen to it once, and then it goes in the bin.

I want to create a record that will mean something to people. If I'm making a record that will get to people's hearts, then I feel that I am doing something that may affect someone in a positive way. I put my whole heart into what I do, whether or not I necessarily like the song or the artist. There is more integrity to mixing than just making money. Otherwise, I'd rather be water skiing!

Although at the time of this interview Ainlay was using an SSL Axiom, he has since replaced it with an SSL 9000J console.

Ed Cherney: Mixing—Persistence Is as Important as Gear

Ed Cherney has distinguished himself as a recording and mixing engineer, as well as a producer. Cherney's background includes the R&B scene in Chicago, where he began as an apprentice engineer in 1976. His R&B roots served as a solid foundation for his later work with such rock and pop artists as the Rolling Stones, Bonnie Raitt, Bob Dylan, Eric Clapton, Elton John, Jackson Browne, Bob Seger, the B-52s, and Roy Orbison. His work with Raitt and Browne earned him Grammy-award nominations, and he received a Grammy award for Engineer of the Year for Raitt's 1994 release, *Longing in Their Hearts*.

Cherney works wherever a project dictates, from Groovemasters, Record Plant, and Ocean Way in Los Angeles to Ocean Way in Nashville. He prefers to mix through SSL 9000 J consoles, as well as Neve 8078s. He typically records to 24-track analog, but uses ADATs, DA-88s, and/or Sony 48-tracks as the project requires.

While his gear may be high-end, his mixing tips and advice are practical.

What's the best approach for building a mix?

Having a great song certainly helps. If you're working with a singer, start with the vocal. What I do, if I haven't heard the song before, is push up all the faders and listen to what's there, to see where the song is. From there I try to eliminate things to find the heart of the song. I start dry, not using any effects or EQ at first, just to find the heart and soul of the song. I strip it down to its barest essentials.

How do you get a vocal to sit in the mix?

Depending on the style of music—if you want a dry vocal or a distorted vocal or a ballady kind of reverb—you just have to see where the vocal frequency range is and try to carve out space in the mix. You have to carve out space where the bass is, or where the guitars might be, or where the keyboards might be.

A vocal that's not loud enough typically isn't a good mix, but a vocal that's too loud is a worse mix. It's important to listen to the vocal on a lot of different speakers. On one set, the vocal may be loud and on another set it may be buried. It's important to reference your mix in other places, like your car, blasters, at friends' houses, at home, and so on.

Placing the vocal is about the hardest thing to do. Typically, the battle is that the vocal is either too loud or too soft—unless you're in Nashville, of course, and then the vocal can never be too loud. Country records really ask for a vocal that's out front because people want to hear all the lyrics.

How do you adjust your mixing approach to fit genre or the tempo of the song?

I don't think you change anything. The most important thing is to listen with your heart, as well as with your ears, and to be able to perceive what the song is asking for, what it needs, what it's supposed to be saying. Then do everything you can to keep it from being boring, which can be the worst sin. The hard part is in recognizing what this thing is supposed to be and what will be effective, and where the performance touches your soul. Once you recognize that—when you have a clear picture of what you want to do— it's easier to pull it off.

How do you mix rock for maximum impact versus mixing R&B for maximum groove?

When you do a rock track, it's really about recognizing that rock is based around the guitars, so it's about getting the guitars to speak. You still certainly have to rock the rhythm, but I don't think the rhythm is in your face as much as the guitars.

When you're mixing a Rolling Stones song, you better make sure that the guitars are forward. If you're mixing a song for Ice Cube, you better make sure that the beat is forward.

Do you compress your stereo mix?

I sure do. We live in an age of volume, and, especially in the digital domain, you have the ability to finalize things and really get the most level possible. Nowadays, dynamics in music aren't that important, at least not in the pop music we listen to. That may change again as we get more into 5.1 and 96kHz, 24-bit sampling.

I came from an era where dynamics could be very important, but now we're in a time where competition on the radio is fierce. You have to make sure that your song pops out of the radio speakers in a car while the listener is driving 90 miles an hour with the windows open. Currently, there are not a lot of subtleties involved in pop music. You get the music forward and you keep it forward, and it better be as loud as the previous song on the radio and hopefully louder than the next one.

Also, in this age of the CD, you do not have the same level constraints that you had trying to get maximum level onto a vinyl LP, especially the inner grooves.

What's your overriding principle or prime directive as a mixer?

I try to make the music speak. I try to be a bulldog about it, to not give up on a song. I get in there and dig and get everything out of it I possibly can, which is a very difficult thing to do, especially because I'm basically a lazy person. But I keep on digging until I get everything I can out of a song.

Bonnie Raitt's song "Thing Called Love" is a good example. It was a big hit for her, but I went back and mixed that song three different times to finally find the pocket and the maximum groove and emotion in it.

Ultimately, mixing is about heart, not equipment. Nobody leaves a session dancing to what kind of gear you use. The tools you use should be as invisible as possible. When someone sees a ditch, they're not thinking about what kind of shovel was used to dig it—just how deep and wide the hole is.

Ultimately, mixing is about heart, not equipment. Nobody leaves a session dancing to what kind of gear you use.

Mick Guzauski: Mixing

In the recording industry, there are a handful of engineers who have distinguished themselves on the merits of their mixing capabilities alone. Mick Guzauski is one such engineer, having mixed No. 1 singles and platinum albums for such artists as LeAnn Rimes, Mariah Carey, Toni Braxton, Eric Clapton, Boyz II Men, Whitney Houston, Kenny G, Madonna, Michael Bolton, Talking Heads, Quincy Jones, and Smokey Robinson.

Mick does most of his mixing from his home studio in New York, Barking Doctor Studio, which is equipped with an SSL 4056-G console, AT&T DISQ digital mixer core, Pro Tools system, and virtually every popular mix format. At the time of this interview, Mick was about to install the country's sixth Sony all-digital Oxford console, as well as a Sony 3348-HR 24-bit, 48-track digital deck.

Although he has access to the best gear money can buy, his insights are applicable to the smallest home studio. Read on as Mick shares his secrets for building the perfect mix.

What have you found to be the best approach for building up a mix?

After I've listened to the song to get an idea how I want to build the mix, I usually mix the rhythm elements first—they're the foundation supporting the vocal. I start with bass, drums, and the main chordal instrument, whether it's piano or synthesizers or guitars. Then I put the lead vocal in and listen, and work all the sweetening stuff around that. Finally, I work on the arrangement elements that really make the song interesting.

How do you adjust your mixing approach to fit the genre of the song?

A ballad, for example, has lots of space and more room for reverb. In an up-tempo groove, I'll use effects with shorter decay times, tight delays, and a lot less reverb-type effects. If you're trying to get definition at a higher tempo, you can't really make it swim in effects. You don't have the space to fill up.

How do you mix a pop, R&B, or dance song for maximum groove?

I concentrate on how the rhythm feels—where each rhythm instrument sets. Groove isn't just about a lot of bottom, or a huge bass drum and snare drum. It's more about listening to what's happening *around* those elements, like hi-hats and percussion. In a well-arranged song, there will be a lot of movement that really contributes to the groove, and it has to be placed right and heard right for it to really work. I think a common mistake people make is to lose the subtleties that really enhance the feel of the groove.

You've worked with some of the greatest vocalists of all times. How do you make a vocal really sit in the mix?

Well, working with some of the greatest vocalists of all times makes it very easy! I usually fit the vocal in the track by shaping the vocal with EQ. Or I'll EQ the track to carve around the vocal, so the vocal doesn't have to sit so far above the track to really be present and be heard. I basically use EQ to eliminate some of the competition between the track and vocal.

> Groove isn't just about a lot of bottom, or a huge bass drum and snare drum. It's more about listening to what's happening *around* those elements, like hi-hats and percussion.

Also, certain notes or parts of a singer's range will be louder than others, even when they're singing at the same dynamic. I'll add compression to smooth that out. The proper reverb, echo, and repeats are important as special elements to place a vocal so it sounds like it's sitting in the mix and not too far in front or too far back.

Do you try to get away from a mix for a while before finalizing it?

Most of the time, I do a song in one day, but before I tear it down and finalize, I take a break for an hour or two. After the break, I usually make some subtle changes.

Do you compress your stereo mix?

I compress it. Mixing with compression changes the balances a little bit, so you want to hear some compression when mixing. How much I compress depends on the type of song. With a ballad, I won't compress a tremendous amount, in order to keep it open and dynamic. If it's a rock song that should be hitting all the way through, I'll use quite a bit of compression.

What versions of a finished mix do you normally print?

I usually print the master mix, which is the one that feels really good at the time. I also print a vocal-up mix, with the vocal up a dB or less. I print a "TV mix" with background vocals and without the lead vocal. Then I do a track mix, with just the track and no background vocals. Sometimes I print an a cappella version, because DJ dance mixers will create a new track around the vocals of the existing record.

Sometimes I'll print stems [submixes] to DA-88—an example would be stereo rhythm section, stereo orchestra, stereo lead vocal with effects, and stereo background vocals with effects. This can save a lot of recalls and remixes if there are a lot of people involved in the decision about a mix. More than half the time, this kind of split-out can satisfy the changes that somebody would want.

What do you think a mix engineer's prime directive should be?

I think the most important thing is to mix for what the song is, and to understand how the music would feel best for the listener. You're not really trying to change what's there; you're trying to enhance what the artist, producer, and musicians have done.

You do this first and foremost with really good balances and good positioning, making sure that every part speaks the way it's supposed to and interacts the way it's supposed to. Nothing is emphasized that really shouldn't be at the time; the focus is always on the important elements of the song.

What projects have you been working on lately?

I just finished three mixes for a Paula Cole album that comes out this fall [1999's *Amen*]. I also mixed several tracks for Marc Anthony, one for Ricky Martin, one for Barbra Streisand, and a Toni Braxton single called "Spanish Guitar," which will be on her new album [2000's *The Heat*].

We talked earlier about varying your mixing techniques to work with each song's tempo. Could you give us a specific example?

Eric Clapton's "My Father's Eyes" comes to mind [from 1998's *Pilgrim*]. That's sort of a medium-tempo song. For the rhythm of that song, there were live drums as well as samples and a loop. I wanted to give the song really good punch, a good dance feel. On the drums, I used a compressor set with a slow attack so the transient attack of the drums would actually be stronger, because the compressor wouldn't reduce the level until the initial attack went through and then came down. In other words, I used the compressor to give a sound a little more attack than it normally had. As for EQ, the track didn't require that much because it was fairly sparse.

Any other tracks you would refer people to as exemplifying your mixing style?

I would say any of my mixes on Eric Clapton's *Pilgrim* album, or the Toni Braxton song "Unbreak My Heart," which is probably one of the best examples of my mixing style on ballads. For something totally different, check out the 1998 Kiss album, *Psycho Circus*. We really worked a lot of effects into that music, electronic kinds of effects. We did a lot of panning and moving things around. As for pop music, I did a lot of mixes on the last 98 Degrees album [1998's *98 and Rising*), as well as the Aaliyah songs "The One I Gave My Heart To" and "Journey to the Past."

Any general advice you would give to aspiring mixers?

The main point is to listen and hear how much something needs to be EQ'ed and processed—and not to use the same amount of processing or the same frequencies all the time. You shouldn't say, "Oh, I'm gonna add 5k to the vocal and pull out 200Hz because that's what I did on the last song." It may not work. Your approach has to be modified somewhat for every song, as each will have different instrumentation, a different singer, a different key, and so on.

Be careful to avoid a frequency buildup in one area and to keep the vocal in the clear. It is possible to have an up-front, intelligible vocal without wiping out the track. If you don't EQ and carve things frequency-wise, then you have to put the vocal up so loud that the track would lose a lot of its immediacy and presence.

Ultimately, you want to achieve a present mix where everything can be heard. You just have to train your ear to know where to carve things out, what to emphasize, to make it all work together.

Another piece of advice I can offer is to listen to a lot of CDs that you like in the room you're going to be mixing in and on the speakers you're going to be using before you start, especially if it's a room you don't know. Also, listen to your current work on a lot of other stereo systems—ones you do and don't know.

When you were starting out, who did you listen to? Who were your influences?

When I was learning in the mid 1970s, I really liked Bruce Swedien's work. He was one of my idols, as was Tommy Vicari. These guys are still doing great stuff. A little later on, I listened to Hugh Padgham—I love what he did with Sting and Phil Collins. I love what Bob Clearmountain does, too. I think he does some of the coolest spatial effects with reverb and echo. Early on, before he was a producer, Phil Ramone was a great engineer, and I listened to a lot of stuff he did.

> Ultimately, you want to achieve a present mix where everything can be heard. You just have to train your ear to know where to carve things out, what to emphasize, to make it all work together.

Of course, I'm always learning. I'm always listening to what other people are doing—listening and experimenting are key to being a great mixer.

Bruce Swedien: Engineering Tips and Techniques

Bruce Swedien is probably best known for his work with producer Quincy Jones and superstar Michael Jackson. The best-selling album, *Thriller,* provides a yet-to-be-matched aural soundscape that takes those who choose to listen closely into an amazing three-dimensional world. However, Bruce's work goes all the way back to the tender age of 10, when his parents gave him his first disc recording device. So began an illustrious career. His voluminous discography includes such musical masters as Duke Ellington, Mick Jagger, Oscar Peterson, B.B. King, and Dinah Washington. His first No. 1 hit came in 1962 with "Big Girls Don't Cry" by Frankie Valli and the Four Seasons. In this multipart interview, 13-time Grammy award winner Bruce Swedien shares some of the most essential fundamentals that any musician or sound engineer must be aware of, regardless of the style of music one performs or records.

Part 1: Swedien on Stereo

How do you view the idea of stereo and stereo image?

Stereophonic sound is a reproduction system consisting of two or more microphones placed in front of a sound pickup area, recorded on two or more channels of a recording device, and played back on two or more loudspeakers placed in front of a listening area. Such a system creates the illusion of the recorded sound having direction, position, and depth. It produces a sound pattern at the listeners' ears that our hearing interprets as indicating direction and depth of sound field in the area between the speakers.

In most cases, accurate localization is the goal of a stereo image. If I were recording a large orchestra, the sound of the players in the middle of the orchestra should appear to come from the space in the middle, between the speakers in the playback system. This is what I call an "unaltered acoustical event," where our audio imagination is largely eliminated from the recording technique, and we simply attempt to recreate an actual acoustic event. Of course, in modern recording, that may not be the case.

In mixing a recording to create a stereo image, the tracks are not necessarily all stereo. Although I use stereo miking techniques in some unexpected places, most of us find that with lead or solo voices, it doesn't work very well. That's where mono is a dramatic tool. It can be placed exactly where you want it in the stereo image.

While these basics seem obvious, many people don't use these concepts when they record. I'm bothered by the number of albums recorded as what I would call "2-channel mono." Some people seem to define stereophonic as "something coming out of the left speaker and something different coming out of the right." This has nothing to do with the reproduction of music.

It's fairly easy to create a left-to-right or two-dimensional image. But how do you achieve depth or that third dimension in a stereo image?

Depth perception in a recording is the result of a combination of values, including the ratio of direct to reverberant sound, the intensity of a sound source relative to others in the same field, and even EQ, especially in the presence area of about 1.5kHz to, say, 5kHz.

Probably the most important factor in creating a feeling of depth is the change in the ratio of direct to reverberant sound. As reverberant energy becomes more prominent, the source appears to move back.

The absence of early reflections in a sound source makes it seem much closer. As you change the quality of early reflections in a sound, they greatly affect the depth of field. These reflections are generally less than 40 milliseconds—once they're longer than that, the ear can pick them out as individual reflections, and below 40 milliseconds, they tend to smear into one sound. That is why intelligent use of predelay with reverb devices can give a tremendous feeling of depth of field.

> Probably the most important factor in creating a feeling of depth is the change in the ratio of direct to reverberant sound.

Here's an example of how I use early reflections to create both presence and depth of field in recording Michael Jackson: First, I'll record a monophonic melody track with Michael fairly close to the microphone. Then I'll have him double the same track at the same position at the mic. Next, I'll have him step back two paces and record a third pass of the same melody with the gain raised to match the level of the previous two. That raises the ratio of early reflections to direct sound. Blended with the first two tracks, this has a wonderful effect. Finally, I might even have him step back further and record a stereo pass of the same line using an X/Y pair setup and blend that track in as well. You can hear the effect for yourself on a song like "Man in the Mirror" on the *Bad* album.

This technique tricks the ear into perceiving a depth of field that isn't really there, through the addition of early reflections. If I'm using any reverb on that vocal, I'll make sure that the predelay doesn't smear those early reflections.

Part 2: Recording Keyboards

Previously, we talked about stereo imaging and ambience, especially with regard to recording vocals. How do you apply these principles to keyboards?

There really are two issues here: recording acoustic instruments like the piano and virtual instruments like synthesizers. The techniques are different but the goals are similar. Let's start with the grand piano.

No matter what you are recording, start by finding the right ambient environment—the right room—to make the instrument sound its best. For example, for a rock 'n' roll band with a big drum sound and incredible guitar players, you'd better find a room or studio big enough to let the drums sound great in the room by themselves. It's very difficult to create the sound of a good room after you've put down tracks in a less-than-ideal space. I have a large family room (25 feet × 30 feet with a cathedral ceiling) that is a nearly perfect room for recording my 7-foot Steinway B piano. It's just large enough to let the instrument really sound, but not so big that you have to deal with cavernous reverberations. I love recording pianos there. So first, look for the right space.

What about miking the piano?

Here's a mistake I frequently see engineers make. They will place one microphone over the low strings inside the piano, and another over the high strings, and think they have stereo. Nothing could be further from the truth. And, if the mics are farther than, say, 40 inches apart, there will be real trouble mixing that to mono, due to angular distortion.

I like to use a coincident pair of mics. Often I'll use a pair of AKG 414s in an X/Y configuration, slightly favoring the high strings of the piano. This sounds so good! Of course, the distance from the microphones to the piano will be dictated by the kind of music you are recording. For rock 'n' roll, you would place the mics quite close; for jazz, further away. For classical music recording, you'll back up quite a bit, and the result will be more of a composite image.

On a rock 'n' roll session, you may not want a beautiful-sounding piano, so experiment for the right effect. Sometimes I use a

> Here's a mistake I frequently see engineers make. They will place one microphone over the low strings inside the piano, and another over the high strings, and think they have stereo. Nothing could be further from the truth.

pressure zone microphone, like the Crown PZM, placed right under the closed lid of the piano. Again, the music dictates the technique.

Try to avoid multiple microphones on a piano, other than a stereo pair. If the recording is likely to be broadcast for mono compatibility, combining mics can be pretty iffy, causing all sorts of phase and cancellation problems.

Recording synthesizers would seem to be an electric, not acoustic technique, true?

We tend to record synthesizers directly. They are, by their nature, virtual electronic devices. Synthesizers and sampling keyboards expand the palette, allowing us to create sounds that didn't previously exist in nature. But that "virtual" sound you get with pickups or direct inputs can often seem dull and uninteresting.

To breathe some life into a dull-sounding synthesizer track, I like to use this technique: I send a composite synthesizer mix through loudspeakers out into a studio or room, and then mic the room sound to add early reflections to the synthesizer tracks. I might also add some reverb, being careful to make sure there is enough predelay in the reverb program to allow those early room reflections to be heard.

The idea is not to mic the loudspeakers but to mic the room. You excite the room with the loudspeakers and capture the early reflections with the microphones. The ideal ratio is about 20 to 25 percent room sound and 75 to 80 percent direct synthesizer. Doing this essentially turns the synthesizer into an acoustic instrument.

Part 3: Recording Strings and Orchestra

Previously we talked about stereo image, depth, and localization. How do these things come into play when recording a string section or an orchestra?

The ability for the listener to localize direction and to sense the spatial relationships between the instruments in a recording gives the music a feeling of depth and expansiveness. In the case of an orchestral recording, it attempts to preserve the auditory perspectives that would be present in a live performance in a fine-sounding concert hall.

The physical data for auditory localization and depth perception lie in the differences in the intensity and arrival time of the sound components at each ear. It is crucial that those components are preserved in orchestral recording by careful recording-room selection, orchestra setup, microphone choice, and microphone placement.

Knowing what the instruments sound like in a traditional music setting is extremely important. Listening to high-quality live music in a good acoustical environment is the ear's best reference or benchmark, especially when it comes to recording orchestral instruments. I feel it is of continuing importance to hear live acoustic music in good acoustical settings on a regular basis to keep that benchmark intact.

Orchestral recording is one area that is poorly understood by many people in the recording industry, simply because there is so little opportunity these days for any of us to record a large orchestra in a fine studio or acoustical space.

That said, what are the factors an engineer must consider when confronted with the challenge of recording a string section or an orchestra?

The acoustic quality of the recording room and the way the studio is set up for the session are the first items to consider. A good-size room with a high ceiling, free of flutter echoes and standing waves, and linear in spectrum response is ideal. Many violins, violas, celli, and basses acoustically blended with the reflected sound of a good room produce the sonic beauty of these sections of the orchestra.

I like to use the "classical" orchestra setup in my sessions: violins left, violas center or slightly right, celli center to right, basses right. The main concern is to have the strings—and horns, if it's a full orchestra—reproduce with as natural a quality as possible.

However, when I recorded the strings for Michael Jackson's recording of Charlie Chaplin's "Smile" on his *History* album, I used a slightly different setup: first violins left, second violins right, violas behind the first violins, celli behind the second violins, and basses in the rear center.

What about microphone technique?

Because of the very nature of orchestral sound, close mic placement with a great many microphones is definitely not the approach for string sections and orchestras. The best way to record an orchestra is with a spaced pair of microphones high above the conductor's head. Then I may use individual microphones for "sweeteners" and for solo parts.

There are three commonly used techniques for recording strings and orchestras: the M/S or mid/side method, the coincident pair or X/Y method, and the A/B or spaced pair method. [For more information on various stereo miking techniques, consult the resources noted at the end of this interview.]

The two methods I prefer are A/B and X/Y. In the A/B technique, the two microphones are spaced 3 to 4 feet apart, pointing at the orchestra, with the axes of their capsules roughly parallel. To enhance the left/right impression by additional intensity and tone-color differences in the A/B method, a small, flat baffle can be placed between the microphones.

The X/Y method uses a pair of carefully matched microphones placed one over the other so that their capsules are as nearly "coincident" as possible. They are pointed so that the axes of their capsules form an "x" of approximately 90–110 degrees, pointing at the orchestra. In both methods I like to place the microphones about 15 or more feet above the floor, roughly over the conductor's head.

The A/B technique will provide a certain degree of left/right intensity to the stereo image, while the X/Y method will result in a more homogenous, blended stereo sound. The music should dictate the choice of microphone technique.

What do you look for in a microphone for recording strings or orchestras?

Over and above the requirement for flat frequency response, low harmonic distortion, and wide dynamic range, the microphones must exhibit almost absolute equality of frequency and phase characteristics; they must be perfectly matched. If these conditions are not met, the resulting impression on the listener will be frequency dependent.

Condenser microphones in nondirectional patterns are particularly suitable for string and orchestral recording. In some cases, cardioid-pattern microphones will be satisfactory because, thanks to the one-sided directional pattern, the direct sound so important for localization can be picked out of the general sound picture from a greater distance.

You discussed the basic setups for recording string sections and traditional orchestras. Once everything is in place, how do you go about getting a great orchestra sound onto tape?

To me, when recording music of this type, the mixing concept actually begins before the conductor's downbeat. I decide on the physical setup of the orchestra in the studio with the recorded aural image of the instruments clearly in mind. In other words, the positioning of the instruments in the stereo panorama of the final mix is precisely the same way I set up the orchestra in the studio for the initial recording. Since the string section is most often recorded on two tracks as a stereo *mix*, this planning is particularly important.

To check for presence when the string section has assembled and is ready to start, I might have each player play the same pitch (note) separately while listening in the control room to make sure that each player sounds equally present. Individual adjustments are made by moving a player closer to the mic if he sounds too far away or having him move back a bit if he sounds too close.

My favorite way to balance a string section is to have a conductor's score in the control room with me. I will ask the string section to rehearse the part, including all dynamics, and as I read the parts on my score I visualize each part in my mind's ear and make sure that each part has equal presence and dynamic level. This method takes into account the dynamic differences that occur in the registers of the various instruments.

With a little practice you can ask the entire string section to play a chord, and when you hear all the notes in the chord with equal presence, you will have a good balance. But there is much more to getting a superb string sound than just getting equal volume level and presence on all parts.

Before we get in over our heads, let's talk a little about microphone selection. For the X/Y or A/B stereo pair, what mics do you prefer?

For a large string section in a good room, I always use two large-capsule condenser microphones. For example, I like the Neumann M 49 and M 50, or a stereo microphone like the Neumann SM 2.

Do you use sweetener microphones for an orchestra?

Certainly, when the music calls for it. My first choice for violins is the AKG 414 EB, but any of the AKG mics of the C 12 or earlier series (C 12, C 412, etc.) would also be excellent choices. For violas and celli, the Neumann U 67 is a good choice, as is the U 87. If the cello section is small, I often use my Telefunken U 47. It has a warm, rich sound on low strings.

How do you determine these microphone choices?

Experience is the great teacher. I let the music dictate the choices. For example, with horns I'll often go for ribbon mics instead of condensers. On percussion, as well, I love the warm clarity of good ribbon microphones. I have a large collection of vintage RCA 44s and 77s, which I use all the time, even on vocals. But there are some really good-sounding, reasonably priced ribbon mics, too. Beyerdynamic, for example, makes two wonderful-sounding ribbon mics: the M 130 and M 160.

> …with horns I'll often go for ribbon mics instead of condensers. On percussion, as well, I love the warm clarity of good ribbon microphones.

What about vocal mics?

Some microphones are very sensitive to vocal sibilance. If you are working with a very sibilant voice, some of the great traditional vocal mics like the Telefunken U 47 can actually be problematic. I might then go for one of the large-capsule Audio-Technica mics, like the A-T 4050 in the cardioid pattern. It manages the sibilance well, sounds terrific, and is a very reasonably priced alternative.

Do you have a preference for vintage and esoteric microphones?

I'm fortunate to be able to try out just about every microphone there is, but often people are surprised by my choices. I consider mics to be like paint brushes. They all do pretty much the same thing, but each has its own characteristics and best applications. Some mics are not very consistent from one serial number to the next, and thus present problems when used in stereo pairs or during more than one session. For example, Shure SM 57s and 58s are notably consistent from microphone to microphone, but of the four SM 57s I own, one sounds remarkably better on snare drums than the others.

In my videos on recording techniques, I use mostly Shure and Audio-Technica mics—nothing esoteric or very pricey. The key is to learn how to use the tools you've got to their best advantage. I love the sound of the superbly engineered—and expensive—Brauner VM 1, but I also love my Shure SM 57s. Used correctly in the right applications, each microphone can help make splendid recordings.

To learn even more from this master recording artist, check our Bruce Swedien's outstanding 2004 book, Make Mine Music, *available from Hal Leonard.*

For More Information...

The Microphone Book, 2nd Edition, by John Eargle (Focal Press, 2004)
The New Stereo Soundbook by Ron Streicher and F. Alton Everest (Audio Engineering Associates, 1999)
For a general overview of mic technology, visit www.josephson.com/mictech.html.

[*Note:* Bruce Swedien was interviewed by Bruce Merley.]

Minimalist Recording: When Less Is Truly More

Ever pause for a moment and wonder how the engineers got such a good balance on some of the classic recordings of the 1950s and 1960s? Amazingly, many of these records were made in one or two live takes and often with just two or three microphones.

Stephen Jarvis is a dedicated audiophile producer, businessman, and recordist intent on using minimalist recording techniques to capture musical performances in a unique way that preserves the subtleties that often get lost in the multitrack process.

Stephen Jarvis (right) prepping his custom Studer 827 2″ 8-track analog recorder with ATR Aria Electonics for display at the 2004 AES Conventions in San Francisco. Also pictured, Morgen Smith, Apple Computer's audio specialist and owner of Ambient Media.

Jarvis knows of what he speaks, having come up through the ranks as a staff engineer more than 30 years ago at the famed Wally Heider Studios. During his career, he has learned recording techniques and communication skills by working with engineers and producers such as Jim Gaines, Glyn Johns, Don Gooch, Ken Hopkins, Mel Tanner, Wally Heider, David Briggs, Betty Cantor-Jackson, Eric Jacobsen, George Massenburg, Nathaniel Kunkel, Eric Dodd (Valentine), Mark Willsher, Cookie Marenco, Jack Crymes, and many others. He is also a very successful entrepreneur, having been instrumental in the launch of a variety of technology companies in and out of the music industry. In addition to his continuing recording experiments, he shares an exceptional collection of audiophile rental equipment with engineers and studios around the world through Stephen Jarvis Audio Consulting.

For Jarvis and others like him, less is certainly more when it comes to minimalist mic and signal path recordings. Jarvis, like Al Schmitt, states that for him, "this business has always been about mentoring and apprenticeship, the sharing of knowledge and insights to improve the art and craft of the recordings that we produce."

Using two or three hand-wired custom microphones and a single hand-wired preamp to record an entire acoustic group may be new to many—but as you will see, it's a time-honored technique that's been used by those in the know for more than three generations.

Let's start at the end of the recording process with the music consumer. If the goal of a minimalist recording technique is to allow the end listener to have a similar experience to being in the room with the performers, how is that listening experience different from a recording done via traditional overdubbing and mixdown?

The short answer to your question is the way I perceive and respond to natural beat frequencies in the air during a live musical performance. Three voices singing on one microphone will sound and blend together differently than the same three individual voices singing [an identical performance] on three separate microphones that are blended inside of a recording desk. It is my belief that many other people can also hear the difference.

A minimal microphone approach is actually the traditional approach to making a recording. For a glimpse of the early days of modern recording with one of the master producer/engineers, Tom Dowd, check out the DVD *Tom Dowd and the Language of Music.* It provides a good primer for any aspiring engineer or producer, and describes many of Tom's early Atlantic recordings, done using just a few mics and a small hand-wired console that he built.

In those days, musicians gathered around one or two microphones and performed the piece. As recording engineers became more creative, the mixing desk was conceived to combine multiple microphone inputs together into the master track of the recording. Later, overdubbing became possible with the development of multichannel tape recorders. My approach is experimenting with techniques passed on from those early days of recording using the best tools of today's technology.

What piqued your interest in this process?

I've been inspired to follow this route by several recordings made in recent years by the talented live-to-2-track engineer/mixer, Gert Palmcratz, from Stockholm, Sweden. Gert has been using the same recording equipment, made by our mutual friend Didrik DeGeer, also of Stockholm. I own and use this same recording equipment here in the US. Gert's results made the effort a worthwhile challenge to see what I could achieve on this side of the Atlantic in one of our modern recording spaces, the Skywalker Scoring Stage, a brilliantly conceived acoustical environment that was created by George Lucas.

So the studio acoustics play a key role in this method of recording?

Absolutely. In addition, the minimalist approach is a simplified process that depends on cooperative participants, quality musicianship, and thoughtful clarity within the arrangements being performed. As part of the necessary preparation to make such an approach work easily, the individual performers should locate themselves in relation to each other to acoustically balance the volumes of their instruments and performances in the studio room. This also allows them to hear each other's performances without the use of headphones. A minimum number of microphones are used in order to reduce phase anomalies. The performance is recorded employing a high-end signal path to the master recording device.

Is it practical to record an ensemble with only one or two microphones?

A single microphone (mono) will capture the relative balances of the performance, based upon the microphone's directional orientation to the sound source(s) and the

Keyboardist Tim Gorman and guitarist Kirk Casey performing live in a minimalist piano and acoustic guitar recording. Note placement of the two hand-wired Didrik mics, and risers used to elevate guitarist. Session at Skywalker Stage, Nicasio, CA.

microphone's individual sensitivities over the range of audible and perceived frequencies. The recording engineer can affect the balance blend by moving musicians and their instruments closer or farther away from the microphone and closer or farther away from each other, within the performance room. This technique can use the natural frequency response curve of various microphones to differentiate the instruments without the use of electronic equalization or combining amplifiers.

The engineer interprets and uses the characteristics of the recording room environment, the individual volumes and performance characteristics of the instruments, and the cooperative musical sensitivity of the performing musicians among one another to create a pleasing blend.

Will such differences be apparent to the listener on any audio playback device or does it require listening back in hi-res, for instance SACD or DVD-A?

Yes, I can hear the differences at 16-bit, 44.1 on CD-quality reference discs. The higher quality formats should make recognition and enjoyment of such dynamic recording even more accessible to the general listening audience.

Can you also get good results if a drummer is in the group?

Yes. Gert recorded a jazz trio in Stockholm using only two microphones on the eponymous album by the Ludvig Berghe Trio. The album graphics include a photograph taken from above the sound stage looking down on the musicians. The two microphones were both omni pickups, located in the curve of the piano. The standup bass was placed on a riser a foot or so away and slightly to the side of the center of the back side of the omni pair. The drums, which have the potential to overpower the other instruments, were located approximately 8 feet away toward the end of the piano with several tall baffles behind the kit.

It was evidence of Gert's genius to see the logic of how he balanced the sound and dynamics of the instruments and players of a very energetic and commercial jazz performance, using only two inputs and no mixer. [*Note:* The full album credits and three streamed examples are available online by clicking on the "Catalog" option at www.moserobie.com. Even via lo-res Web streaming, the separation and clarity of the instruments is evident!]

Is it possible to use less expensive mics, in a similar setting, and still get good results, or must you use truly exceptional and expensive mics and hand-wired preamps? As you know, *hand-wired Didrik DeGeer mics and preamps are built on a special-order basis only and retail for approximately $20,000 US each.*

The better the tools, the more flexibility the engineer will have to perfect the recording. But we all do the best we can with the tools at hand. A cooperative group of creative people can do a lot with very modest gear. It is really about creating good sounds with the instruments and then balancing the music in the room where it is being performed.

You mentioned the importance of selecting the optimum combination of mic and preamp for each new situation. Could you give a few more examples of particular combinations that have worked well for you?

I tend to prefer noncoloring microphone preamps in most situations. D.W. Fearn and Doug Sax's Mastering Labs have given us two wonderful choices of tube preamps with clarity. I have been using GML equipment for most of my own recordings since the mid-1980s. Millennia Media HV3 8-channel units and Millennia's high-voltage preamps used with a matched pair of DPA 4009 omni microphones is great on most pianos. To complete the high-end analog signal path system with accurate conversion on necessary multichannel digital recordings (PCM and DSD) and for film/video work, I use 32 channels of Genex GXA8 and GXD8 converters, a Lucid master clock, and 30 channels of GML HRT9100 analog line mixers for monitoring and transfers.

One of Stephen Jarvis's hand-made Didrik DeGeer variable pattern microphones.

With respect to the performers, listen to the source of the sound first. The sound of the instrument may change your choice of microphone. If possible, try to arrange for some time to experiment in advance of the session.

My most recent piano recording sessions have been with my friend, Tim Gorman, on a forthcoming release with a working title of "Cowboy." We have been coproducing the sessions at the Skywalker Stage. For this record, I wanted something very special and sensitive. I've been using the Didrik DeGeer tube microphones and Didrik's hand-wired preamp almost exclusively with the Yamaha and Bluthner pianos, recording live to 2-track through Euphonix/Pacific Microsonics HDCD converters to an Alesis Masterlink recorder. We feed the audio signals and the master clock from the Pacific Microsonics into the Masterlink via the AES interface.

In the case of recording pianos, more often than not, removing the lid, or at the very least, propping the lid open to a vertical

Here is the minimalist recording station used by Stephen Jarvis. Pictured on the work table are (left top) Alesis Masterlink, below it, Pacific Microsonics HDCD converters, to the right with the copper-colored front, the Didrik hand-wired preamp, and to the right of the table, a second Masterlink and HDCD converter.

position, will eliminate much of the mud in the sound swirling in the lower registers of the instrument. The sound from the instrument, as it is heard by the microphones above the piano, tends to become much more even.

A pair of Didrik mics are placed about 10–12 feet away from the instrument to capture both the sound of the piano and the rich acoustics of the Skywalker sound stage.

Pianist Tim Gorman is captured by a much closer-spaced pair of Didrik mics. Note the piano lid has been propped completely open to reduce the low-end "mud."

Could you suggest a few setups that might help enhance the timbre of a dull sounding instrument or voice? Conversely, how about a setup that might minimize a sibilant or overly bright instrument or voice?

The short answer is to locate a better instrument and/or find another singer! Having said that, don't try to record in a padded room that sounds like you're standing inside of a pillow. The performance room's ambience should sound natural. A good test to determine if the room has sufficient diffusion for articulation of the voice or instrument is to go out in the studio and have the musician play or sing. If they can be clearly understood some distance away, then you have sufficient natural diffusion.

The piercing edge of a voice can be hard to overcome. It may not be just sibilance that

An excellent but overlooked rock vocal mic, the Shure SM 7B. Photo courtesy of Shure.

can be removed with a de-esser. I will usually set up several mics and listen for the one that works best with that vocalist. One of the most overlooked rock 'n' roll vocal mics is the Shure SM 7. For strident voices, I reach for a smooth Neumann M 49, M 249, or even a Sennheiser 441 in a live situation. My experience is that the AKG C 12, Tele 251, 414 type of microphone products appear to be brighter to my ears and would only increase the strident element of the sound. I've found the new Brauner VM 1 KHE tube microphones to have the smoothness of the Neumann sound combined with the apparent brightness of the AKG microphone products (www.braunerusa.com/vm1kh.html).

Alternatively, I've watched producer/engineer Nathaniel Kunkel, in this type of situation, grab some knobs and work his magic using a couple of GML 2020s to create a great filter EQ and multiband dynamics processor that would tame those errant frequencies in a matter of moments to the smoothness of a baby's bottom. Sometimes in the heat of a performance, the singer is ready to perform and there's no time for experimentation. That's why talented engineers who can get results quickly get the big bucks. They get it fixed immediately and don't get in the way of capturing an inspired performance.

How do you start a session using this approach?

Initially, I just walk around in the recording room and clap my hands to listen to the room ambience and for obvious problem areas in the space. I listen to my voice and to others talking in the room to locate the point of best articulation, where one can hear things most clearly, to initially place the microphones. Then I go back and forth, referencing the musical balance in the control room monitors [or headphones] to adjust the distances of the individual performers from the microphones being used. The performance volumes of each instrument must also be balanced by the musicians themselves during the performance.

Traditional equalization done via a console or outboard unit introduces some element of phase shift to a recorded signal. You suggest that by using "organic EQ" one can eliminate that phase shift, resulting in a more realistic recording that captures the natural sound of the performance. Will the listener hear this on one or two tracks of a multichannel recording that has, say, 24 or more tracks of information?

Every microphone has its own natural frequency response curve. Organic EQ, if you will. If you move a microphone closer to a performer, generally the bottom-end response of the microphone is increased, although less so when using an omni pattern. The use of minimal microphone techniques doesn't usually call for close-proximity mic placement to most instruments. In fact, as you move any sound source *away* from a microphone, you will hear the timbre change. For instance, using an AKG C 12, you can position a vocalist up to 2 feet away from the mic and achieve a very smooth, balanced sound.

Proper musical arrangement would allow for the use of minimalist techniques during the recording of any commercial project. For example, the Aaron Neville album *Warm Your Heart* (A&M catalog no. 5354, reissued in 2004 by Classic Compact Disc 53645), produced by Linda Ronstadt and George Massenburg, used this type of technique for an effect in the production of track 5, "Don't Go, Please Stay." The Boys Choir of Grace Cathedral in San Francisco was recorded [on location] as an overdub, using four microphones to a 48-channel digital recorder.

I provided a portable six-input Sonosax mixer to monitor the track with four input channels for the mics. The natural reverb of the church is captured and blended into the mix within the chorus sections of the song. It was well worth the effort of moving the equipment to the location to gather the unique sonic signature of the overdub performance in the real acoustic space.

For More Information...

Stephen Jarvis Audio Consulting. E-mail s.g.jarvis@worldnet.att.net

Tay Music. Indie label managed by Tim Gorman and Kirk Casey—www.taymusic.net. Casey was one of the composers of the music for by the megahit "Sims" games, and Gorman recorded and performed with the Who over several years, recorded with the Rolling Stones, and worked for producer Glyn Johns production company in England in the 1980s.

Didrik DeGeer mics and preamps. Didrik DeGeer, Idungaten 1B, 11345 Stockholm, Sweden

Moserobie Records (including the Ludvig Berghe Trio). www.moserobie.com

Tom Dowd and the Language of Music. www.thelanguageofmusic.com

For those interested, there is also an informative background article on the differences in how we perceive music in the November 2004 issue of *Electronic Musician,* titled "Can You Believe Your Ears? Psychoacoustics explores our response to sound," by Mark Ballora (http://emusician.com/mag/emusic_believe_ears/).

Is New Technology Short-Changing Music Listeners?

Jarvis on the sonic image of compressed audio formats

As recording engineers developed techniques and refined the sound of popular recordings, listeners were moved by certain blends of instruments, including the Motown sound, the Beatles sound, and others. This concept of the "commercial mix" has always driven engineers' search for musical balance and technologies to extend their control over those elusive elements of the so-called "magical hit" mix. The delivery medium and the technology used for playback by the listening public has brought us to the age of digital downloads and compressed files using codecs, in an effort to fit 10 pounds of audio into a 5-pound box.

In my opinion, listeners have lost something in the exchange for miniaturization and convenience. I have had the opportunity to hear 16-track, 2-inch tape playback vs. the MP3 compressed files over accurate monitors. The general listening public may not know what they are missing unless they have heard such a comparison for themselves. It's like using Cliffs Notes instead of reading the novel. You get the basic idea of the composition, but the personal listening experience and potential impact of the music has been reduced. Music lite.

Chapter 2
Tech Tips

All about Mic Preamps

A rguably one of the hottest areas of recording technology is the continually expanding universe of microphone preamps—also referred to as mic/pres, micamps, pre's, and preamps. It seems that at every Audio Engineering Society and International Music Production Association show, there are a few more companies new to the mic preamp realm and one or two established companies who now offer mic preamplifiers. From his home in the Sierra Nevada mountains, three and a half hours east of San Francisco, John La Grou, founder and president of Millennia Media, one of the most respected manufacturers of high-end mic preamps and signal processors, offers this "refresher course" in mic preamp function and utilization.

When he's not designing products or managing the thriving business, you'll find him in the studio or concert hall, since he's an active audiophile engineer for classical and acoustical music. The same enthusiasm John shows when discussing what makes a great mic preamp comes through when playing back an excerpt from one of his latest recording projects, a new high-resolution recording of Handel's *Messiah* captured at the Mondavi Center for the Arts. It's due out later this year from the American Bach Soloists, and if what I heard is any indicator, it may set a new standard in clarity and realism for this Baroque masterpiece. The album is due out in late 2005 on the Delos label.

Let's start at the beginning, why do we need mic preamps?

A mic preamp is necessary because microphones generally have very low-voltage output, and most recording devices require relatively high-voltage input. The mic pre is the link between the microphone and the recording device. It boosts the voltage level as much as 5000:1 or more. Another reason is that a microphone typically has very low current-sourcing potential. By placing a mic preamp near the microphone, you can then run long high-capacitance cables to the recording device without loss of frequency or signal.

Where do you find mic preamps in the recording world?

Everywhere! Anywhere a microphone is being used, you will usually find a mic preamp—typically inside a mixing console, but more and more engineers select outboard mic pre's because they can offer sound, function, and quality that console mic preamps can't match.

Aren't there two general philosophies guiding the design and use of outboard mic preamps? One is to design a sort of "invisible" or transparent preamp that has no coloration of the sound source, and the second being to come up with a pre that will *color, fatten, or enhance the sound source?*

That's a pretty good perception. I would say there are two schools of mic preamp design—one might be called "accurate" and the other night be called "colorful." The accurate camp tends to be made up of classical music and critical acoustical recording engineers, while the colorful group tends to be the rock, pop, and alternative engineers. They use the mic preamp color to achieve a greater sonic palette and to give them more creativity in the final sound. Sort of the way a painter interprets the colors of a painting, whereas the acoustic music engineer is more like a photographer who wants to precisely record a visual event.

So both types really have a role to play in the sound engineering world?

Absolutely.

In addition to the classical and critical acoustical uses, where else might the accurate preamps be useful?

Other areas would be live sound, film scoring, Foley, ADR, and voiceover work. Anywhere an engineer desires to capture the event as it happens in real-time acoustic space without adding any acoustic coloration. The White House uses some of our preamps for that reason.

How about applications for the colorful preamps?

Well, given that the rock and pop market makes up 90 percent of the [studio] music market, there's a lot of opportunity for coloration preamp sales and use there. You'll actually find that the preamp market generally follows those numbers. A much higher percentage of

Millennia HV-3D 8-channel preamp.

mic preamps are known for some type of coloration, versus a smaller number that are known for their accuracy.

For a home or project studio based around a Mac or PC workstation, what functions are essential in a mic preamp?

The watchword is simplicity. For instance, if you're doing a vocal at your studio, you need a mic, a preamp, and a recording device. That gets you into the system. And on the other end, you'll need some kind of mixing environment, analog or digital, in the box (workstation) or out of the box, an amplifier and speakers to monitor, and a way to store your mix.

Preamps are pretty simple. There are really only two functions that are required. One is phantom power, to power your condenser mics. The other is gain control, to boost the signal to the necessary level.

After that, there are a number of enhancements that may or may not come in handy. One would be a pad to attenuate a hot signal; another would be a polarity reversal switch to flip polarity 180 degrees. Some preamps have continuously variable potentiometers, good for setting vocals just right, while others offer stepped click switches that allow exact repeatability of a setting—ideal, say, if you are trying to precisely match a stereo pair of channels. The user has to determine which features will be advantageous for their uses.

What about the so-called specifications that each manufacturer lists for their various pre-amps? Is that the best way to determine how a preamp will perform?

Well, I don't see specs as being the best indicator of how any audio device will perform. The numbers that are absolute measurements, such as voltage gain, input noise, common mode rejection, distortion, and frequency response, are measured and reported objectively. But from my experience, these numbers are not always reliable indicators of sonic performance. Specs such as these should always be treated with respect, but your ears should be the final judge of any preamp's performance.

Would it be a stretch to say that there's no way to be sure what a preamp is going to sound like by simply checking out the specs?

Right. You have to use the particular preamp in your studio, with your microphones and your talent and program sources, with your production goals, and your monitoring equipment. That's the only way to see if a particular piece of gear will meet your needs.

A lot of people say, "I'm not that experienced. I have no way of knowing for sure if it's going to work for me." For those engineers, I suggest starting with two or three mic preamps in their price range that they think may be suitable. Contact a reputable dealer and ask if you may test them at your studio. Many local dealers understand the situation and are happy to accommodate the request.

One of the areas of research you've delved into is the difference in tonal quality that results when you use different brands of tubes in a mic preamp. Can there really be a dramatic difference if one exchanges a tube with the same model made at a different factory?

Yes, there can be a dramatic difference in sound. It all depends on the tube. There are a number of tubes that sound very similar and there are a number of tubes that impart a very distinct character. If fact, this interested me so much, I did a bit of research and testing to try to document the specific sonic differences and describe them so users could have more reliable information on specific tube performance.

I collaborated with Mark Franklin, and we spent a lot of time just swapping out tubes, listening, and trying to write down what we heard in subjective terms. It's the same for many rock guitarists, who will swap out their tubes to get a very specific tone, so they certainly hear the difference. It's really a question of what's best for you and your particular recording situation. [John's white paper can be found online at http://www.mil-media.com/docs/articles/tubetest.shtml.]

Another vintage recording tool, analog tape, has been going through a crisis, with the two main suppliers stopping and starting production. Outside of music, tubes don't seem to be in many other products any more. Are we facing a similar crisis with diminishing sources for new tube supply?

That's a good question. In the last few years there's been a bit of resurgence in tube making. So I have a feeling that as long as demand is there for vacuum tubes, which I think is growing, then there will be tube makers. It's just economics.

I don't think there's a problem with current tube supply. The problem we get into is the environmental issue of making tubes, which is a very, very dirty business. That's why no one makes tubes anymore in the US. Instead, they are made in overseas countries that have less stringent requirements. I don't see tubes becoming extinct any time soon.

Would you share an overview on transformer vs. transformerless mic preamps? What are the differences in performance?

Before we talk transformers, let me touch on pads. [*Note:* Pads are used in a circuit to reduce or attenuate an input signal so that it does not overload the preamp.] The Millennia HV-3 preamp has the highest input headroom specification of any mic preamp I'm aware of. It will handle +23dBu before clipping, so you can basically use them at line level without any overload. No pad is really needed in the design. There's also no transformer on the HV-3. However, for some applications, a transformer might be useful, so we developed the Origin, which allows the engineer to switch a transformer in or out of the circuit, depending on the needs of the moment.

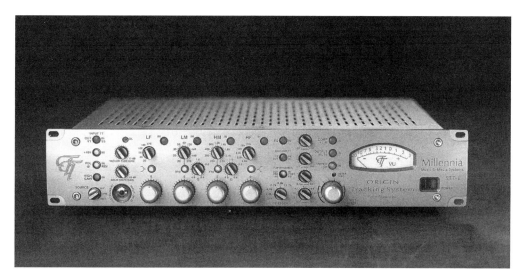

Millennia STT-1 Origin preamp.

There must be real benefits to including a transformer in a preamp's design.

Rather than benefits, I'd say there are trade-offs. A transformer will improve certain specifications, while others will deteriorate. Transformers are generally known for coloration. I'll share an anecdote to illustrate.

Many years ago I was talking with [legendary audio designer] Rupert Neve about his renowned 1000 (1073, 1081) series mic preamps, and why they sounded so distinctly good for rock music. He told me that 80 percent of that sound is because of the transformers. They impart a type of distortion that happens to be really musical sounding. It makes music sound bigger than life. It provides sparkle and presence and roundness that is completely unnatural, but very nice for rock music. It just happens to be something that people love.

You'll find that most other mic preamps that use transformers have some degree of coloration. Some are trying to be more accurate than others, and have done a pretty good job. But there are two places where transformers show their weakness. One is with high dynamic input. You could never put +23dBu into a mic pre with a transformer. It would fall apart way before that. The other is low-frequency performance. Let's say you're recording a pipe organ way down at 20–30Hz, and if you try to feed it even +5dBu, you would likely see 0.1 percent to 1 percent distortion, along with ringing and saturation. In fact, the lower the frequency, the quicker they saturate. So there's a couple of the trade-offs when you decide whether to use a mic preamp with transformers.

My personal preference when going for an accurate sound image is to avoid transformers, but if I ever wanted to design a preamp that had lots of coloration and character, a transformer would be the first place I'd start.

Millennia's Other Secret Weapon

Throughout our interview, which paused from time to time as John helped manage the day's work, I was struck by the extremely smooth flow of ideas, product, and information among the staff. The atmosphere was professional, but decidedly laid-back, fittingly underscored by various musical selections humming at a pleasant level in the facility. As the phone rang, I found out many of the callers were end users and dealers on a first-name basis with Millennia staff. The easy banter of the employees on the shop floor varied between discussing the acoustic guitar recording playing in the background (such CDs come in each week from a wide variety of users eager to demonstrate their results using Millennia products) to whether or not snow was in the forecast that evening.

Meanwhile, a special shipment completed bench testing and was soon carefully packed, awaiting that evening's

UPS pickup. The shipment was due to arrive in time for a specific client's weekend recording in another state. Beyond the outstanding sonic performance of their products, the Millennia Media team has one other secret weapon—an overriding passion for exceeding the needs of some of the most demanding engineers and musicians in the world in terms of performance, product knowledge, and service. John La Grou's dedicated staff, combined with products that deliver, continue to make lifelong friends every day.

—KH

Prior to shipping, each Millennia unit goes through a burn-in to ensure all components are functioning properly.

The success of your line of high-end mic preamps has been amazing—more than 20,000 HV-3s are in use today—with so many top users swearing by your products. After these accomplishments, how do you top yourself? What do you see on the horizon for the evolution of mic preamps?

At Millennia, we're going to continue to push the envelope on audio performance and quality when it comes to professional recording. I know that all of the good companies in high-end pro audio, like ourselves, are growing steadily. I don't see us entering the low-priced mic preamp market. That's not what we do.

As the industry grows, more and more people are realizing the benefit of having these kinds of tools available to them. They hear that they can improve their work and gain a sonic advantage over others. I see tremendous potential to high-end pro audio, which I believe will continue for many years into the future.

Portions of this interview were informed by John La Grou's excellent tutorial on mic preamps given at the 117th Audio Engineering Society convention in San Francisco in October 2004. For lots more good information on mic preamps and high-end audio gear, visit www.mil-media.com. An interesting white paper on microphone preamp design may be found at: http://www.mil-media.com/docs/articles/preamps.shtml.

John La Grou's Personal Preamp Collection

In my personal studio, I have a really nice selection of mic preamps. If I desire neutrality and accuracy, I'll use my own HV-3 preamps. But if I want thickness, brightness, or other kinds of coloration, I'll turn to my collection of vintage and modern transformer-coupled mic amps—which are anything but neutral.

When putting together a studio, there are two major acquisitions that will pay back with the broadest range of sonic texture and personality—microphones and mic preamps. If you're looking to build or expand a studio, you should plan on investing a significant chunk of time listening to the range of mic preamps available. I assure you, it will be time well spent.

Over the years, I've done a fair bit of listening comparisons with vintage and modern mic preamps. For my personal studio, I've acquired a nice selection of my all-time favorites. I'll try to describe each mic amp and give a little historical background.

Telefunken V72 and V76

Perhaps the oldest mic amp in my collection was made by the German Telefunken Corporation. There are actually two versions. One mic amp is called the V72 and the other is called the V76. These modules were designed by Dr. Nestler, who was head of Telefunken's

A pair of V76 preamps in a custom rack.

audio research and development labs in the 1940s and 1950s.

Two V72s in a rack mount configuration.

Actually, the V72 was largely modeled after an earlier Telefunken mic preamp called the V41, which was in production from 1928 through the Nazi era. The V72 was the standard mic preamp in German radio stations and many European recording companies, such as Decca and EMI. Even today, in the Mideast, Africa, and South America, thousands of V72 preamps are still in use. It's estimated that Telefunken and others built over 40,000 V72s.

In 1958, a new design called the V76 began to displace the V72. The V76 had a wider gain range, lower noise, better frequency response, selectable filter controls, and so forth. It was also about three times larger than the V72 and had gain up to 76dB—hence its name. Both V72 and V76 preamps require 220V, so if you use them in the States, you'll need a step up power transformer.

If you're wondering what these preamps sound like, go listen to the Beatles' *Sgt. Peppers Lonely Hearts Club Band*—it was recorded by George Martin using V72 and V76 mic preamps on every instrument and voice.

Keep in mind that if you stumble upon an old mic amp like the V72 or V76, chances are it is at least 40 years old and will need refurbishing. The electrolytic capacitors will have dried out and need replacing, and the silk wire may be rotted, among other problems. When I bought my V76s, the transformer mounts were also rotted and required replacement.

I did all the racking on the V76 pair. My V72 pair was racked and modified by a really fine local technician named James Gwanger.

API 312

API gear was first made in 1966 by Saul Walker. It basically evolved from audio products made by an earlier company called Melcor. It was Melcor, or possibly Burr Brown or Philbrick, who probably first used the original 1 in. × 1 in. discrete amplifier module, later becoming the API 2520 footprint. It's said that API built 700 mixing consoles before closing their doors in 1978, which means there were probably at least 15,000 of the original 312 mic preamp modules built.

The venerable API mic preamp is still being made today by Larry Droppa at Audio Toys. I've not heard his version, but I understand he's doing a pretty good job at keeping the original specifications and sound of the vintage API gear. My own

An early spec sheet for the 2520.

pair of API 312 mic preamps is original vintage from an early API console. They've been racked by Brent Averill in Los Angeles. Brent is one of the industry's most knowledgeable resources for racking and refurbishing vintage audio gear, and I would encourage you to look him up.

API 312 custom rack mount.

The API is a discrete solid-state design, and is probably the simplest mic amp schematic I've ever seen. It has an input transformer, an output transformer, and the API 2520 op-amp in between. Add a few feedback resistors and that's basically it. Some have characterized the API sound as cutting, scooped, present, chalky, bright, forward, 1970s, and electronic. Some of my favorite applications for the API are drums and guitar cabinets.

Helios Channel Strip

I recently acquired some Helios channel strips from Vintage King Audio in Michigan. Richard Swettingham started building custom consoles under the Helios name in England around 1969, and was in business for about ten years. Some of the early Led Zeppelin and Rolling Stones records were made on Helios consoles, including *Beggar's Banquet.* Jimi Hendrix and Led Zeppelin also made a number of records on Helios electronics.

Helios managed to build about one console per month during their ten-year history and most were installed in European studios, which is probably why we don't hear too much about them here in the States. Many of these consoles have been gutted for their input modules, so I'm guessing that only a few dozen complete Helios mixers remain intact.

Tony Arnold, probably best known for his work with Robert Fripp and King Crimson dating back to the 1960s, acquired what was left of Helios, including all the original parts and circuit diagrams. Tony has been repairing and maintaining some of the remaining consoles and modules. Tony is the force behind this remake of the original Helios 3-band EQ input modules.

These reissues are said to be a faithful reproduction of the originals, with all bipolar discrete circuitry, and a custom Sowter input transformer that's said to precisely mimic the original iron made by Lustraphone.

A pair of Helios channel strips.

What I like about these Helios modules is that they don't sound like anything else in my collection. They have a very unusual personality that's extremely colored and manipulated, yet retains a clear focus on the program being recorded. I think it's the mid-range that really intrigues me the most—it does remarkable things to male vocals. So far, I've only played around with recording guitar and voice, but I can already tell that I'll be using these a lot more on pop recording.

Geoff Daking 52270H Modules

Here's another piece of great audio equipment that I can't live without. A British studio called Trident was formed around the same time as Helios. The Beatles recorded "Hey Jude" at Trident Studios. "Hey Jude" went on to be the biggest selling song the Beatles ever wrote.

Geoff Daking 52270H modules are based on the legendary Trident A-Range electronics.

Trident was a forward-looking studio that designed their own mixing console. They called it the "A-Range" and it wasn't long before other studios were putting in orders for their own A-Range mixers. Trident continued as a company for many years, but the A-Range was only built for three years—which is a shame. Many have called A-Range the best-sounding electronics that Trident ever developed.

A few years ago, Geoff Daking updated the old Trident A-Range electronics into a reissue called the 52270H. I have a pair of these racked up in my studio. I've never used the original transformer-coupled A-Range electronics, so I can't compare them. Even so, Geoff's modules have a sound like nothing else. The 4-band EQ is both sweet and aggressive. This is a perfect tool for sonically rich portraits of acoustic guitars and vocals.

By the way, Geoff is also making complete consoles based on this A-Range module. If I were looking for an analog rock 'n' roll console, this would certainly be on my shortlist.

Neve 1272 Modules

I think by now that everyone has probably used a 1970s Neve module at one time or another. Rupert Neve's designs have become one of the classic and unmistakable signatures in pop recording.

A lot of people have converted the Neve 1272 module into a microphone preamplifier—which sounds strange at first because Rupert never intended the 1272 as a mic preamp. The 1272 was designed as a general-purpose amplifier. In old Neve consoles, you would find 1272 modules used for headphones, line output, summing, talkback, and a lot more.

A rack of Neve 1272 amplifiers.

But remember—Rupert said that transformers account for 80 percent of his sonic signature. It turns out that the 1272 modules employed the identical output circuit and transformer as found on Neve's dedicated microphone preamps. And on many 1272 modules, the input transformer is likewise identical to Rupert's dedicated mic preamp.

So, really, about the only difference between a 1272 and a dedicated Neve mic preamp is the gain circuitry—the 1272 has a single gain stage, whereas many of Neve's dedicated mic preamps had additional gain circuitry. So don't expect as much gain from a 1272 as you would get from a 1073 or 1081, or other dedicated Neve channel strips from that era.

Also keep in mind that Neve had a nonstandard gain-staging method. If you ever want to rack up some 1272s, be careful on your gain switching. I had Brent Averill build some custom rotary gain switches for these 1272s, and that made life a lot easier. I also added 48-volt phantom switching to each input.

Neve 1073 Modules

Okay, here's what many engineers consider the Holy Grail of pop music mic preamps. For me personally, the Neve 1073 ranks among my first picks for a pop-music attitude generator. The 1073 was Neve's most widely installed console module through the mid 1970s.

Neve 1073 console modules in a custom rack.

There was also a number of other nearly identical "10-series" modules made in this period, such as the 1066, 1081, and quite a few others. They were all built with essentially the same mic preamp circuit—same transformers, same gain circuit, and so forth.

A pair of newly made 1081 channel strips. Photo courtesy of *Sound on Sound* March 2004 review (www.soundonsound.com).

As a bonus, all the 10-series mic preamps came with a really great-sounding inductive EQ. Most console EQs today are designed around resistors, capacitors, and IC opamps. The 10-series Neves were designed using passive inductors and discrete amplifiers, which gave them a very unique and distinctive sound, especially when used on percussive instruments.

The 10-series Neves have an uncanny knack for keeping instruments highly defined within a thick pop mix. They give a sense of presence and immediacy without getting overly bright or strident. If you've used a 10-series signal path, you know what I'm talking about.

Not surprisingly, over the last few years, there have been at least a half-dozen companies who have released their own versions of the 10-series Neve signal path. Some have copied it part for part, and some have attempted to change various aspects of the sonic signature while retaining Neve's essential nature.

A Primer on Monitors for the Home Studio

By John Eargle, JBL Professional

All of you have monitor speakers in your home project studio, and sooner or later, virtually all of you will be replacing these speakers as part of a general equipment upgrade as you expand your business horizons. So, I'd like to address the twin topics of how to care and feed your present monitors as well as what to look for when the time comes to replace them.

What is a monitor speaker? Unfortunately, the term is used very loosely throughout our profession. However, most recording engineers will agree on the following general requirements:

Ruggedness with high output capability

A monitor speaker should be able to produce levels in the 90 to 100dB range comfortably and with low distortion. How low in frequency the system's response will go is basically dependent on its size. A pair of monitors for use in the typical home project studio should be able to make it down to about 40Hz.

How loud your speaker will play (Sound pressure level, SPL) is given roughly by the following mathematical relationship:

SPL at 1 meter (3.3 feet) = sensitivity (1 watt at 1 meter) + 10 log power rating

Here, the sensitivity is the on-axis output at one meter with an input of 1 watt to the loudspeaker. The power rating is the amplifier power value recommended by the manufacturer. If you have a semi-scientific pocket calculator, you can determine the value of the above expression directly. If you don't, just remember that for each 10-times increase in power applied, the loudspeaker's output will rise 10 decibels. For example, if your monitor is rated at 89dB, 1 watt at one meter, 10 watts will produce a level of 99dB at one meter, and an input of 100 watts will produce a level of 109dB.

Some of these levels may seem a bit loud, but remember that as you double your distance from the loudspeaker, the SPL will drop about 6dB. At a distance of about 10 feet (about 3 meters) the direct sound field level will drop about 10dB.

You should know the limits of your monitors. If you hear any signs of distress, pull back the level. Do not let a client push you into playing at higher levels than you know to be safe. Also, a simple accident in signal patching can blow out a tweeter or other component, so turn down the monitor level when you are rerouting signals. If you are into electronic music, watch out for high-frequency signals at high levels that may be inadvertently routed to your monitors, even momentarily.

Uniform dispersion over the forward listening angle

For several reasons it is important that monitors cover a fairly uniform listening angle in the forward direction. Assume that you are seated in the "sweet spot" where the response is ideal. What about a client who is positioned next to you? If your monitors have uniform coverage over a 30-degree horizontal angle, then you will both hear essentially the same response. If you are seated, and your client is standing up, you will both very likely perceive different signals. A seated position is of course preferred.

Uniform on-axis frequency response

Most good monitor loudspeakers today have fairly uniform frequency response along the primary axis of the system. It wasn't always this way, and some early monitors were fairly aberrated in their frequency response. Digital recording has raised the bar for all manufacturers, and today most speaker systems will exhibit response that is flat within + or –3dB from about 40Hz to 8kHz. It is customary for the high end to roll off slightly—and, of course, response below 40Hz with reasonable level capability comes with a higher price tag.

> Digital recording has raised the bar for all speaker manufacturers, and today most systems will exhibit response that is flat within plus or minus 3dB from about 40Hz to 8kHz.

Accurate stereo imaging

Many monitor systems today come in left/right mirror-imaged models, and this is primarily for precise balancing of system response for accurate stereo imaging. If your speakers are not exact mirror images of each other, then you run a good risk of having your center-panned phantom images compromised to a greater or lesser degree. You can determine this by panning a wide-band pink noise signal to the center of the monitor array. If everything is properly balanced, you will clearly hear a center image that has no fuzziness to it at all. It should be a clear, narrow image from bottom to top of the frequency range. If your monitors have individual level controls for mid and high components, you may be able to tweak the response a bit, improving the imaging.

What to look for when the time comes to upgrade your monitors

The next step up in monitor quality may be getting a pair of powered monitors. These are invariably bi-amped, which means that highs and lows are separately amplified. Bi-amping will result in cleaner overall sound, since intermodulation distortion is virtually eliminated. Most bi-amped systems have component protection built in, and the systems are thus guarded from stupid accidents. Other benefits may include low-frequency boundary equalization, which allows you to mount these systems in either free-standing mode or against a wall with optimized response.

If you are making the big step from stereo to surround sound, powered systems will facilitate things a great deal. A number of small powered monitors are now available that require a matching subwoofer, and five such monitors are often combined with a single subwoofer channel in a so-called 5.1 configuration. In these systems, the main channels are generally limited to low-frequency response down to about 40Hz, with the sub taking over below that point. These sub-sat systems can be conveniently mounted on stands in a circle surrounding your workspace, taking up much less space than full-range systems.

John Eargle is author of a number of reference audio books including Loudspeaker Handbook, The Microphone Book, *and* Audio Engineering for Sound Reinforcement. *He has been associated with JBL, Incorporated for more than 25 years and has made more than 260 records, many of which can be heard on the Delos label. For more information on JBL products, visit www.jblpro.com.*

How to Get the Most Out of Your Studio Cabling: An Interview with Phil Tennison

One of the most important but most overlooked components of any recording studio is the cabling. Most of us walk into a studio and take the hundreds or thousands of feet of cable for granted until a problem arises. Phil Tennison, Technical Support Manager for Mogami Cable, shares valuable insights into what cable can do in our studios.

What's the real difference between high-end and everyday cable?

The term "high end" always gives me pause, just because there is so much stuff touted as high-end cable that performs no better, sometimes *worse*, than far less expensive but well-designed cable. High price doesn't necessarily mean higher performance. So let's just say we will compare better cables with the plain-wrap variety.

Build quality is generally much better in the good stuff. They have superior dielectrics like crosslinked or foamed polyethylene, higher purity oxygen-free copper (OFC), and simply more care in the manufacturing process. In balanced cables, the twisting of the conductors functions to reject noise. Here, even the precision of the conductor's insulation diameter can have a big difference in noise rejection, as can the consistency and pitch of the twists. Consistency of manufacture means that sound quality of a given product will be the same every time, which is not the case with el cheapo cables. In an assembled cable, better soldering and care assure that the quality in the raw materials actually function as designed.

Just beneath the jacket of your favorite microphone cable you will find the shield. It is the shield's job to convert any stray electrical field into a voltage signal, which is then sent to ground. Shield materials are foil or stranded copper, which is either spiraled or braided around the cable. The better the coverage of the shield, the less RFI (radio frequency interference), EMI (electromagnetic interference), and other nasties can sneak through. Generic cables use a single layer of foil, which opens up gaps when handled, or spiral or copper shield with rather poor coverage. Any good cable will give specs for the percentage of copper shield coverage. Typical cheapo cables will be 80–85 percent coverage. The good stuff will be 98 percent or better coverage for spiral shields, 95 percent for braid.

Can you hear the difference between the two?

In a decent system, most people who pay attention can and do hear differences between cables. I don't think it takes a pair of golden ears—just reasonably careful listening and an open mind. Cable construction can cause highs to be brighter or duller, bass to be fattened up or rolled off, with audible differences in low-level detail. These interactions alter the way we hear dynamics in music. It isn't always so subtle, either. Many, many sound engineers have approached me at AES [Audio Engineering Society] conventions to say that after rewiring their studios, it sounded like they had upgraded all their equipment.

I should talk a minute about what I mean by "good sound." There is a plethora of processors, effects, plug-ins, etc. that are designed to alter signals we feed them. A cable, on the other hand, should *never* change what is sent through it! The role of cable is to convey signals as accurately as possible without allowing noise to enter. That's it! If a cable is consistently more full, bright, smooth, soft, up front, or you name it, on all types of gear, there is something wrong with it! The problem with this approach to cable design is that it might be pleasant coloration on some equipment, bad on others, and will inevitably mask or damage musical information that should be left intact.

A good test for those who want to experiment more with what a cable is doing, try a very short length and compare what happens with a long length. The longer a cable, the more its sonic signature becomes apparent.

What should we expect from a cable upgrade?

More silent background, detailed and extended, but not harsh or edgy highs, bass that is clean and extended. Sometimes people say it just sounds more natural.

Most obviously, better cables will have less noise. It is very common for people to tell me that they changed out a single cable and a particular background hum, hiss, or buzz that they put up with because they thought that was just part of their equipment simply vanished. Often we don't even really notice low-level noise until it is suddenly absent. The wonderful signal-to-noise of digital recording systems makes this more beneficial than ever.

What's a basic cable upgrade going to cost?

For a simple Pro Tools–based studio, an hour or so of time and a few hundred dollars can do wonders. A really good 8-channel db25 to ¼ inch or XLR harness can be $100–200, depending on length. Add in $40–50 each for a few really good mic cables, similar pricing for quality instrument or keyboard cables. If you are using passive monitors, a speaker cable upgrade for as little as $50 can make it easier to hear what you are doing in your mix.

What do you recommend for digital signals?

Lots more affordable equipment is offering AES interfaces. This is a far more stable digital medium than the common consumer-equipment derived S/PDIF, evidenced by the fact that a good AES cable can run almost 500 feet without trouble. AES cables use XLR connectors and look just like analog line and microphone cables. But you should invest in a genuine AES cable, because the capacitance in these is lower than standard mic cable and the shielding is generally better. You might get by using generic XLR cable in a pinch, but doing so can cause all kinds of problems later on.

What should you look for when shopping for cables?

When shopping for premade or bulk cable to make your own, doing a bit of homework makes good sense. There are lots of products out there, with wildly differing quality. You can't tell anything from looking at them. If you know an engineer at a large studio, you might ask what they use.

Compare the specifications. They really do mean something. Lower capacitance is better, 22–24 pf/foot or lower is typical for a good analog cable. I recommend looking for oxygen-free conductors, and 95–100 percent copper shield coverage. I personally avoid silver conductors in an analog cable, especially combinations of silver and copper in the same cable. Despite having slightly better conductivity than copper, silver conductors always seem to exhibit an unnaturally bright, etched, high-frequency characteristic. A short-cable comparison reveals this. This is the type of coloration that can sound attractive when first heard, but remember: cables should transparently convey, *not* change, the sound. If a cable brand does not have published specifications—just glowing ad hype— you should probably pass on it.

If you are working mainly in the studio, cables with the best spiral wrapped shields are better sounding than those with braided shield. Braided shields hold up better in the more hard-core live situations, though.

For ruggedness in patch cables, I prefer molded ends. Molding is typically associated with cheap cable, but some very good ones come this way, too. Molded ends can take constant handling and keep air away from the connection and copper inside the cable.

Any cable handling tips?

Once you've spent good money on quality cables it makes sense to take care of them. If cables are coiled and uncoiled a lot, use the standard industrial wrap, sometimes called the "over/under," for the longer cables every time you store them. If you do this they won't become damaged by getting twisted up or wound too tightly. They'll just spring into use with very little tangling.

Phil Tennison is Technical Support Manager for Mogami Professional Cable Products, which are distributed in the US by Marshall Electronics. Visit their Web site at www.mars-cam.com for more information. Mogami cable can be purchased at a wide variety of pro audio dealers.

Why Use External Digital Converters?

By Richard Elen

The topic of digital converters often makes people's eyes glaze over. The purpose of dedicated external converters can be even less clear. If digital audio is just numbers, and digital gear already has built-in analog-to-digital (A/D) and digital-to-analog (D/A) converters, why pay for additional external devices? Indeed, external converter units don't record audio, or mix, or add any effects to the sound, so why do they exist?

What Do Converters Do?

All digital recorders, digital mixers, and digital processors must use either built-in converters or outboard "dedicated" converters somewhere in the audio chain to input analog audio and play it back.

To understand the advantages of high-quality conversion, let's start by exploring what converters do. Very simply put, an audio A/D (analog-to-digital) converter converts analog audio signals into digital data so they can be stored, mixed with other digital signals, manipulated by digital signal processors, and transferred across interconnects as numerical information. D/A (digital-to-analog) converters do the same thing in reverse—they accurately reconstruct an analog signal from the digital data stream of numbers.

High-quality converters are difficult to make. As a result, you will quite often find that the converters built into a piece of equipment such as a recorder or a PC-based audio card are cheap and relatively nasty as far as quality is concerned. This is hardly surprising, because in a complex system the converters are just one part of the whole. Yet the converter—especially the analog-to-digital converter—determines the maximum level of quality that any digital system can attain.

If the converter is poor, the results will be poor—whatever the quality of the rest of the chain.

The solution is to use a high-quality external A/D converter to ensure that the maximum digital quality is delivered to the rest of the system. The question of exactly what makes a high-quality converter is what this article covers.

One reason an outboard converter can make a huge difference is that all the effort has gone into producing only the converter. Most of the stand-alone converters available today are made by companies that do nothing else.

In his widely respected book, *The Art of Digital Audio* (Focal Press, 1994), John Watkinson writes, "The quality of reproduction of a well-engineered digital audio system is independent of the medium [tape, disk, etc.] and depends only on the quality of the conversion processes." So, clearly, the primary reason for the existence of external converters is better sound quality. Whereas the internal converters of most audio equipment are just one part of the overall design picture, external converter manufacturers focus solely on the quality of the conversion process itself.

When it comes to money, you can pay a lot or relatively little for external converters. By and large, the axiom "you get what you pay for" applies to almost all electronic equipment at any given time, and it applies to conversion systems—up to a point. Certainly, cheap converters (under $1,000 or so for a stereo unit) sound cheap. But above a certain point—around, say, $3,000–4,000 for a stereo, 96kHz A/D+D/A—you may not be able to hear the difference, even at double the price. These price points change as the technology develops, however, and newer units often offer better performance at the same price—or less—than earlier designs.

Therefore, there is only one sure way to tell whether a converter is worth the money: use your ears. Consider what you can afford and listen to how much better it sounds than what you're using now. Try other units, either side of that price point, and be sure you can hear the difference. There is little point in buying super-expensive converters if they sound no better than something half the price—unless you think the name will buy you prestige and clients. (It won't, and there are some very well-respected brand names around that won't cost you an arm and a leg.)

What do external converters do better than on-board converters? The main thing that an external converter offers is improved conversion quality. But there are several factors that determine the quality of the A/D and D/A conversion process. Among these are:

Analog Design

The analog stage of a digital converter system is one of its most important design aspects. Self-noise, for example, can instantly reduce the resolution of an A/D converter. For every 3dB of self-noise, a signal through an A/D loses one bit of resolution. (Did you ever wonder why 18- and 20-bit converters existed when the only available recording resolution was 16-bit?) The low-level resolution will be lost in noise.

Be careful when you read specifications. The theoretical performance of the converter chip itself is never the real-world performance of the entire unit in use. A 24-bit converter will have smaller quantization steps than a 20-bit unit, but whether you can hear the difference in the noise floor is a different matter. A 24-bit converter can theoretically offer around 144dB signal-to-noise ratio, but that's below the thermal noise of almost any active component, and as a result you may be lucky to do better than a little over 100dB. There is debate about whether we can hear as much detail as 24-bit offers, anyway. A properly dithered 20-bit signal roughly matches the resolution of human hearing, so there is no point, by the way, in 32-bit converters. However, DSP within a mixer or signal processor will require more bits—often significantly more—than the input and output specifications.

Most people believe that the important part of a converter is the converter chip itself, and often ask, "Which converter chips does a particular manufacturer use?" The inference is that this is the primary factor in determining conversion quality. In fact, this is not the case. Most converter chips from the small number of major manufacturers offer similar performance for similar price as far as conversion is concerned. Designers choose one over another because of price, availability, and specific features that suit their designs. Of course, they'll measure the chip to see how it performs and to ensure it lives up to its claims, but in general the quality of a converter does not lie in the chip. It lies in how the manufacturer uses it. In other words, quality rests in good design.

In that arena, analog design is the most often overlooked, yet it can make all the difference. Additionally, poor analog design can produce noise on the clock lines, which, along with bad cabling between units and other factors, adds jitter to the signal, blurring the timing of samples and leading to loss of detail and stereo imaging, and other problems. This brings us to the second important design consideration: the system's clock or phase-lock-loop (PLL).

Clock Design

The accuracy and stability of the clock is vital in reducing jitter. This is true whether the clock is running on its own or is being locked to an external source. In the latter case, it's important that the synchronizing signal is reclocked to remove incoming jitter—a particular problem when synchronizing to video. This is approached in a number of ways. An innovative approach is to use two PLLs, one to handle gross timing errors and a second to really lock the timing down. A good clock, either inside the converter or a separate unit providing sync for the whole system, makes a surprising, audible difference.

Power Supplies

It's also important to ensure that both digital and analog parts of the converter receive the highest quality, most stable, most interference-free power supply. Regulators, filters, and smoothing must also be of the highest quality, with the minimum of ripple or other unwanted signals superimposed on the DC supply. RF (radio frequency) signals in the power lines from the digital part of the system can induce noise (or noises) in the analog part, reducing the noise floor and introducing artifacts that must be attenuated as much as possible. This is a particular problem in computer environments, where RF interference is one reason that converters on PC sound cards often lack quality. In addition, they have to fit into a small, unshrouded card space. Instead, use a digital I/O card and external converters, or perhaps better, use an external converter with FireWire (IEEE 1394) I/O running direct to the computer.

Digital Design

Because of their high frequency, digital signals behave in some ways like radio broadcasts, and the traces on the printed circuit board act as antennae. As a result, digital signals can easily leak into other circuits in a converter, again creating noise and significantly degrading performance—unless digital circuitry and boards are laid out carefully, and the right relationship is established between analog and digital areas.

Other Features

There are other features that an external converter can offer. One is multiple interfaces, and conversion between them. There are relatively few industry standard interfaces—such as AES, S/PDIF, ADAT Optical, and MADI, among others. Several of these are proprietary and a given manufacturer's system may only include interfaces from that manufacturer. Outboard converters often offer format conversion, taking digital signals from a number of different interfaces and allowing them to talk to your system, without the need for expensive additional pieces of equipment. Some converters use plug-in interface cards, enabling you to buy only the interfaces you need, swapping or adding extra cards when the need arises.

Increasingly, converters also offer some degree of analog or digital signal processing. This might take the form of a compression system on the input that minimizes the likelihood of digital "overs" or distortion during recording, and/or conventional compression capabilities. Alternatively, a converter may offer different output resolutions for different applications. Most converters today are 24-bit, but soundtracks found on DVD-Video are often 20-bit, while consumer CDs are 16-bit. A good "dither" scheme can reduce the 24-bit resolution of a modern converter to 16 or 20 bits with very little loss of quality or detail. Dither is an essential part of digital audio, converting quantization errors into innocuous noise and allowing you to hear signals below the noise floor, as is the case with analog. However, what is technically the best way of doing this—a type of dither called "TPDF"—may not sound the best, particularly when you are working at 44.1kHz (CD sample rate). As a result there are other schemes that can sound better, such as Apogee's UV22HR.

Some conversion systems may offer additional capabilities on the analog side, such as built-in mic preamps, instrument-level inputs, and other features that can be useful if you need them and you like their sound.

Conclusions

A good converter manufacturer can pay much more attention to audio quality and system flexibility than the manufacturer of an all-in-one digital system, where the converters are usually as inexpensive as possible and may not be that manufacturer's specialty. It's reminiscent of those old-fashioned "music systems:" a given brand might include a decent CD player, an acceptable cassette player, a good amp and tuner, and dreadful speakers. But because it's an all-in-one system, you can't pick and choose components.

When it comes to digital audio, however, you can choose to invest in external converters from a specialist manufacturer. If you care about the quality of your end product, it's something you may want to consider. Just use your ears before you buy to ensure that you are going to get the audible improvements you're paying for.

At the time this article was written, Richard Elen was Vice President of Marketing at Santa Monica–based Apogee Digital. This article is based on The Apogee Guide to Digital Audio, *by Richard Elen and Julio Alvarez. A copy can be requested from Apogee at www.apogeedigital.com. The article was specially updated for this edition. Richard Elen is now Director of Creative Services at Meridian Audio Ltd., Huntingdon, UK.*

Console Care: Getting the Most from Your Analog or Digital Mixer

By Jimmy Robinson

New or used, analog or digital, the mixing console at the heart of your studio is probably the most expensive piece of gear you own. As the nerve center of the whole system, the console's performance will have a direct impact on the efficiency of your work, the comfort of your performers, and the quality of the sound you record and mix. It only stands to reason, then, that maximizing the performance and longevity of this investment should be high on your list of studio maintenance priorities.

Fortunately, there are a number of common-sense things you can do yourself to get the most out of your mixer.

Before You Buy

Let's assume you haven't purchased the console yet. My first suggestion is this: Buy the best-quality mixer you can afford. If you have a fixed budget, and sacrificing a couple of cool features would allow you to move up a whole level in manufacturing quality, consider it seriously. While the features may seem important, four years down the road when the faders won't even pass audio, the extra aux sends won't matter very much. Look for quality brands, quality parts, and quality workmanship.

If you are purchasing a used mixer, have it thoroughly inspected by a qualified, impartial technician. That unbelievable deal may harbor dying switches, dirty pots, a sagging frame, vintage cappuccino, or worse. And don't let history blur your objectivity—just because Mick Jagger slept on it doesn't mean it's a great desk. A good tech can tell you much about the condition of the desk. At the very least, an inspection will prepare you for some of the future maintenance you are likely to face.

Be sure to check on the availability of replacement parts. An otherwise wonderful deal can become a real headache if you discover too late that many component-level parts can no longer be obtained.

After You Purchase

Now that you own the beast, you have the honor of taking care of it. The goal is to get the best sound and most reliable performance from your console for the longest possible time and most reasonable cost.

Keeping most electronic devices running at peak performance boils down to two simple guidelines: clean and cool. If you have a large-format console, odds are that the console can heat the room in the dead of winter. Cooling, most likely all year round, is important. Ideally, the temperature around the console should be maintained at 68–72 degrees Fahrenheit. But more important than the actual temperature is its stability. Try to keep the room temperature within a 10-degree range, 24 hours a day.

If heavy-duty cooling is out of the question, then stability is even more important. A console maintained at a *constant* 80 degrees Fahrenheit may perform impeccably for many years, while one that is cooled during the day to 65 degrees and warmed to 85 overnight may show component failure after just a few years. In general, a stable temperature is very good, a cool, stable temperature is way better, and a cool, stable, *clean* environment is an audiophile's dream.

> Keeping most electronic devices running at peak performance boils down to two simple guidelines: clean and cool.

A clean environment means both clean air and clean physical surroundings. Perhaps the most insidious threat to a mixing console is cigarette smoke. Smoke particles are small enough to penetrate the tiniest openings in electronic hardware, large enough to wreak havoc with audio quality, and sticky enough to stay glued to your faders, switches, and pots for as long as you own them. Unlike your lungs, your console will not heal itself even if you stop smoking in the control room. The best advice is not to smoke in the control room. Adding an air filtration system to your air conditioner may help, but no smoke is the best solution.

Larger contaminants may seem obvious (cigarette ashes, crumbs, and pet hair), but the audio annals are filled with tails of dead mice, oatmeal, illegal substances, and the like discovered by technicians repairing a "broken" console. Cappuccino is also a well-known console enemy. Even more than the liquid, the sugar in coffee and soda is particularly damaging to electronics. Its ability to promote corrosion is extraordinary, and its electrical properties can be mystifying. Keep beverages away from your mixer!

Now that we've covered a few don'ts, what can you *do* to help your console?

AC Power

First, power your console with a good AC source. You want clean, interference-free power. That means, first of all, a separate branch for your audio equipment—ideally, a separate subpanel from your building's main AC panel, but at the bare minimum, a separate circuit or circuits for your studio equipment.

That power should have an isolated ground separate from the rest of the building. There are specific outlet fixtures that accommodate isolated grounds and specific electrical codes that apply to their use. You should use a licensed, qualified electrician to handle this work.

A good grounding plan for your whole studio also will go a long way to maximizing the audio performance of your console and all your studio equipment. Again, if you don't have experience in this area, a qualified technician is worth the investment.

If you have the means, and especially if your AC power is subject to a lot of interference and irregularities, power conditioners and even a balancing power conditioner may be called for. Start with a good ground scheme, and, with luck, you won't have to go the whole route to balanced power.

With analog mixers, poor AC power may create some distortion or other artifacts in your audio system or crash your console automation. With digital boards, dirty AC or irregular line voltages can crash computers, mute audio, blow speakers, or even damage the console. If line conditioning is not an option, at least monitor your AC power (your tech can help you set this up) so you know what the problems are. If there is always a voltage dip at 4 P.M. because of a generator switchover at the power plant, at least you know to work around a critical mix at that time. Save the mix at 3:50 and take a coffee break for 20 minutes.

Routine Cleaning

Keep the console clean. Vacuum the control surface regularly. If you can see a layer of dust between the knobs, you're not doing it often enough. Keep cover panels in place and doors closed. Have the cat sleep on the sofa, not on the console.

Exercise all pots and switches regularly, especially with an older mixer. This helps keep contact surfaces free of dust and debris, and burnishes off any oxidation that may be forming. Only about half of the pots and switches get regular use, leaving the others to accumulate dirt, creating static, unstable levels, and distortion when they are called on to perform. Make sure you exercise *all* switches and pots, turning pots from end point to end point on a regular basis.

If you live in a particularly humid area, you also may want to consider a dehumidifier for your control room. High humidity can accelerate oxidation at an exponential rate.

The patch bay is another vulnerable area of your console. A mass of mechanical connections with hundreds of openings exposed to your working environment, it is usually placed dangerously close to desktops holding food and ashtrays.

> Make sure you exercise *all* switches and pots, turning pots from end point to end point on a regular basis.

Patch cords should be cleaned periodically. They are typically brass connectors, so a good brass cleaner that leaves no residue can be used. The jack fields themselves can be burnished with a tool designed especially for this purpose. Don't overburnish, however. This is an abrasive process that will eventually increase the diameter of the opening, creating a looser fit and potentially poorer connection with the patch cord.

Here's another don't: Don't ever use any off-the-shelf home cleaning product on any part of your mixing console. Very few such products, especially sprays, are safe to use on electronic equipment, and most are likely to contain cleansers, solvents, and other chemicals that may damage console parts.

A Few More Do's

Always use the right cable for the right application and connection. Whether analog or digital, mic or line level, T/DIF or S/PDIF, making sure you have the right cable—in addition to the right connectors—will maximize the quality of the audio that passes through the console and the entire studio. Be sure to follow correct guidelines on cable length, especially with digital cables.

Follow the manufacturer's instructions for installation and operation of your console. These instructions were written for good reason and can save you costly repairs and tedious inconveniences down the road.

Be sure to use the correct boot-up and shutdown procedures, especially with digital consoles. Thousands of hours of engineering time have been squandered looking for missing devices in software, trying to correct corrupted configurations, and attempting to recover lost mix data because of an ignored procedure. What appears to be a defective mixer often turns out to be operator error.

Jimmy Robinson, a long-time audio veteran, has spent more than 20 years as a recording/mixing engineer, a record producer, and an audio technician, with facilities such as Sony Studios and Right Track in New York City, and console manufacturer AMS Neve.

When a Console Disaster Strikes

Now, let's assume disaster does strike and someone pours a soda into a bucket of faders. What do you do?

❏ Dive for the power switch and **turn off the power** to all parts of the console, and possibly most devices connected to it.

❏ Call your qualified technician immediately and ask for his/her directions until he/she can arrive on site.

❏ If there is liquid in the mixer, and it is a small or portable type of console, tip the unit so that the liquid runs **away** from the electronics of the mixer and pours out of the console.

❏ Don't squirt anything into the console.

❏ Don't turn the power back on until the console has been thoroughly examined by a qualified technician.

❏ Follow your technician's instructions completely before powering up again.

❏ Do not attempt to clean the faders yourself. Have your technician handle this task or supervise you. Faders are very delicate and vulnerable to contamination. They should be maintained by trained, qualified personnel only.

Following these basic guidelines and using common sense should provide you with excellent sound and years of reliable performance from your console. Good luck and happy mixing!

Ensure a Long Life for Your Studio Condenser Mics

By Karl Winkler

As home and project recording have exploded over the last decade, a wide range of studio condenser microphones has been developed to meet the needs of studios. Many musicians and engineers, however, grew up using dynamic microphones, which, unlike studio condensers, can take the dirt, dust, saliva, and rough handling dished out in clubs and rehearsal halls.

Now, many engineers are investing in their first studio condenser mics. This article will tell you how to get the longest life and best-quality recordings from your condenser.

High-quality studio microphones are designed for many years, even decades, of use. However, many engineers are unaware that microphone diaphragms are "working" even when the mic is not plugged in. Thus, the designs of these mics have to take into account that mechanical movement will occur at the diaphragms 24 hours a day, 365 days a year. In some cases, the life expectancy of a microphone has been shortened due to improper handling and care.

By design, condenser mic capsules as well as the amplifier circuit are of an extremely high impedance. Pollution with dust, ash, smoke, and so on can degrade the insulating properties of the materials used for this part of the microphone.

Also, interfering noises can be produced at the capsule and amplifier of the mic under damp conditions (like close-miking of vocals or high humidity). To avoid these noises, and, in general, to keep your condenser mic in tip-top shape, take the following precautionary measures.

- **Use a dust cover.** Microphones not in operation should never be left on the stand unprotected. With a nonfluffy dust cover, the mic can be protected from dust settling on the capsule. When not in use for a longer period of time, the mic should be stored in a case of some kind. One specific recommendation is to store condenser mics in sealed plastic boxes (like Tupperware) along with a silica gel desiccant pack.

- **Use a pop screen.** The pop screen does more than eliminate the plosive noises in vocal recordings. In close-miked vocal applications, such screens also can efficiently protect the diaphragm from almost anything, including breath humidity and food particles.

- **Discard aging windscreens.** Foam material used in mic windscreens ages and degrades over time. With very old windscreens, the material decays, becomes brittle, and sheds. The particles can then settle on the diaphragm. To test for this, hold the windscreen over a flat surface and wring it in your hands. If particles show up on the surface, you should discard the windscreen.

- **Perform functional testing.** Modern condenser mics cannot be harmed by high sound-pressure levels (SPLs) found in the studio. Still, there is no need for "pop" testing to see if a microphone is working and present on the console. Normal speech is the best test, as only "scratching" the mics may not show a dropped cable leg or even gross distortion. Also, pop testing can produce SPLs at the capsule that exceed 140dB, which may damage studio speakers.

  With older mic types, be aware that some diaphragms can indeed be damaged by excessively high SPLs. The Neumann M 50, KM 53, KM 54, KM 56, SM 2, SM 23, KM 88, and TLM 50 all have nickel diaphragms that can be damaged by high SPLs. Also, older U 47s and M 49s may still have PVC diaphragms, which become brittle with age. Even transporting mics from one part of the studio to another and the subsequent rush of air over the capsules can cause huge SPLs at the diaphragms. When moving the mics, enclose them in a case, a box, or even a plastic bag.

- **Service regularly.** Sending in mics for servicing can help detect potential damage early. Slight soiling can be removed much more easily than a layer of nicotine embedded firmly in the diaphragm. Regular checkups of mics on loan or those used in dusty or smoky environments can prove especially beneficial, as the cost is small compared to that of a major overhaul.

- **Recognize the potential expense of do-it-yourself.** Attempting your own repairs on a delicate condenser mic can often do more harm than good. For cleaning soiled capsules, consider referring the work to a trained and experienced professional. Also, certain parts of condenser mics may be specifically selected and cannot be replaced with standard components. Once you've invested in a studio condenser mic, it's wise to send any defective or damaged microphones directly to the manufacturer or authorized service centers for repairs. These providers offer both a full stock of spare parts and experienced technicians who can accomplish repairs in a timely, professional manner.

Following the tips in this column and exercising some common sense, you should enjoy a long life of excellent service from your studio condenser microphones.

Karl Winkler is currently Director of Business Development for Lectrosonics, Inc., a leader in the design and manufacture of audio products including DSP systems and wireless microphones (www.lectrosonics.com). Prior to joining Lectrosonics, he was an executive for Sennheiser USA, which represents the Neumann microphone line in the US.

The Need for Speed: FireWire, USB Open New Doors for Portable Audio and MIDI Recording

By Paul de Benedictis

One thing is certain in the recording business—every year things get faster, better, and more affordable. Ever since the Portastudio became popular more than 25 years ago, musicians have been looking for ways to do increasingly higher-quality recordings and music composition wherever they may be. Likewise, the MIDI and digital audio revolution put tremendous creative power in the hands of musicians but sometimes required a steep learning curve in the Zen of keeping your computer happy. In this article, we'll hear about how FireWire and the universal serial bus (USB) are changing the way music and recordings are made. The original article, inked in the late 1990s, emphasized developments in MIDI and SMPTE sync and issues with early USB interfaces, plus then-revolutionary "card cages" for laptops. How quickly things change. As Paul reports, in 2005, SMPTE is less of an issue, and inexpensive FireWire, USB audio, and MIDI interfaces have replaced "card cages" in every studio—and outside the studio anywhere a musician can travel.

Just as writers can take their laptops anywhere they travel and draw inspiration, FireWire and USB interfaces are making master-quality recording and MIDI composition from just about anywhere a reality. You don't have to be in the studio to make music anymore.

MIDI (Musical Instrument Digital Interface) was designed to allow synthesizer keyboards to send information to each other. MIDI provides a language that allows one musician using a computer and a variety of electronic instruments to compose and perform music that used to require an entire band to realize. With the addition of audio recording in practically every music software system available, live tracks of singers, guitarists, and other acoustic instruments are now common.

As the technology for MIDI and audio recording have converged in the studio, more and more demands have been made on the computer at the heart of many control rooms. Fortunately we are at the beginning of a new level of speed with USB 2.0 at 480 megabits per second, and FireWire 800 (IEEE 1394b) doubling its speed to 800 megabits per second—plenty fast enough for serious 24-bit, 96kHz professional audio recording with ample bandwidth for accurate MIDI recording and playback. Recording rigs have become much more portable, as well, with the advent of improved USB, FireWire audio, and MIDI interfaces that connect right to a laptop.

One area of concern as music technology continues to evolve is compatibility between the computer hardware and operating system software, the music recording software, and the external audio and MIDI interface. Fortunately, in the last five years, manufacturers have begun to make both the recording software and the interface, and test them for both the latest Windows OS and Macintosh OS. This makes everything easier for the recording musician.

However, if you do decide to put a custom system together with recording software from one manufacturer and audio and MIDI hardware from another, be sure to get some guidance before buying. With the variety of prices and suppliers ushered in by the Internet, one great benefit has emerged for the musician—retail stores must offer great service if they want repeat customers.

Start by finding a knowledgeable recording salesperson at a nearby store. Get the salesperson's advice as to what type of rig will fit your needs and budget. Then hold him or her to it. Often problems arise from conflicting system files that are created by different companies and not necessarily "tested together"—a good sales associate should know which way to steer you to put together a functional system that's right for you.

Quite a few audio and MIDI interfaces are completely powered from FireWire or USB. This allows you to make your next record on your tour bus, or on the top of a mountain— no AC adaptor necessary! There are also "interfaces" built right into the musical keyboard controller itself. Plug in the keyboard to the laptop and you never even use a MIDI cable. Plug in audio to the *input* of the keyboard to record your vocal or guitar. If you are using software "virtual instruments," just plug in headphones and you have—literally—a complete studio in a box. What was a dream a decade ago is reality today.

Getting the most from your recording system continues to get a lot easier. With a few well-planned system choices, you'll have all the speed you need to make your music anywhere your career may take you.

Paul de Benedictis is a composer living in the San Francisco Bay Area. He's putting the finishing touches on a follow-up to his first CD, Power of One. *He also provides marketing and artist-relations services for music technology companies.*

TLC for Your ADAT

By Robert Stevens

With more than 100,000 recorders at work around the world in studios both small and large, the Alesis ADAT is still an integral part of today's recording environment. Odds are, someone you know has an ADAT or two reliably working away in their recording rig. Unlike an effects unit or MIDI tone module, however, this piece of technology requires some regular care.

Why? Unlike most technology in your studio, an ADAT is full of moving parts. A spinning drum rotates record and playback heads past the tape 3,000 times a second, which wears the heads down over time. Gears and levers load the tape into the mechanism, rubber pulleys pull the tape past the heads, arms, and shafts, and belts move to keep the music flowing. Add to this the fact that magnetic tape leaves behind a residue of microscopic particles, and it's clear the ADAT needs your help to continue functioning reliably.

Deep Cleaning

The best thing you can do to keep your ADAT functioning reliably and minimize head wear is to clean the heads and transport regularly. Alesis recommends cleaning the ADAT after every 250 to 500 drum-on hours (during which the tape is engaged against the heads). You can check your deck's total drum-on hours by simultaneously pressing the Stop and Set Locate buttons on the front panel of the ADAT. Depending on the environment, ADAT heads should last between 1,500 and 5,000 hours before requiring replacement.

Power users who use their ADATs eight to twelve hours a day will need to clean heads every three to five days. Project studio users who log 20–40 hours a week with their ADAT should plan on cleaning the deck every two to three weeks. Musicians and "bedroom studio" users who use their ADATs one to two hours a day will need to clean the heads every four to six weeks. Keeping a written log of head-on hours and cleanings will help you keep things on track.

Wet or dry head-cleaning cassettes are recommended only as a short-term solution to a specific problem, and should never replace regular manual cleaning. If you do run a cleaning tape through your ADAT, the ADAT's faster tape speed makes it necessary to play the tape for only 15 to 30 seconds. When done, never rewind the tape, as this can throw debris back into the transport. Unlike manual cleaning—which actually removes debris— a cleaning tape may simply move debris from one part of the transport to another.

The best solution is manual cleaning, which involves removing the top panel and tape carriage for easier access to the deck's transport. If you're inexperienced or uncomfortable with that prospect, leave the cleaning to a professional.

A basic tutorial on how to safely clean your ADAT heads may be found at: http://www.alesis.com/support/faqs/adat_cleaning.html. If you still feel shaky after reading this, take your ADAT to a qualified service technician for cleaning.

Here are some general ADAT cleaning do's and don'ts:

- Use a long cotton swab for cleaning all tape-path components, but never use it for cleaning the actual heads, because a swab's cotton fibers can snag and displace the heads. Heads should be cleaned with a small piece of lint-free cloth.

- Use 91 percent, 99 percent, or denatured alcohol only. Rubbing alcohol (71 percent) is nearly one-third water, which can leave behind impurities and debris after it evaporates. Cleaning solutions designed for electronics and tape heads will work fine, as will premoistened head cleaning tissues.

- Don't use alcohol to clean the rubber pinch roller, as it can dry out the roller and shorten its life. Formula 409, Fantastic, or even plain water are preferred for this application.

- Tape oxide usually builds up on the bottom of rollers, pins, and other components in the tape path. Keep cleaning these areas until no discoloration is visible on the swab.

- Always clean components in the same order each time, and follow the direction of tape travel inside the transport. This will help you avoid missing any components.

Other ADAT Tips

- Make a "golden" tape by formatting a virgin cassette when your machine is new or freshly serviced. When ADAT errors occur, put this tape in to locate the source of the problems. If the errors go away when playing back the golden tape, the problem may be with your work cassette. If errors persist, your ADAT may be in need of cleaning or service.

- Don't start recording right at 00:00 on the counter. Start your recordings at 00:10 or 00:20 for more reliable synchronization.

- Back up your tapes frequently by making digital clones between two ADATs. All that's required is a nine-pin sync and LightPipe cable.

- The ADAT's interpolation light indicates that error correction is taking place, but it doesn't necessarily imply a serious problem. Only when the interpolation light is lit frequently should you clean or service your ADAT.

- Cleaning your ADAT is not particularly time consuming or difficult, but it *is* crucial to keeping your recorder working reliably for the long haul.

Robert Stevens is a customer service representative for Alesis Corp. in California. You can get a lot more information on the care and feeding of your ADAT at http://www.alesis.com/support/faqs/index.html.

Protecting Your ADAT Masters

Like the recorder itself, ADAT tapes perform best when treated with care. Here are several ways you can ensure a long life from your ADAT master tapes:

- Handle cassettes with care, and never touch the tape itself.
- Use a library case instead of a slip case for better dust protection.
- Store tapes vertically, to avoid edge damage.
- Rewind tapes before ejecting, to avoid potential data loss on reinsertion.
- Exercise new tapes by fully fast-forwarding and rewinding before formatting.
- Store tapes between 60 and 75 degrees Fahrenheit, at a humidity of 40 to 50 percent. Do not subject tapes to extremes in temperature or humidity.
- Store tapes in a dust-free environment.
- Keep tapes away from magnetic fields. Avoid placing tapes by motors, speakers, computer monitors, or televisions.

Source: Michael Ryan, formerly of EMTEC Multimedia

16-bit or 24-bit: What's in a Word?

Tom Jung, recording engineer and founder/president of the pioneering digital jazz label dmp (Digital Music Products, Inc.), has been working at the cutting edge of digital audio technology for nearly 20 years. A perfectionist and advocate of the use of technology to improve the quality of recorded sound, Jung is sought out by manufacturers for beta tests and evaluations of their state-of-the-art audio developments. We went to Jung to learn more about 24-bit equipment.

What does the newer, 24-bit digital recording equipment do to the sound in a digital recording?

When you increase the word length (or the sampling rate), you break down the audio into smaller particles, so to speak. It would be akin to higher resolution in a video monitor—greater detail. One obvious change is wider dynamic range. But the thing that I think is most apparent is detail in the music, particularly in acoustic music where you are hearing the room and reverb tails and the little finite reflection patterns. These are audible clues that come from hearing more of the reverberant characteristics of the performance. The increased resolution gives you greater, more continuous depth of field in the stereo image.

Does this mean we should junk all our 16-bit gear and replace it with 24-bit equipment?

Not at all. I think you can do really good work in the 16-bit, 44.1kHz world. In fact, I believe we really haven't even scratched the surface on how good we can make 16-bit, 44.1kHz recording.

It's ludicrous to talk about DVD, higher sampling rates, and word lengths in a technology like PCM (pulse code modulation), which I believe could possibly be flawed. There is so much that we still do not know about digital audio, I would prefer to see a lot more work and research done before we commit to future formats without a good understanding of what we're dealing with. The best thing to do now is to continue to improve the current technology while thoroughly investigating the new generation of carriers.

Nevertheless, careful use of higher resolution can yield a superior-sounding project. If attention is paid to redithering, a critical process, you can realize greater-than-16-bit resolution, even though you ultimately are recording 16-bit. For example, with the Yamaha O2R mixer, you can take advantage of the 20-bit converters and then dither down to 16-bit before you transfer to a 16-bit medium.

Are you saying we can mix 16-bit and 24-bit gear and get a better recording?

With care, yes. But often people don't pay attention. They'll use 20-bit converters, and everything might even be 24-bit inside the console. But they'll record to a 16-bit recorder without redithering and *bam*—the 24-bit audio is truncated to 16-bit. They've lost the advantage of the 24-bit resolution, and the truncated data will likely contain some real nasty distortion. A straight 16-bit recording would probably sound better. Redithering is critical when interfacing signals or processors using differing word lengths. Digital technology is misused as much as it is used properly, largely from lack of knowledge or understanding.

What are some other things to look out for?

With digital gear we tend to assume that if it passes audio, the sound is fine. With analog, things like wiring problems are pretty obvious—we can spot a single-ended signal or a ground loop immediately. But digital gear is not immune to setup problems.

Clock jitter is a major problem in digital recording and easily induced by sloppy setups. For example, running AES/EBU (Audio Engineering Society/European Broadcasting Union) digital audio through a 25-foot microphone cable is not a good idea. It might work, but you probably introduce so much jitter that you would be better off going back to analog.

Check setups carefully. Know the internal word-length structure of all the digital gear you are interfacing. Redithering to match the word length of the device to which you are sending the signal is very important. Know the manufacturer's specifications and recommendations for each piece of digital gear. And listen carefully at every stage. Our ears are not yet as well trained to hear problem signs in digital audio as they are in analog.

How do you get the best, then, out of 16-bit digital recording?

Take care—in every step. If you're recording a vocal, get the best microphone you can, the best preamp, the best cable, the best A/D converter, etc. Always analyze what you are doing and ask yourself, "Is this the very best I can do at this stage?" In the entire scope of recording, processing, and mixing, there are hundreds of little decisions to make. Any one of them could be the reason why something doesn't sound so good.

If there is a way to stay digital, do so. Going back to analog to use a great-sounding tube EQ might be tempting, but remember that the D/A and A/D processes could be far more devastating than the benefits of the analog EQ.

Do you use house sync or some common reference clock to drive the digital equipment in your recordings?

I have a very fine house clock, but I didn't always like the results I was getting. Phase-lock-loop circuits of some gear are not all that good and can actually create jitter. In theory, house sync is better, but if your experience doesn't support this, try the internal clocks, or use the piece of gear with the weakest phase-lock-loop circuit as the master, with the better-designed phase-lock-loop gear locking to it. What is recommended in the manual is not always the best thing. Try something and listen.

How important is monitoring in maximizing your digital recordings?

Many of the things we have discussed are subtle and can only be heard on accurate monitoring systems. I'm not sure how many of the subtleties of resolution, depth, and jitter can be heard on a crummy monitoring system. Room acoustics are equally important. If you're going after quality, I think you can do really good work in the 16-bit, 44.1kHz world. But you have to pay attention to detail and you need a monitoring tool to let you know when something isn't quite right. Get the best monitoring system and listening environment you can achieve within your means. And listen.

If you'd like to know more about high-resolution digital recording, visit the Tech Talk page on the dmp Web site at http://www.dmprecords.com.

[*Note:* Tom Jung was interviewed by Bruce Merley.]

Redithering? What's Redithering?

By Bruce Merley

The word *redithering* has been popping up a lot lately, with the introduction of high-resolution digital audio equipment, such as 20- and 24-bit A/D converters, mixers, and processors. What *is* redithering, and what does it mean to the recording engineer or recording musician?

In order to *redither*, apparently something has already been dithered, so let's look at dithering first. In 16-bit digital audio, the quality of quiet or very low-level signals degrades dramatically as one approaches "1 bit of amplitude." The process of dithering improves the quality of low-level signals through some internal extra number crunching, which adds a broadband noise to the signal at an extremely low level. The result is that distortion of low-level signals is significantly reduced and, remarkably, we can actually hear components of the signal that are below the theoretical limits of the system. Dithering is a process that actually adds noise to allow us to hear low-level signals better.

Dithering is employed when reducing the number of digital bits used to represent a signal. Until recently, most digital audio gear was 16-bit, but calculations inside the processors result in word lengths much greater than 16 bits. This increase occurs any time there is a gain change, EQ, or almost any kind of digital processing. In the end, these longer words must come out as 16-bit words that contain the information provided by the additional bits in some meaningful fashion. Dithering is used to accomplish that task internally within the device.

Now, with the introduction of 20- and 24-bit equipment, we have the opportunity for higher resolution, better imaging, smoother digital signals, and generally improved digital sound. Indeed, the dynamic range, distortion, and general resolution of the new 24-bit gear is so great that dithering might not be necessary at all. Well, not quite yet…

For the time being, we live in a world where 16-, 20-, and 24-bit equipment and systems, not to mention multiple sampling rates, must coexist and interface with one another. Your new A/D converter is 24-bit, but your recorder is 16-bit. You might even deliver a 24-bit digital mix to the mastering engineer, but the CD is still 16-bit. What happens to your music in this mixed-word-length world?

When you connect the output of a 20- or 24-bit device to a 16-bit device, you lose those extra 4 to 8 bits of information—much of that extra resolution, subtlety, imaging, transparency, and so on. Until the entire audio production and delivery chain is consistently

24-bit from the first A/D converter to the home CD player D/A converter, it will not be possible to realize all the sonic benefits of high-resolution gear. Enter *redithering*.

Remember that any time you reduce the word length of a digital audio signal, dithering is necessary to minimize the distortion and losses of simply truncating or cutting off the extra bits. So when you connect the output of your 24-bit digital mixer to your 16-bit recorder, the signal should be dithered again. And when the mastering engineer sends the output of his digital console to burn your reference CD, it should be dithered again—that is, *redithered*.

Much of the new high-resolution gear with 16-bit outputs has built-in redithering; some of the equipment does not. Most mastering engineers will automatically redither before generating the final 16-bit audio master. Some don't.

These days the mastering engineers have to cope with the collective noise, word-length changes, and format conversions of lots of digital gear, as well as accumulated dithering and redithering performed in converters, processors, and workstations. Mastering engineers surveyed said that redithering is standard for them, as they all tend to use high-resolution digital processing gear and to output to 16 bits. But most also said that there are times when an undithered master is the final choice. They listen to the final mix dithered and undithered, and choose based on what they hear.

While there are many redithering devices using different algorithms and techniques, the engineer generally picks the device with effects that best suit the program being mastered. In the hands of a good mastering engineer, redithering is not simply a technology housekeeping process but becomes a part of his or her artistic palette.

Bruce Merley is a business consultant to the audio, video, and entertainment industry and past president of the Society of Professional Audio Recording Services (SPARS). In an earlier life, he cofounded Clinton Recording, one of New York City's premiere music recording studios.

Phase: Part 1

How Subtle Aspects of Time Can Enhance or Distort Your Recordings

*P*hase—it's one of those audio terms that we often hear but rarely understand well. Roger Wiersema, Chief Engineer at Polarity Post Studios in San Francisco, who has more than 25 years experience in music recording technology, explains phase.

Roger, what is phase and what does it mean to people in audio recording?

Essentially, phase is the time relationship between two sounds, waveforms, or signals in a circuit. When this time relationship is coincident, we say the two signals or sounds are "in phase" and their amplitudes are additive. When the time relationship is not coincident, they are "out of phase" and their amplitudes are subtractive. This has ramifications both acoustically and electronically.

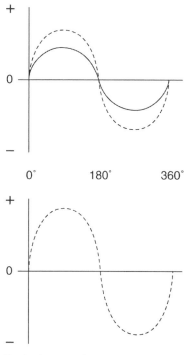

Two in-phase waveforms (top). Sum of the waves is additive (bottom).

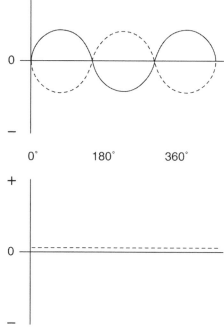

Two 180-degree out-of-phase waveforms (top). Sum of the wave is subtractive (bottom).

How do acoustics affect phase?

Let's take the example of close-miking a piano with two microphones. When you strike a key, the sound from the string will reach the closer mic sooner than the mic that is farther away, creating a slight timing or phase difference in the microphone signals. If those two signals are played on a stereo system, the effect should be a stereo "image" of some sort. Indeed, our ears capture the same kind of timing or phase differences, and the brain uses these differences for sound localization.

Now, if the signals from the two piano mics are summed to mono, the phase difference between them could result in phase cancellation. In that case, certain frequencies, depending on the music content and the microphone distances, are reduced in volume as a result of the subtractive amplitude of the out-of-phase signals. (Conversely, if certain frequencies are in phase, the volume will increase.) The result could be a change in timbre of the piano, a decrease in volume of certain notes, or even a kind of distorted, dirty sound.

Whenever you are miking in stereo, especially close miking, it's a good idea to listen, then sum the two channels to mono and listen again. Then reverse the phase of one channel and listen again. This should tell you what frequencies are being canceled when you sum to mono. If you don't like what you hear, reconsider your microphone placement; phase is working against you.

Sound reflections in a room can create similar cancellation effects, which recording engineers must consider in the room setup for a recording session.

We often hear about speakers being out of phase. How does phase work in audio gear?

If your speakers are out of phase, it generally means that one of the two speakers has its polarity reversed. This has the effect of putting the signal 180 degrees out of phase, which, theoretically, could mean total signal cancellation. Normally with a stereo signal we notice a loss of stereo image. When you play a mono program through out-of-phase monitors, you will notice a loss of bass and a loss of mono or center image.

In a studio setup, it is critical that all wiring is carefully done to maintain polarity and phase consistency. In a balanced system, maintain absolute pin and color-code consistency with respect to hot (or high), cold (or low), and ground. When mixing unbalanced and balanced gear, always be consistent—normally unbalanced hot to balanced hot (or high). It's also a good idea to verify the internal connector wiring of all outboard gear; not all manufacturers use the same XLR pin standards.

How do you track down a phase wiring problem?

I take the balanced output of an oscillator and put a diode across one side, either high or low, and wire this to an XLR connector or a patch cord. Then I'll look at the oscillator signal on an oscilloscope. It will display a half-wave form, either positive or negative (top or bottom side of scope zero line). Next, I hook the scope to the output of the device or system I am checking and the oscillator to the input. If the system or device is in phase, the half-wave form will appear on the same side of the scope zero line as originally noted. If it's out of phase, the half wave will appear on the opposite side of the scope zero line.

There are also commercially made phase-checking devices that use an LED indicator to replace the oscilloscope.

Are there other sources of phase problems in audio?

There can be many. For example, most digital gear (like analog-to-digital converters) introduces minute amounts of delay in the signal it processes. While generally insignificant, these delays can accumulate, especially in an elaborately processed mix. Mixers must be aware of these minute delay-induced phase shifts, since the accumulation of a number of these could have detrimental effects on the music.

Any final thoughts?

Avoiding phase problems and using it to advantage is a lifetime study, of both science and art. Ultimately, your ears are the final test.

Phase: Part 2

Using Phase in the Studio

Fred Guarino, owner and chief engineer of Tiki Recording, just outside Manhattan in Glen Cove, New York, explains how phase affects both the acoustical sounds and electrical audio signals in our music.

Fred, how does phase affect the sound of music?

First of all, if the sounds the listener hears are all "in phase," there will be no effect, negative or otherwise. But if the sounds are "out of phase," depending on the degree, the effect could be a lack of definition, poor imaging or placement of sounds, lack of bass or low-frequency energy, an overall thinness or weakness of sound level, or combinations of these in varying degrees. The actual effect is dependent on the degree of phase shift and at what frequencies it occurs, as well as the nature of the source sounds and the relative loudness of each.

Is music always supposed to be "in phase?"

Not necessarily. In music, phase simply represents a time relationship between two related sound sources. Generally, we seek to keep everything in phase for maximum clarity, fullness of sound, and most realistic sonic image. But room sound or ambience is actually a complex mixture of reflections in and out of phase in varying degrees. Other times we intentionally manipulate phase for a musical effect.

Here's an example. Sometimes in recording rock band guitar amps, we'll use an out-of-phase signal to create a particular hollow-sounding effect. First, we'll place a mic fairly close to the amp's speaker. Then we'll put up another mic, say, about a foot further away, and blend the signals from the two. By altering the distance of the second mic, we change the phase relationship of the two signals and vary the degree of the "hollow" effect.

So you can use phase as an effect?

Oh yes. Sometimes it's dramatic, as I just described. Other times it can be more musically subtle. If the second, rear mic in the example above were moved back 6 or 8 feet and up in the air 8 to 10 feet, in a large room it might result in a big, spacious guitar sound, very different from the first effect. Phase can serve as an equalizer or a dramatic effect, creating definition and spaciousness in music.

It seems like phase is everywhere. How do you control it?

We're always checking for phase, listening, checking what our ears hear against the phase meter, reversing the phase switch on the console, and listening some more. The opportunities for phase shift and reversals are everywhere—mic placement, room reflections, processor delays, miswired cables, outboard effects, operator error—you name it. Learning to hear how phase shifts affect sound is a fundamental skill for engineers. Not just hearing an obvious single-ended signal, but also smaller, subtle shifts in specific frequency bands.

Here's an odd example. In some DTRS machines (DA-88 format), when you monitor in input, you actually are listening through the A/D and D/A converters, which have a slight processing delay. If you blend this signal with the actual source in your monitor mix, the delayed signal creates a phase shift, which alters the EQ and imaging of the original source. Of course, only the original source goes to tape, but if, for some reason, you had been monitoring in this fashion, you would have a false impression of the source, which could adversely affect your recording decisions.

It seems like slight phase shifts result in useful or manageable effects. What about radical phase shifts?

A theoretically perfect, 180-degree out-of-phase signal would result in total cancellation of the original source. Few things in acoustics approach theoretical perfection, but radical phase shifts cause dramatic changes. Going back to our guitar amp example, some people like to take a guitar amp with an open back and place one mic in front of, and another in back of, the speaker. Because of the motion of the speaker cone, the rear mic picks up sound that is almost exactly 180 degrees out of phase with the front microphone. The result, if the speaker-to-mic distances are similar, is radical low-end loss and reduced level in the blended signal. You either have to vary the microphone distances or reverse the phase of one mic so it is in phase with the other. The console's phase reverse switch comes in handy here.

The same thing happens when you mic a snare drum above and below. The sound captured by the two mics is so close to being 180 degrees out of phase that the result is thin and weak. Reverse the phase of one mic, and the snare sounds full and punchy.

What about dramatic electronic phase shifts?

Phasers, flangers, spatializers, and digital delays all create frequency-related phase shifts for dramatic effect. More problematic is incorrect wiring in a balanced circuit. Whether inside a piece of gear or in your studio wiring system, whenever hot and neutral are reversed in the circuit, the resulting phase shift causes a loss of level and low-end signal—a thin-sounding signal. You can't be too careful in wiring equipment, cables, patch bays, etc. If that new piece of gear I'm trying out just doesn't perform the way people claim, before I send it back to the dealer for a refund, I check for a phase problem. Sometimes the solution is that simple.

You have to be vigilant in avoiding phase problems, and creative in using phase in recording. But hey, don't let it *phase* you! [?#%!]

Demystifying Time Code

Did you ever have a lock-up problem or a synchronizer that went ballistic? And just what is "drop frame" anyway? Sooner or later, if you have a studio, you'll use time code. For many, dealing with time code is one of recording's black arts.

Here's an article to help you better understand time code. It is excerpted from the *Time Code Primer*, written by Steve Davis of Crawford Communications in Atlanta and published by the Society of Professional Audio Recording Services (SPARS).

What Is Time Code?

SMPTE/EBU time code is a binary code, which becomes an embedded part of a picture or sound recording and assigns a specific address to each moment of time in a recording. It also provides a means of resolving the running speed of a recording. Each frame of time code contains all the information about that frame, including address data that can be displayed as a digital clock:

HOURS : MINUTES : SECONDS : FRAMES

The Hours field is incremented from 00 through 23 hours, and the Minutes and Seconds fields from 00 through 59. The Frames field takes the numbering down to the smallest increment that can be cut, a single image or frame. Time code frames can be subdivided into bits (1/80 frame) or sub-frames (1/100 frame).

Time Code Types

All time code is based on two parameters:

- reference frequency, which determines frame rate or speed at which frames are rolling
- the method of counting frames (the number of frames considered to be in one second of time code)

Reference Frequencies

EBU time code

In European and other countries with 50Hz AC power, 50Hz is the reference frequency. These countries use EBU (European Broadcast Union) time code, which runs at 25 frames per second (fps).

SMPTE time code

North America and Japan, with 60Hz AC power, use a 60Hz reference frequency and SMPTE (Society of Motion Picture and Television Engineers) time code. Because film and video have different frame counts and run at different speeds in these countries, SMPTE time code has three versions: non-drop frame and drop frame (based on a frame count of 30fps) and 24 frame (developed for film and based on a frame count of 24fps).

NTSC video

For broadcast, the National Television Standards Committee (NTSC) uses a reference of 59.94Hz. This slowed the frame rate slightly to 29.97fps. In NTSC video frames are still counted as 30fps, but they actually roll by in real-time at the rate of 29.97fps.

Frame Count

The four frame-counting methods for time code are:

* non-drop frame SMPTE (30 frame)
* drop frame SMPTE (28–30 frame)
* 24-frame SMPTE (24 frame)
* 25-frame EBU (25 frame)

Address data in these four versions is basically the same except in the frames field. Time code was originally developed to edit film and video, which run at differing frame counts. There are versions of time code to match every format.

Non-drop frame SMPTE

Non-drop frame SMPTE time code has a base of 30 frames; the frames field increments from 00 through 29 before returning to 00. When non-drop frame time code is referenced to 60Hz, it runs at a true 30fps and agrees perfectly with real elapsed time. This is the ideal tool for editing audio-only projects. When applied to NTSC video, the 30-frame code runs at the NTSC rate of 29.97fps, or 0.1 percent more slowly.

Drop frame SMPTE

Because NTSC video counts 30 frames in each second but actually runs at a rate of 29.97 frames per second, a readout of this code applied to NTSC video will lag farther and farther behind a real-time clock by a factor of 0.1 percent. But broadcasters need the hours, minutes, and seconds of NTSC rate time code to read out at the same rate as real-time. If we omit or "drop" 0.1 percent of the frame *numbers*, then on average, the readout will agree with real elapsed time. So, in drop frame code the first two frames of every minute, *except* the top of the hour and the tens of minutes are "dropped" from the numbering system. In this way, the numerical readout *appears* to be running 0.1 percent faster than it really is, and, with NTSC video, appears to increment at the same rate as a real-time clock.

Remember, no frames of actual video or audio are dropped, nor is the recording speed altered.

25-frame EBU, 24-frame SMPTE

Much less frequently encountered are 25-frame EBU, designed for PAL and SECAM systems used in other countries, and 24-frame SMPTE, which was developed to accommodate motion picture projectors that operate at the rate of 24fps.

Wiring Time Code

Longitudinal time code (LTC) is intended to be distributed the same way as ordinary audio signals. All wiring practices pertinent to good audio apply equally to time code. Time code is made of square waves, which are notorious for their tendency to leak (crosstalk) into other signals if not handled properly.

Time code is inherently insensitive to absolute phase. Therefore, in fully balanced installations, hot and cold (phase and antiphase) may be reversed without operational penalty. However, reversing them in an unbalanced installation will result in shorting out time code signals, increasing leakage and rendering operation impossible.

Wiring Recommendations

- Use high-quality, shielded, twisted-pair cable.
- Tie the shield at one end only.
- Make sure that the equipment you connect to the shield is grounded. Draining the shield into a floating ground or chassis is not a good idea.
- Respect polarity, especially if using adapters.
- Some types of "balanced" outputs are not "floating." These outputs do not lend themselves to unbalancing, as doing so short-circuits half the line, increasing crosstalk.
- If time code disappears when plugged into an unbalanced input, try reversing the phase of the wire.
- In unbalanced installations, use short cables in order to maintain signal integrity.

Recording Time Code

Because of the mid-range, chattery quality of the time code signal, it can be heard even below the noise floor if it crosstalks into other audio channels. On the other hand, if an adjacent audio track leaks into the time code track, it can corrupt the time code. When there is no concern of time code leaking into the program, it is common practice to print code at the standard operating level of the tape (0VU), or even higher.

On machines that print time code on a standard audio track, such as analog multitracks, or when using one of the audio tracks on ¾-inch or VHS video tapes, code must be recorded at a much lower level to avoid crosstalk in the audio program. Typical time code levels for such tapes are –7 to –10dB below standard operating level (0VU).

Copying Time Code

Because time code has a square waveform, it is difficult for analog audio tape to record and reproduce. This means that whenever time code is copied, it should be reshaped. When time code is copied without reshaping, the waveform becomes more rounded and within a few generations becomes unreadable. Recorders with time code capability typically have built-in reshaping circuits on their address track. However, if you are recording code to a standard audio track, it is good practice to patch the code through a time code reader. The Reader In/Reader Out path usually reshapes the waveform. This restores the readability of a rounded time code waveform without altering the sync information.

Time Code Do's and Don'ts

- **Don't** pass off or ignore time code problems. If they are not addressed, all subsequent elements will probably be useless.
- **Do** establish "house sync" based on a video sync reference. Distribute this reference to all time code devices.
- **Don't** cross midnight. Never allow time code to cross midnight (frame address 00:00:00:00) during the program, pre-roll, or post-roll of a recording.
- **Don't** mix drop frame with non-drop frame time code. That is, don't use different time code types on separate audio recordings that are intended to synchronize with each other.
- **Don't** put more than one type of time code on any single reel.
- **Do** listen to code through an audio channel. Often just listening can identify problem code.

- **Don't** ever restripe a time-coded analog tape once sync audio has been recorded. If you try to replace problem time code with "good" code on any analog audio tape, you will destroy the original speed reference as well as the frame addresses.

- **Do** avoid having the same frame address more than once on the same reel. It leaves the machinery very confused about where it is on the reel.

We have barely scratched the surface here, but you can learn all about time code from the SPARS Time Code Primer, *available directly from the Society of Professional Audio Recording Services. Contact the SPARS National Office at (800) 771-7727, or on the Internet at www.spars.com and then click on the link for "Publications."*

Eliminate Hum and Buzz

By Jim Furman

Like most engineers, you've probably had the maddening experience of an annoying hum or buzz disrupting one of your sessions. You may not know that ridding your studio of these nuisances is only a matter of taking the time to learn how to condition your power properly.

Hum and buzz are primarily caused by irregularities in voltage supply, and can even result in physical damage to your equipment. Aside from the bothersome noise, other hazards include radio frequency (RFI) and electromagnetic interference (EMI), power surges, brownouts, and even blackouts. Even relatively low-energy disturbances can cause data loss in computers and digital circuits and create noise in your audio and analog circuits.

Another culprit: ground loops. These are usually the consequence of powering components in different locations from different electrical circuits, grounding rack units both through AC cords and metal rack connections, or connecting audio signal grounds to the chassis. With so many variables, tracking down the source of your troubles can be tricky.

Protecting your studio from harmful effects of transient irregularities is easy. Two pieces of equipment combat power problems: power conditioners, which protect your equipment from voltage irregularities like spikes and surges; and voltage regulators (VRs), which provide a stable output voltage by compensating for a range of incoming voltages.

Both types of gear provide protection and reliable operation, but neither dispels low-frequency noises like hum or buzz. Balanced AC power lines can reduce the radiation of hum at the source: the AC wiring abundant in a typical studio. Unfortunately, electrical power in North America is not delivered in a balanced manner. To balance it on the receiving end, you must invest in a center-tapped isolation transformer. This apparatus, also called a balanced power line, consists of two out-of-phase 60V lines that provide the necessary 120V to power your equipment. The result: ground currents are all but eliminated, dispensing with the need to adopt cumbersome and expensive star-ground systems or to use massive bus bars or heavy ground rods to minimize hum. Though not inexpensive, balancing the AC supply with a balanced power line is simpler, cheaper, and more effective than the other solutions. Plus, balanced power is the safest way to go because there is no need to "lift grounds" or compromise the integrity of the safety ground wire.

If you are reluctant to install a center-tapped isolation transformer, audio isolation transformers can provide a quick fix. These economical devices are available in several convenient formats. Some are small and can be patched in wherever and whenever needed. Others are wired as an integral part of patch bay, isolating everything patched through it.

The latter option lets you experimentally patch a transformer isolator into key interconnections (such as mixer outs and amplifier ins) as needed. If the patch succeeds in eliminating the hum or buzz, you can permanently connect the mixer and amp by accessing the isolator via rear jacks, thereby modifying the wiring rather than relying on patch cords. One caveat: Most audio isolators are for high-level, low-impedance lines only, so they cannot be used directly with microphones or guitar pickups. If curing your studio's electrical ills sounds daunting, don't worry. You don't need a bevy of new gadgets or an army of electric company experts to fix power-related troubles. Keep it simple, and tailor the solution to the problem. To recap:

- For basic protection from spikes and EMI, install the best power conditioner you can afford.

- If AC voltage fluctuation is a problem, consider getting a VR, which usually also provides power conditioning features.

- If hum and buzz are the main concern, look into acquiring a balanced power isolation transformer.

- For a quick-and-dirty hum fix, carry a toolbox-sized audio isolation transformer or two, or try an isolated patch bay.

You'll be surprised at how much you can do to clean up your power with a little research and a modest investment in the right tools.

Jim Furman is founder of Furman Sound, which manufactures a variety of power conditioners, voltage regulators, isolation transformers, and many other studio tools. He also plays bass. There is an excellent detailed white paper delving further into issues of studio power management, titled "Safe, Quiet and In Control," available online at Furman Sound's Tech Corner, http://www.furmansound.com/pdfdata/ whitepaper.pdf.

Keeping Tube Mics Alive

By Klaus Heyne

You finally saved enough money to purchase a great old tube microphone that could be the crown jewel for your studio, but you're slightly terrified about the idea of buying a 40-year-old device that costs more than a used car. You wonder whether you would ever actually dare to use it in a session with live musicians, lest it crumble into a pile of copper wire and carbon powder.

Fear not. Splurge on your dream—but follow these tips from Klaus Heyne, a master microphone technician, whose ability to upgrade and optimize the performance of vintage condenser microphones is legendary.

Unless you are truly a tube microphone aficionado with ample knowledge of the sonic subtleties of the hundreds of fine recording mics in existence, stick with the "big five" microphones (AKG C 12, Telefunken ELA M 250 or 251, and Neumann M 49, U 67, and U 47). All of these large-capsule tube microphones are admired around the world for their unique character (each one noticeably different), their warm, spacious sound, and their ability to capture complex sound textures because of their high degree of resolution.

Contact several vendors as well as completed auction results on eBay, to establish the current market price for the vintage microphone you are interested in to ensure you don't pay above market for your investment. When buying the mic of your choice, make sure the item is "stock," meaning all of its relevant components should be original: housing, capsule, mic amp, tube type, cable, and power supply. If the mic has had repairs, these should have been performed either by an authorized service station of the brand in question or one of only a few competent, well-respected restoration facilities. (Use an Internet search engine to research the company name, for testimonials.) In either case, there should be detailed documentation of the work performed. Otherwise, the mic's collectible value may be compromised.

Buy from a reputable dealer or broker. Almost all of them will allow for an independent prepurchase evaluation by a third party. These sellers will be willing to fully refund the purchase price (minus shipping costs) if the mic is returned within a few days of purchase. Therefore, immediately take the candidate to a qualified service technician to verify its operational condition and degree of originality.

Once the microphone is yours, you'll want to keep it in optimum working condition. If the microphone has been meticulously cared for up to the time of the purchase, preventive maintenance should cost you little or nothing.

High-quality condenser microphones (like the "big five") built after about 1958 have virtually no deteriorating components. So, if you follow the steps outlined below and handle the microphone and its power supply with care, they should last almost indefinitely.

Aside from the classic "big five," there are some very fine modern condenser microphones, both tube and solid state. I recommend that [first-time] buyers stay with the "bread and butter" microphones of the major manufacturers. Mics like the Neumann U 87A and the AKG C 414 are excellent large-capsule condensers with wide applications, and they hold their value very well. The U 87 has been in production since around 1967 and has been continually improved and upgraded over the years. All of the suggestions I make below for care of vintage mics apply equally to the modern condensers.

Dynamic microphones may be a little more rugged, and ribbon mics require some special care. However, with a little bit of common sense and preventive maintenance, condenser microphones can perform flawlessly for many, many years without the need for expensive repairs.

Golden Rules of Preventative Maintenance

The three most important steps to guarantee a long life and undiminished performance from your condenser mic are easy to perform and cost almost nothing.

1. Minimum Distance

Stretch your hand—from the tip of your thumb to the tip of your pinkie. That's the minimum distance to any sound source a microphone capsule should be without getting mechanically "tired" and eventually losing its original diaphragm tension and performance.

2. Pop Screen

Always use a stocking screen for vocal work, since the head grille over your capsule offers little protection against saliva spraying onto the diaphragm. Saliva is starch, starch is sugar, and sugar is sticky. Since the capsule is electrostatically charged (from the mic's polarization voltage), airborne dust particles fly straight to the diaphragm, from as far as 6 feet away. These tiny bits of debris become lodged on the now sticky membrane; soon, the movement of the membrane is slowed down by the weight of the dirt. High frequencies go first. Eventually so much dust and dirt collects that it electrically shorts to the capsule's backplate, resulting in thundering discharges.

When the bitter end is near, the output of the mic starts to cut out completely.

3. Plastic Bag

To minimize the static attraction of dust to the capsule, pull a plastic bag (from your grocer's produce department) over your mic if you need to leave it on the stand, as during overnight breaks in your recording sessions. When the session is over, wrap the mic in the same bag before transporting or storing it in its case.

A plastic bag is also effective and inexpensive protection against moisture buildup in the capsule—for example, when you are traveling in rainy weather.

Klaus Heyne is proprietor of German Masterworks, and has been customizing condenser microphones for artists, producers, and engineers in the recording and film industry throughout the world for two decades. He can be reached via e-mail at GM@germanmasterworks.com.

Sound Storage Advice for Your Master Tapes

The convenience and ease of operation of various recording media make it easy to forget that the tapes you have recorded on hold priceless and irreplaceable information. As a result, more and more people are forgetting or are unaware of the proper methods for storing digital or analog audio tapes, especially for long periods of time. How many of us are guilty of storing valuable masters on a dusty bookcase or in a musty garage or closet?

Michael Ryan, formerly the Technical Support Manager for EMTEC Multimedia's studio and broadcast media products, offers some advice on tape storage.

Storage Conditions

The best climate for long-term storage of any type of magnetic tape is one that is comfortable for a person. The temperature should be between 60–75 degrees Fahrenheit and the relative humidity should be between 40–60 percent. The storage area should be free of magnetic fields as well as dust and debris. Places to avoid are attics, basements, and garages, all of which can be subject to excessive heat and/or humidity. It's also important to remember that when moving tapes between environments with different climatic conditions, one should allow adequate time (up to 24 hours) for the tapes to acclimate to the new environment before use.

Preparation

One of the most critical aspects in preparing magnetic tapes for storage is in winding the tape. This should be done on a machine that has been thoroughly cleaned and is in good working order. Winding should be done at low speeds (library wind mode) to avoid edge damage and prevent any part of the tape from protruding above the rest.

In addition, analog tapes should be wound "tails out" to minimize the effect of print-through echo (a phenomenon where the material on one part of the tape transfers to another).

Proper Storage

Magnetic tapes should be stored vertically (or upright) so the weight of the tape is supported by the hub or reel. The tapes should be in plastic boxes or ones made with acid-free materials, because acids help decompose bonding agents in the tape. The tapes should be stored off the ground on sturdy shelves or racks to support their weight.

Digital Tape Considerations

The guidelines we discussed apply equally to all magnetic tapes, both analog and digital. But remember, while a badly stored analog tape might be largely retrievable, a damaged digital tape is likely to be useless. DAT, ADAT, and DTRS formats must be cared for properly if they are to last.

Michael Ryan was formerly Technical Support Engineer for EMTEC Multimedia, one of the world's leading suppliers of magnetic and optical recording media.

Chapter 3
Studio Acoustics

Tips on Studio Acoustics

By Bob Skye

Sound is a highly subjective experience and there is no such thing as a perfect monitoring environment. But when it comes to mixing, the acoustical geometry and setup of your studio control room has tremendous impact on your ability to get the sound you want—and create a mix that will transfer to other listening environments.

Every studio represents a number of compromises in terms of acoustics and noise. However, by clarifying the issues affecting monitoring room quality and accuracy, you can take practical and not-too-costly steps to best deal with those compromises.

Noise vs. Acoustics

Being clear on the difference between noise and acoustics is important. Noise may refer to how nonmusical sounds outside and inside your studio affect your environment, and also, how your music affects others on the outside of your studio space. Acoustics, on the other hand, refers to how sound is perceived in a given environment.

If you are designing a new studio but haven't dealt with noise issues—whether they stem from a refrigerator in the next room, buses on the street outside, or neighbors complaining about your "noise"—then you may be wasting your time and money.

Noise has a lot to do with the construction of your space. Physical elements such as wood or concrete floors, thick walls or thin, and many or few wall "penetrations"—such as doors, windows, and electrical plugs— will affect the success of your studio space. The idea of soundproofing is a misnomer. *Reducing* the amount of sound or noise that gets in and out of your space is the more practical way to look at it.

For many studios, the amount of noise they can let loose outside usually is determined by the point at which a neighbor complains. Every city has ordinances governing noise levels and every studio owner should be aware of them. Many such ordinances limit noise to 5dBA above the ambient noise level, which depends on the neighborhood and the time of day. 5dBA above the ambient noise level at 3 A.M. is a much lower ambient noise level than at 3 P.M.

The amount of noise you can accept in your studio depends on what you can live with and what kind of work—demos or final mixes, for instance—you do. Typically, a noise-floor level rating of NC-20 (approximately 20dBA) is considered reasonable for mixing. [*Note:* The noise control or NC rating system is one of a variety of single-number rating systems used to measure noise in occupied spaces. For more information, visit www.noisecontrol.net.] On the other hand, many successful recordings are made in what I would call "hostile environments" from a noise standpoint. It depends on the type of work that you are doing.

The other noise floor is determined by the limitations of your recording equipment. Most of us have done the subjective equipment noise floor test by cranking up the volume in the quiet passages of something we've mixed and listening to the thermal noise and other things that hiss and crackle below the level of the music. This may give you an indication of the noise limitations of your recording and playback system.

Now, back to acoustics. A basic analog sound-level meter can help you sort out some of these issues. If your room is too leaky, your lowest-cost alternative is to cover up or improve the coverings on the penetrations (windows, door seals, and so on) on your walls, where most problems usually come from. Gypsum board (AKA sheetrock) is typically used to cover up these leaks, as it is relatively cheap and has the mass necessary to be an effective sound barrier.

As for your room's acoustics, there are certain rules of thumb that will help you alleviate the problems that cause many of the undesirable effects in mixes.

1. Set your speakers in a symmetrical configuration, side to side, so that they are equidistant from your right and left ears, and equidistant from the sidewalls.

2. Use a matched set of speakers.

3. Determine where early reflections will occur and make adjustments to diffuse them.

4. The oldest rule of thumb, of course, is to listen to your mix on as many systems in other environments as you can. This will help you determine if your mix stands on its own, and may indicate problems deriving from your monitoring environment.

A fine basic explanation of control room monitoring may be found in *Practical Recording Techiques, 3rd Edition,* by Bruce and Jenny Bartlett (Focal Press, 2002).

Geometry vs. Soft Stuff

An early reflection is anything that reflects off a surface and hits your ear 10 milliseconds or less after the direct sound from the speaker. The goal is to push the reflection time out 15 milliseconds or more. That's why having a back wall 10 or more feet behind where you sit is one good rule of thumb. The console and ceiling should never be ignored as potential sources of early reflections.

An easy way to locate early reflections is to have someone slide a hand mirror along the surfaces of your console and any other potential reflector, while you sit in the chair where you'll do your monitoring. Whenever a speaker comes into view in the mirror, that's a reflective spot. Mark it with a piece of tape. Then measure from the loudspeaker to that piece of tape to your nose. Then measure straight from the loudspeaker to your nose. Now calculate the difference in path length. Take the half-wave of that, and that is the range where you're going to have challenges in your room's frequency response.

For example, if you have a path length of 4 feet from your right loudspeaker to your nose, and you measure an early reflection off the console at 5 feet, then the path length difference is 1 foot. A 1-foot wavelength represents a frequency of about 1.1k. Half of that is around 550Hz. You can expect an equalization problem around 500Hz based on this measurement. Now, check the side wall, the opposite side wall, the ceiling, the console, and so on—get the picture? If you are able to arrange the geometry of the room by angling walls (angle your mirror to see the desired results), you can send the energy to the back wall, where it becomes easier to deal with, by virtue of arriving later to your ear and the ability of diffusing those rear-wall reflections. [*Note:* A handy wavelength to frequency calculator may be found online at: http://www.sengpielaudio.com/calculator-wavelength.htm.]

In dealing with early reflection, I choose geometry and diffusion over soft stuff every time. If you can move your speakers just enough so that the early reflections bypass you and go all the way to the back wall, you're better off than putting up soft stuff. Diffusion means dividing the energy so that it's a lesser amount in a particular direction, but it still sums out to a lot of energy in the room. Soft stuff absorbs the energy, especially in the high end. Although putting soft stuff all over the place is an easy fix, it will cause more coloration problems and mix imbalance issues than using diffusion and geometry.

RPG Diffusion Systems (www.rpginc.com) and a few other companies sell off-the-shelf products for diffusing surface reflections. While not always inexpensive, they give good, predictable results and are worth the investment. Bass traps have their place, but review the product carefully to be sure it will accomplish what you need.

Once you understand some of these issues, good horse sense can take you a long way. Low-end buildup in corners, for instance, is predictable. Mother Nature says so. There are tools you can spend money on to alleviate that, but my recommendation is to save the money. Just be sure you're not sitting in a corner trying to listen to a mix.

In 1974, musician and engineer Bob Skye founded Skyelabs, Inc. Over the past 30 years, he has specialized in location sound recording, live broadcast, acoustical and system design, and forensic audio/video (www.skyelabs.com). Mr. Skye also owned and operated major world-class recording studios from 1983 to 2004, and has earned engineering credits for gold, platinum, and Grammy award–winning records. His credits include work with a diverse range of artists such as Dave Matthews Band, Van Morrison, U2, the Russian National Orchestra, Herbie Hancock, and AC/DC. He has also been an audio and acoustical consultant with Charles Salter and Associates.

Cost-Effective Acoustical Treatments for Your Home Studio

By Nick Colleran

Acoustic treatments for studios and control rooms fall into three categories: absorbers, barriers, and diffusers.

Acoustical absorbing materials are often called "fuzz," slang for open, airy, fluffy, and light materials that do not reflect sound. Perhaps the most common absorber is open-cell urethane acoustical foam. This material is highly efficient and yields absorption coefficients above the theoretical limit, due to the sculpted surface pattern. Although the flat surface area absorption may be limited to 1.00, the total surface is increased, producing more total absorption than would otherwise be possible. While sound will not bounce back from absorbing materials, it will pass though them with minimal loss.

Barriers to sound transmission are heavy, dense, and massive materials. They include multiple layers of drywall (sheetrock), acoustical lead, and, most recently, mass-loaded vinyl. The latter two materials are thin (⅛ inch) but have sound transmission losses that exceed those of a 2-inch solid core oak door. They offer the advantage of retrofitting an existing wall without heavy construction or loss of space. Barriers do little to absorb sound.

Diffusers (or diffusors, if you prefer) are a means of acoustical crowd control. The object is to scatter the sound, not kill it. They are particularly useful for increasing the apparent acoustical size of a room and for broadening the "sweet spot" for mixing. Early diffuser designs, such as the polycylindrical seen on film scoring stages, take this a step further as they become bass traps below 500Hz. This is particularly useful to small control rooms, where sound can hit the rear wall at the midpoint of its cycle and return to cancel itself in the middle of the room.

Other odds and ends that are quite useful include sound sealant caulk and neoprene isolation pads. A crack at the intersection of a wall can cause a loss of 8 to 16dB. If air or light passes through, then sound sneaks through as well. Resilient pads are necessary to decouple structures, float floors, and walls. Sound travels through structures particularly well below 100Hz, and isolating the structure by floating may be the only way to prevent this.

While acoustical foams are generally low cost and safe for home use, there are some other effective options. Moving pads work well to attenuate high-end leakage. Absorber panels can be made from compressed fiberglass ceiling tiles. When placed across a corner and lined with rock wool, they make an effective bass trap. These materials should be covered with an acoustically transparent fabric to prevent glass particles from entering the breathing space. Chair cushions and pillows are also useful. In the past, budget studios have used egg cartons; however, the acoustical properties are not that good, and an open paper wall covering won't lower your fire insurance premiums.

There is little that can be done to stop sound transmission through walls other than increasing their mass with extra drywall or barrier. If the walls are solid, however, door seals (including the gap at the bottom) and caulking will sometimes provide significant improvement.

Diffusers, particularly the polycylindricals, can be a good do-it-yourself project. A piece of ³⁄₁₆-inch Masonite placed between two strips of 1 in. × 2 in. wood across a corner or centered on your rear control room wall will provide both high-end diffusion and bass trapping. A full 4 ft. × 8 ft. sheet that bows out at the center 6 to 7 inches will scatter sound over 180 degrees and have a center frequency of absorption at 63Hz. The back of the panel should have absorbing material to dampen the resonance, while the front surface will benefit from acoustical fabric such as Guilford of Maine FR701. The hard surface without the cloth produces a scraping fingernails-on-the-blackboard sound (not a lot, but very unpleasant).

Other styles of diffusers, such as the quadratic, can be approximated by use of a bookcase filled with different sizes and shapes in a symmetrical left-and-right pattern. A good selection of books can also impress your clients.

For isolation, if you can't float the room, float the musician! During the polyester period of disco, it was often necessary to record live drums and acoustical piano. To avoid heavy kick drum in the piano, the drums were floated. This was achieved with a sand-filled floor (heavy, dense, and massive) floating on truck tires (resilient, decoupling). This effect can be accomplished on a less grand scale by using a heavy platform with neoprene pads.

If your session is starting before you have time to build, there are ways to maximize what you have. First, find a room that sounds good and use it. If there is leakage between mics, arrange the performers as they will appear in the stereo mix to have it work for you. Place microphones flat on the floor (with a pad) to avoid interfering reflections. If you sing better in the shower, set up a mic there and try it.

In mixing, decouple the monitors from the console surface. (Mouse pads will work.) Use absorbers to eliminate close-order early reflections ("comb filtering"), add diffusion to broaden the listening position, install bass traps, or open the door to the rest of the house to avoid cancellations in the bottom.

Trust your ears. Listen on different systems in different surroundings. Listen in mono for phase problems. Get a good night's rest and listen again with fresh ears.

Nick Colleran began his career in audio in the 1960s as a writer, musician, and producer for CBS records. He is cofounder of Alpha Audio, Virginia's first large-scale recording studio, and Acoustics First. Colleran still gets his "studio fix," most recently producing an educational rap record. You can find information about acoustic treatments at www.acousticsfirst.com.

Chapter 4
Microphone Magic

How do you get amazing sounds from everyday, affordable microphones in the sub-$400 range? A wide range of top engineers share their favorite tips and techniques using mics that anyone can afford.

Joe Barresi

Joe Barresi, known for his eclectic collection of studio gear and his big guitar sound, has produced and/or engineered projects for such artists as Fu Manchu, Fastball, L7, Queens of the Stone Age, Hole, the Jesus Lizard, Anthrax, Loudmouth, and Bauhaus. At the time of this interview, he was in the studio with Veruca Salt.

Joe Barresi with a few of his studio "toys." Photo by Mr. Bonzai, courtesy of McDonough Management.

Altec saltshaker (63 A) mic. Photo courtesy of Airbone Audio Microphone Museum.

Do you have any reasonably priced microphones that you're especially fond of?

Actually, there are two that I think are extremely cool. One is the Altec saltshaker microphone, and the other is an Electro-Voice 666 (EV 666), which I call "the mic of the beast."

Both are pretty old. The saltshaker came from the United Nations. If you see old pictures of the UN, there are these little saltshaker mics with tabletop stands on them that were placed in front of each speaker. The 666 is fairly old as well. My friend John Travis loaned me his 666 once, and I liked it so much that I went out and found a few of them in a pawn shop.

Neither mic is new, obviously, but you can still find them. People advertise saltshakers all the time.

How do you normally use each of them?

I use them on just about everything. I use the EV 666 on vocals, guitar, bass, piano, and snare drum. I always have these mics with me, and I pull them out if I want a unique sound or effect. If I'm looking for a slightly weird bass tone or a boing-ier snare tone or a really unusual-sounding vocal, I'll use the 666.

I won't use the Altec on vocals because it doesn't sound very good, but I use it on the kick drum all the time and it sounds great. I've also used it in front of bass amps and electric guitars. It handles EQ very well. It's kind of mid-rangey and doesn't have a lot of bottom, but you can add tons of bottom to it and it doesn't get nasty sounding.

Electro-Voice 666 cardioid dynamic mic.
Photo courtesy of www.coutant.org.

Sometimes I just put it on the floor in front of the kick using the original base that came with it, like it was sitting on a table.

On what albums or tracks have you used these mics?

I used the saltshaker on a band called Queens of the Stone Age. It's all over that record, on the drums and on the guitars. You can also hear it on the kick drum on *King of the Road*, the album I just finished for Fu Manchu.

I used the 666 on a song called "Off the Wagon" on an L7 record. It's on the guitar solo, the piano, and the lead vocal. Using the 666 was an inspirational moment. I told the band, "Hey, this is the mic of the beast—it's the devil mic," and they said, "Cool!" I swear the guitar solo was one take, the piano was one take, and the vocal was one take. It's a highly inspirational microphone.

Do you have any unusual uses for either mic?

Because the saltshaker was a tabletop microphone, I pull it off the stand a lot, strap it to a regular boom stand, and use it as a regular mic, but nothing highly unusual.

They're more unique-sounding mics, as opposed to using an SM 57 in a garden hose or something. They have their own EQ to them because of their limited bandwidth. Plus, they look cool. Sometimes when you throw weird equipment in front of people, it inspires them to do something strange or react differently.

David Luke

Independent engineer/producer David Luke has been in the recording business for 20 years and spends much of his time at Fantasy Studios in Berkeley, California, in addition to occasional remote recordings around the country. His credits include work with a diverse group of artists, such as Bruce Hornsby and the Range, Booker T. and the MGs, the Johnny Nocturne Band, Otis Redding, the Delfonics, the Oakland Interfaith Gospel Choir, and bluegrass band New Grange.

Do you have a favorite affordable microphone?

It's definitely the AKG D 112. I haven't used anything else for kick drum for the past ten years. Most people use a D 112, Sennheiser 421, or Electro-Voice RE 20 for kick; I prefer the D 112. It sounds closest to what I want. I don't have to EQ it too dramatically; it just gives a good basic sound. Most people I work with don't want me to spend hours in an expensive recording studio A/B testing five different microphones for a drum sound. They want me to put the mics up, get a good sound, and go.

How do you use the D 112?

I use it mostly on drums, although you could use it on bass amp as well. I've recorded live drums my whole career, and I have a standard setup that I almost always use: SM 57 on the snare and D 112 on the kick. For everything else—tom-toms, overheads, hi-hats—I use condenser mics.

For live recordings, I have used the D 112 as the low mic on a Leslie speaker. You want a setup that's safe and will help you can get a good, clean recording. I would use a dynamic mic like the D 112 on the low end of the organ and get it pretty close, and then have two mics on the high end of the organ as well. It's a matter of being practical.

AKG D 112 cardioid dynamic mic.

How do you get the best possible sound out of the D 112?

It's made to pick up high sound-pressure levels. Putting it up on an amplifier would probably be a good choice because it wouldn't overload. The D 112 is meant for applications like tight-miking a kick drum, right on the beater. It can tolerate that. It's meant as a bass drum microphone, primarily, or for any kind of loud, percussive instrument.

Could you name some albums on which you've used the D 112?

I used the D 112 on drums for both the Oakland Interfaith Gospel Choir album I just finished, as well as the fourth album I produced for the Johnny Nocturne Band. It'll be the kick drum mic for a Booker T. album I'm working on. If I'm recording live drums, I'll definitely use the D 112.

Mitch Easter

Mitch Easter's production and engineering credits include work with R.E.M., Suzanne Vega, Pavement, Dinosaur Jr., Velvet Crush, and the Hang Ups. He sings, too—check out "Pillow Talk" on the Sixths' album *Wasps Nests*. His unique studio, Brickhenge Fidelatorium, is profiled later in the book.

Is there an affordable microphone that you prefer?

Actually, there are two I use every session. One of them is the EV 635 A, which has been around forever and was probably designed for television reporters. I bought mine new for $65—although I'm sure it costs more now—and I've had it for almost 20 years. It's indestructible. The other is a Beyerdynamic M 201, a skinny, hypercardioid dynamic microphone that probably costs about $150.

How do you use each of them?

The 635 is great on electric guitar amps. It's omnidirectional, and I think omnis are sometimes overlooked—because if you're recording a rock band, you have to think about isolation, so you think about a directional mic. What you gain with an omnidirectional is a real natural sound.

The positioning of this mic is not so critical. You can stick it right up on an instrument and the sound character doesn't change that much. You can take a 635 A, stick it inside an upright bass, and it will sound terrific—it won't sound like it's inside a can.

At the same time, it's really good on loud noises, like on a drum set if you want a roomy, 1960s, more realistic jazzy drum sound. It doesn't have a super-wide frequency response, which I find useful. It's got the information you need with no extra stuff. I always pull out the 635 A, and it tends to sound good on somebody's guitar or somewhere else in the session.

The Beyerdynamic M 201 is my standard snare drum microphone. When I start a session and don't know the drummer, I'll put that on the snare and it almost always works. I think the difference between it and a Shure SM 57 is that it's not as fat sounding, but it's a little more hi-fi–sounding. It seems a bit brighter and clearer. It's also a hypercardioid, so it's good if you need a little more isolation to keep the hi-hat out of the snare mic or something like that.

Have you had any unusual uses for either mic?

I suppose I've used them both on some goofy things. I do remember many years ago having to record the sound of frying bacon, and I almost certainly would have used the 635 on that to pick up the omnidirectional sound. I probably used it because I knew that if it got bacon grease on it, it probably wouldn't kill it.

Beyer M 201 hypercardioid mic.

On what specific tracks did you use either or both of these mics?

Probably on everything I've done, but among the well-known things are the early R.E.M. records. Both microphones were around for those sessions. I distinctly remember using the 635 A on most of the electric guitars. A couple years ago I worked on a Pavement record, and I was using the Beyerdynamic on the snare drums in those sessions.

How do you get the best sound with them? It seems like whatever you do with them, they sound good.

Well, the 635 A is a microphone that doesn't really care what you do with it. I think it all has to do with the attitude you bring to the microphone. A lot of people think that you use a [AKG] D 112 for a bass drum and a [Shure] SM 57 for a snare drum, like these are

Electro-Voice 635 A omni-directional dynamic mic.

some sort of rules. When you think that way, it is hard to get good results with something else. But if you're open to listening to what the microphone does and then figuring out where to go from there, these microphones can be used in all kinds of ways.

The 635 A wouldn't be the vocal mic for a super hi-fi ballad, where it needed to sound sparklingly clear, but it might be the definitive vocal mic for a real screamer or a real soul man or a punk rock guy. It's more about *considering* that it might work.

Fred Catero

Long-time engineer and teacher Fred Catero has worked with an extensive list of diverse artists, including Santana, Simon and Garfunkel, Janis Joplin, Chicago, Herbie Hancock, the Pointer Sisters, Barbra Streisand, Taj Mahal, Bob Dylan, Sly Stone, Dave Brubeck, and Aaron Copland.

Do you have a favorite affordable microphone?

First, let me say that no equipment, whether it's expensive or inexpensive, will make you a better musician. If you sound bad, then that's what the microphone will pick up.

That being said, one of my favorite less expensive mics is the Audix CX 111. They list for $600, but I found one for $400. As far as I'm concerned, it compares favorably to a Neumann U 47. I actually put them together at one point and tried different things with them, and I couldn't hear the difference. The CX 111 is the quietest mic that I've ever dealt with.

How have you used the CX 111?

I've used it to do vocals, and it's a wonderful microphone for acoustic instruments. I recorded a great-sounding acoustic piano with it. I also used the CX 111 to record a string quartet. These musicians play for the San Francisco Symphony, and they're very fussy about the quality of their instruments when recorded. Afterwards, they had nothing but praise for the quality of the sound and the faithfulness that the CX 111 gave them.

I bought my CX 111s on the recommendation of Greg Errico, who used to be with Sly Stone. He uses CX 111s with his drum set and loved the way his drums sounded with them. In fact, I recorded his drums with the CX 111s, and they sounded wonderful. I tried out one CX 111 and liked it so much that I bought three more.

How do you get the best sound out of this microphone?

The trick, as with any mic, is to use it within its range and within its limit capability. Don't put it an inch away from an extremely loud amp or drum and expect it to sound as good as a mic specifically designed for close miking. The finer the mic, the more careful you should be to use it the way it was designed to be used. Improper use of a high-quality microphone can make it sound no better than a cheap, poor-quality mic.

Any parting thoughts?

You should buy yourself one really good microphone. Now, I don't mean spend $5,000, but if you're generally looking for $150 mics and you can splurge on one $400–500 microphone, for instance, then you should. There will be times when you need super quality for a lead vocal or something acoustic that has real subtleties of sound, so you should buy a higher-end microphone—and then take good care of it.

Audix CX 111 cardioid condenser mic.

Elliot Scheiner

A well-known engineer/producer, Elliot Scheiner has worked with some of the biggest names in the business, including Aretha Franklin, John Fogerty, the Eagles, Steely Dan, Jimmy Buffet, Boz Scaggs, Natalie Cole, the Foo Fighters, and Fleetwood Mac. He's won five Grammy awards, including Best Engineered Recording for Steely Dan's *AJA* and *Gaucho,* and 20 Grammy nominations, including a nomina-

tion for Best Pop Album for the coproduced 1998 Fleetwood Mac *The Dance.* He has received two Emmy award nominations for Outstanding Achievement in Sound Mixing for Television, and won the Surround Pioneer Award in 2002. He has been instrumental in collaborating with Panasonic to develop the ELS Surround system found in Acura TL vehicles, drawing rave reviews from music and audio aficionados. Recently, he has been remixing classic albums in surround sound, including Queen's *A Night at the Opera* and several of R.E.M.'s albums.

Tell us about a mic costing around $300 that you like to use.

To be honest, I don't use many mics in that price range because I don't have to. But one I do use is the Audio-Technica M 25, which is a dynamic, hypercardioid mic. It takes an enormous amount of sound pressure.

How do you use the A-T M 25?

I use it primarily for tom-toms. Some people use it on kick, but I never have. The A-T M 25 is my main tom-tom mic. I use it consistently, just about any time I have to record drums.

Is its ability to take sound pressure the reason you use the A-T M 25?

Actually, there are quite a few mics that will take that kind of pressure. The really great thing about the A-T M 25 is that it has a tremendous amount of rejection. When I focus it on a tom-tom, that's pretty much what I get. I get very little snare drum and very little kick, which is incredibly important to me. It gives me the ability to leave the tom tracks in the mix a lot higher than I would normally. I don't have to ride them. I can just leave them static.

Do you have any tips on getting the best sound from the A-T M 25?

In terms of drums, I don't have to EQ the A-T M 25 much or at all. I can record with it flat off the toms. So my advice is to get the toms to sound exactly like you want and just put the mics in place.

Since you don't have to use "affordable" mics, what turned you on to the A-T M 25?

I had to record Fleetwood Mac live in a last-minute situation. I do a lot of live events, and normally I have to use pretty much what the front-of-house (FOH) guys use, except when it comes to drums. FOH guys have different considerations and objectives, and they need other mics than I would normally use for drums. In this case, the FOH guy was using SM 91s, and I just didn't find that suitable. I ended up calling Audio-Technica and they sent me the 25s. They worked out great. Now the A-T M 25 is part of my regular complement.

What tracks could someone listen to if he wanted to check out the A-T M 25's drum sound?

Check out anything on Fleetwood Mac's *The Dance* [released on CD and video in 1997, now available on DVD]. There's a lot of tom-tom stuff with Mick Fleetwood and, on *The Dance*, there are no replacements, no samples. You can hear exactly what those mics sound like.

Audio-Technica A-T M 25 hypercardioid dynamic mic.

Bil VornDick

Bil VornDick is an award-winning acoustic music recording specialist. His many producing and engineering credits include Bela Fleck and the Flecktones, Alison Krauss, Ralph Stanley, Mark O'Connor, Doc Watson, Bob Dylan, James Taylor, Maura O'Connell, and Jerry Douglas. He produced Alison Krauss's 1990 *I've Got That Old Feeling*, which won the Grammy award for best bluegrass recording, and Ralph Stanley's 1998 *Clinch Mountain Country*, which was nominated for a Grammy award and named album of the year by *Rolling Stone*.

What's your favorite affordable mic?

My favorite low-priced mic is the Audio-Technica 4033 SM. It costs about $399 new but you can get one used for $300.

How do you use the 4033?

I use it for mandolins, acoustic guitars, and vocals. It's clean and has a warmth for wood instruments. Mostly, I like to use it on mandolins, along with a KM 84. The 4033 helps bring out the woody tone of a fine classic instrument like the mandolin.

When do you use it for guitars and vocals?

I usually use the 4033 on guitars if I'm overdubbing. If you position the mic straight out in front about 12–18 inches, and angled in front of the musicians, chin down, you can get a very large guitar sound. With vocals, it depends on the timbre of the vocalist. Every voice is different. Usually, I put the 4033 as one of the mics to shoot out against others if I'm working with a new vocalist or background vocalist. When I was recording and producing *Clinch Mountain Country*, I used the 4033 on [guest artist] Bob Dylan's vocal. With so many vintage tube mics to choose from, I stuck the 4033 up. There was no time to try out various mics on Bob in this session, but my hunch proved right. The 4033 did just fine.

Any tips for getting best sound out of the A-T 4033?

Use it with a really good mic preamp. Depending on the application, I vary the mic pre I use with the 4033. Think of the microphone as your paintbrush and the mic pre as the paint. Every combination will be different, so get to know them very well.

Audio-Technica cardioid condenser 4033.

What tracks would you recommend to someone who wanted to check out the sound of the 4033?

Listen to Dylan's vocal on *Clinch Mountain Country* from Rebel Records. I also used the 4033 on Sam Bush's mandolin for the Bela Fleck album, *Tales of the Acoustic Planet, Vol. 2.*

Barry Rudolph

Barry Rudolph is a Los Angeles–based recording engineer who has worked with artists such as BB Mak, Rod Stewart, and the Corrs. His Web site, www.barryrudolph.com, is full of useful information for engineers and recording musicians. He regularly reviews new equipment for *Mix* and *Music Connection*.

What's one of your favorite mics these days?

I've been using the Royer R 121 ribbon microphone, which has a figure-8 pickup pattern in an interesting way.

I've been taking two 4 × 12 Marshall cabinets and facing them at each

Royer R 121 figure-8 ribbon mic.

other—as close together as 6 inches—to record electric guitar. I put the Royer in the middle, set up so that one lobe is aimed at each cabinet. The first trick to this is that you have to wire one of the speakers out of phase. Just split the wire on the back of the speaker in one of the cabinets and plug it in backwards.

Both of the cabinets are run from the same head, often a 100-watt Marshall top. It's important not to use two amps because then the phase might flip.

You can get a lot of great guitar sounds by varying how close the speakers are to each other, and where you put the mic. For instance, for a bright sound, you can put the mic between the center of two of the speakers. If you want more of the cabinet sound, pull the cabinets further apart and put the mic near the center of the grille cloth.

That's the trick, and it's really a cool sound because it really couples the low end and the air—a really good coupling of the speaker and the mic.

Is there a particular session where you used this technique?

You can hear it on the soundtrack for *Mission Impossible 2*. I did a lot of the rock tracks you hear in the movie, especially the guitars and drums on those cuts.

John Cuniberti

John's production and recording credits include the first five Joe Satriani albums, all of the Dead Kennedys' albums, George Lynch's solo album, a live recording with the Neville Brothers, the Kevin Gilbert catalog, and a steady stream of alternative and rock artists.

What's your favorite affordable microphone?

The Shure SM 57. If there has ever been a microphone that could be called a "workhorse," this would be it. It's probably the only dynamic microphone you could use on virtually everything and get a good recording.

How do you use the SM 57?

I would say the two most common uses for the mic are snare drum and electric guitar. The SM 57, put in front of a Marshall amplifier, is a *classic* sound. You can have a guitar player listen to a dozen different microphones, and chances are he'll pick the SM 57 over mics that are considered to be of better quality. People have grown accustomed to the way this microphone sounds when it's in front of a loud guitar amp.

Snare drum is another application in which the SM 57 excels. It has the ability to handle high sound-pressure levels, and it has a bit of a peak around 6kHz, which is nice for snare. If I had to mic an entire drum kit with SM 57s, I could live with it—with some skillful EQ, the sound would be perfectly fine.

Can you think of any specific tracks that feature the SM 57?

The lead guitar and melody for Joe Satriani's *Flying in a Blue Dream* was recorded with the SM 57. With Joe, we'll listen to maybe half a dozen microphones, trying to find the one that best conveys what's going on in the studio. Chances are, when he says, "That one," it will be an SM 57.

Do you have any tips for getting the best sound out of the SM 57?

Because the microphone rolls off bass, you can use proximity effect to make up the difference [meaning: the closer the diaphragm is to the source, the more low-frequency response is emphasized]. The SM 57 on electric guitar sounds best when it's up close—about a ½-inch off the grille cloth. I record it flat, and just move the microphone around the speakers to emphasize different frequencies.

For snare drum, get the mic close—I usually tuck it in between the hi-hat and the snare drum so it's off-axis to the hi-hat. This way, any EQ you're adding to the snare drum mic won't pull in as much hi-hat.

Shure SM 57 dynamic cardioid mic. Photo courtesy of Shure.

Any parting shots?

Don't be afraid to use anything. Experiment. The project studio is where you can outdo the guys who are strapped into $2,000-a-day rooms filled with expensive microphones they feel they *have* to use. It's very difficult to go into a big room with big money and high expectations and be experimental.

Shure has a number of siblings to the venerable SM 57, so check out their Web site at: www.shure.com/microphones/ to learn more about the various models now available.

Joe Chiccarelli

With a recording career spanning 20 years, Joe Chiccarelli has produced and/or engineered such artists as Tori Amos, Beck, U2, Hole, Etta James, Bob Seger, Frank Zappa, and many others.

Is there any affordable mic you use regularly?

The Audio-Technica 4041. I've used it on acoustic guitar, hi-hats, drum overheads, hand percussion, Leslie organ speakers, dobro, and as a room mic. It's gotten a lot of use, now that I think about it. As an inexpensive, small-diaphragm condenser microphone, in my mind, it's equal to a Neumann KM 84, an AKG 451, or an Audix SCX One. All these other mics sell for more.

What drew you to the A-T 4041?

I like it because it's fast as a condenser goes—it picks up transients very well. It definitely excels on string instruments, transient percussion instruments, things like that. It can be a little warmer than some of the other condensers I've mentioned. It's bright, but the A-T 4041 doesn't have the "spit" that some other mics have. There's something in the bottom that I really like. It's a little warmer.

On what specific projects have you used this mic?

I used the A-T 4041 a lot on Laura Love's album *Shum Tickey* on Mercury Records. I used it on dobro and acoustic guitar. I used the mic last year for John Michael Montgomery's

Leave a Mark album, primarily on acoustic guitar and Leslie cabinet. On Beck's [untitled] EP, I used the A-T 4041 on acoustic guitars.

How do you mic up an acoustic guitar with the A-T 4041?

I place it all by itself near where the fret board joins the body of the guitar, maybe 6 to 12 inches away from the guitar. A lot of times I'll use it in combination with a bigger condenser in that position. Then the A-T 4041 might be up near the player's fretboard hand, firing down the neck towards the sound hole.

Audio-Technica 4041 cardioid condenser mic.

Found any interesting applications for the A-T 4041?

I've used the A-T 4041 really close on a dobro, almost right in the resonator. A lot of times I'll put two mics on top of the snare drum, taping an A-T 4041 alongside an SM 57. The SM 57 will be my main snare drum mic. I'll send the A-T 4041 to a compressor and compress it a fair amount, then blend a little bit of it in with the SM 57. I get a lot of the snap from the condenser, and the tone from the SM 57.

What's next for you and your mics?

I'm doing an atmospheric rock 'n' roll record with Ian Moore on BMG, recording at the Hit Shack in Austin, Texas. After that, I'm recording a punk band called Foul in San Francisco. I'm sure the A-T 4041 will see quite a bit of use on both of these projects.

Chapter 5

G^3—Gear, Gadgets, and Gizmos

All engineers have tricks up their sleeves to use in certain situations. It might be a piece of off-the-wall gear, a dime-store toy, or a weird use for a standard recording tool. Any way you slice it, our G^3 contributors push the envelope with their tips.

Tony Hodson: Stomp Boxes Rule!

There are about as many different recorded guitar tones and textures as there are guitarists on the planet. Find out how to make your guitar tracks stand out in this interview with engineer, producer, songwriter, and guitarist Tony Hodson. Tony has an extensive collection of vintage and custom, limited-edition stomp boxes that he uses to craft his sounds. These days, Tony wears two hats, dividing his time between his role as Studio Manager/Chief Engineer at Stockton, California, Studio C, and commuting each week for sessions in Los Angeles at a number of composers' home studios. He recently mixed the song "I'm Ready" on Disney's hot-selling *Kim Possible* CD, and contributed guitar tracks and postproduction

engineering for 2002's *Baywatch* reunion movie. Songwriting credits include work with Thunderbugs, Aura, and Roger Smith. Additional television music credits include cues for *Diagnosis Murder*, *Head 2 Toe*, *Martial Law*, *E! Entertainment*, and *Fox News*.

What do you like to use when you're recording electric guitar?

I always like to use a [stomp box] compressor in front of everything I do, and I try to get the cheapest one I can find, like a Roland CS-3. I set a fast attack and a very slow release, which allows me to really play hard, but smoothes out how the distortion box behind it reacts. I've found that this keeps the guitar sound much bigger in the final track, rather than recording just through the fuzz box and then compressing it later on.

I own a few different esoteric fuzz boxes, one of which I'll put right behind the CS-3. One I like now is just labeled "Jack." I don't even know who made it, but I bought it one day and it has a really great fuzz/overdrive sound all its own. Another one I'm partial to is the Fuzz Factory by ZVex (www.zvex.com). It's actually very unstable. It has a knob called "stability" and if you turn that all the way down, you just get pure feedback, even at micro-volumes.

So quality is not the key?

Right. Actually, the worse they sound, the better they sound when mixed into the track. What I'll generally do is track the guitars that make up the texture in a song, and then I'll replay (double) the parts using any of these "filtery" fuzz boxes. Then, when I'm ready to mix, I can bring them in and out, say for a chorus, to give a nice build to the song.

What others do you use?

I have an old A/DA Flanger that allows you to use a velocity control pedal to adjust the flange effect. I first heard it on Steve Stevens' guitar solo on Billy Idol's classic "Rebel Yell." It's a sort of 1950s ray-gun sound. I may use that as a sound effect on a track; it's not clocked to anything, but its random quality can give a tune a touch of something special.

I'm thinking, "How am I going to bring one special thing to a chorus that is going to make you stop and listen to it?" Instead of doing something predictable, like a string orchestration for the chorus, or a standard lead guitar sound, or adding a canned drum loop, I prefer to create something unique on the fly with these effects boxes.

Can you give us an example?

On the *Baywatch* reunion movie, I had every keyboard player who came in to play wondering, "What's that patch from?" I had used my Roland GP-100—the rack mount "big brother" to the GT-5 effects stomp box—which provides a great variety of synth sounds, all driven by strumming a chord. Again, it's unique, because rather than the waveforms generated by keyboard synths, you have all the harmonics and overtones that the guitar creates, so it was a big hit on that movie soundtrack.

What's your current amp of choice?

I'm using a Fender Deluxe, which is often right in the control room with me, with an SM 57 hung over the front and a blanket covering it. Keep the control room monitors at a moderate level, and there's absolutely no bleed.

Where can readers shop for these stomp boxes?

The Roland products can be found at most guitar shops. For the esoteric ones, there are a number of more boutique-y music stores that carry them, like the Boogie Store on Ventura in Los Angeles, or Bananas at Large in Marin County. Also, the Guitar Center in Sacramento carries ZVex. I'm looking for new boxes all the time, and quite a few of the smaller companies have Web sites that list their dealers. Be sure to check out www.tonefrenzy.com, as they have a great Web site, with lots of downloadable samples of different effects, and offer a mix of vintage and esoteric stomp boxes.

Any parting thoughts?

If you're playing on a session or are called on to add a guitar part when engineering—even if you aren't the most schooled player—if you come in with some unique sounds, more than likely you'll get the job…and you'll get called back. There may be guys with more licks, but you'll have all the sounds. And sounds help make great rock records.

Using Logic in the Studio

On any given day you may find Oakland, California–based engineer/producer Dale Everingham at one of two locations: behind a large-format console at a top studio laying down tracks with a wide variety of artists, or at his home studio, where he uses the latest digital systems to produce, compose, and record pop, hip-hop, and film and television soundtracks. His talent can be heard on E-40's smash CD *Grit & Grind,* albums by Destiny's Child, Boyz II Men, En Vogue, and Mazzy Star, plus an upcoming pop-punk version of *I Wanna Be Like You*, tracked with Smashmouth.

Tell us a little bit about your home studio setup.

I've built my main system around an accelerated, fully loaded NuBus Power Mac. It's a big system with three drives, CD burner, extra large monitors, and racks of modules and processing. I use it mainly for composing and production work. But it's not practical to move, so I recently got a 667 G4 PowerBook with FireWire interface.

What software are you running?

I run MIDI and hard-disc recording at the same time, so I use Logic. I have Pro Tools on both my systems. I've got Logic 5.0 running on the PowerBook and an Mbox (Digidesign's desktop USB interface) for instant Pro Tools compatibility wherever I go. I also added the MOTU 8/96 FireWire interface so that I can get in or out via XLR, TRS, or Lightpipe.

Sounds like you're ready to travel at a moment's notice.

Yeah, when I get a call, I grab my PowerBook and whichever interface is needed, and head to the studio ready to work. I just scored a new station ID for Channel 26 in San Francisco on it. I've been busy loading up all of my samples on the PowerBook with Logic's EXS 24, a multisample player. I had thousands of samples I've used over the years, stored as Akai, SampleCell, or Emulator sound files, but they were too cumbersome to access. With the EXS 24, I have them all available to me in banks on a pull-down menu.

Are you using any of the virtual instruments available for your system?

I have quite a few running including the PPG Wave, JunoX, Pro 52, which gives you the classic sound of a Prophet 5 synth, B4 Hammond organ, FM Heaven, and Native Instruments' electric piano. These new virtual instrument plug-ins give you all the parameters of the original instrument. It's great to have something really close to the original that you can always access without the weight.

Any novel applications for these plug-ins?

I can reprocess any sound from a session file through any virtual instrument. For instance, I can take a vocal and run it into the Pro 52 plug-in, giving me the ability to do some analog filtering and processing. I've been experimenting with a couple of plug-ins called Pitch Blender and the Orange Vocoder. With Logic 5, they have simplified virtual instrument and plug use by including many plug-ins and instruments. But even better, these new plug-ins and instrument types work without cumbersome shells or second-party software, giving me more time to write music!

Reviving the Classic Sound of Beatles-Era Gear

John Paterno is a Los Angeles–based recording engineer who has worked with a wide variety of artists including Los Lobos, Tim McGraw, Badly Drawn Boy, and Joan Osborne, and just before this interview, he had completed a new album for Jeffrey Gaines on Artemis Records.

Did you use any new gear on the Jeffrey Gaines project?

Well, I've recently picked up three Chandler LTD-1 preamp/EQs that I used extensively on this album. They are like Neve 1073 modules on steroids! Of all the 1073-style things out there, the Chandler is the only one that sounds like the "real deal" to me. Plus there are extra EQ points, phantom power, and a built-in instrument input on the front panel.

What makes them different?

It's what makes them the same that is worth mentioning! They are made with the same construction techniques, grounding, wire gauges, and, whenever available, original components as the original 1073. Some of the cards in my LTD-1s are, in fact, original Neve cards that have been pulled from disassembled consoles. They are run off of a remote power supply, which will power up to four modules.

How do you use them?

I originally bought them to record drums, but I basically use them in any situation where I would reach for a Neve module. Since it also has a DI input on the front panel, I have been running bass, guitars, and keyboards directly into it as well. On Jeffrey's album, we cut all the vocals through the LTD-1. I also used them quite a bit on the upcoming Badly Drawn Boy record.

I heard you also scored an EMI TG-1/TG-3—AKA "Beatles compressor."

Yeah, I asked Chandler to send me one when I heard they were making them. The first thing I tried it on was piano, and as soon as I got it going, it just sounded like "Hey Jude" to me! It was pretty stunning. They based it on a few of the original EMI compressor/limiters they had access to. It has a six-position Fairchild-like attack/release switch, and in limit mode with the switch in position 1 or 2, it just pumps like nothing I'd ever heard before. Definitely not for the faint hearted!

Any other uses for the Beatles compressor?

Of course I had to try it on drums! I put up a mono mic in front of a kit, which was in a small iso booth, and ran it through in limit mode. I used it on a few of the Jeffrey Gaines songs. It pumps so much that it sounds like there is reverb on the drums—but there isn't! I've also used it on DI guitar, vocal, and assorted other things with great success. The folks at Chandler are not kidding around!

For more information, check out www.chandlerlimited.com.

Creative Compression

Paradise Studios is located in a suburban Sacramento, California, neighborhood in what was once the corner convenience store. Co-owners Kirt Shearer and Craig Long have worked on a wide assortment of projects with artists as diverse as Cake, Tony! Toni! Toné!, Hillary Stagg, Mumbo Gumbo, Tesla, and Beer Dawgs. The studio is outfitted with a Trident Series 80B, Digital Performer, and a veritable treasure trove of new and vintage processing, mics, and gadgets. (Be sure to also check out the Studio Profile on Paradise found later in this book.)

Any recent projects on which you pushed the engineering envelope?

I was working with a band called Deathray that was started by former Cake guitarist Greg Brown. As we were tracking one particular song, they asked for a Beatles-esque mantle over the whole mix. They envisioned that smooth, balanced, gently compressed sound that was the hallmark of the *Sgt. Pepper's*–era Beatles tracks. Much of that sound resulted from the unique English tube gear used to record the Beatles.

So you had already mixed down the song?

No, we inserted the "tube gear from hell" setup into the stereo bus as we mixed. That was the way we decided to get that throwback, nostalgic sound in terms of the dynamics and presence. It made for a pretty exciting mix session.

How did you tackle the job?

I took the feed from the stereo bus insert and fed it into a gadget called the Eclair Evil Twin/Model 92 direct box. It's basically a low-noise, high-bandwidth, line-level Class A tube direct box that allows you to bypass the console either while recording or when doing some audio trailblazing. Although many people use it to record bass, the combination of tube harmonics, Class A electronics throughout, and Jensen transformers give a fat, natural, "bigger than life" sound to just about anything you run through it.

Next, I ran the output from the Evil Twin into a pair of Telefunken V 76 mic preamps that we normally use for our tube mics. From there, I fed the track into an ART Pro VLA-1 stereo compressor. It's an opto-compressor that gives a soft, knee-leveling control to tracks, while maintaining a smooth, musically transparent sound. Knowing what the band was looking for, I set very slow attack and release times on the compressor. The compressor's output was then patched back into the stereo bus, going to the DAT.

By using the gain controls at the front of the signal chain on the Evil Twin, I was able to adjust both the tonal character and intensity of compression we were hearing at the compressor's output. I just played back the whole song a number of times, tweaking the gain on the Evil Twin until we got the sound they were looking for.

Can you describe the sound?

One of the hallmarks is that the attack and release on transients like the cymbals is slower than normal, giving the track a bit of an ethereal sound. The other instruments and vocals still sound transparent, not overly squashed, the way some solid-state compressors or plug-ins can sound. Also, by running the mix through three different stages of tube electronics, the song had a much warmer and richer sound than the original tracks.

Big Bass Tips: Using the Bass Pod in the Studio

The discography for engineer/producer Tom Size is just as diverse as his own musical tastes. His skills have added to albums by Laurie Anderson, Tommy Castro, Pete Escovedo, Huey Lewis and the News, Ray Obiedo, Todd Rundgren, Joe Satriani, and Psychograss. He describes Tomland, his Northern California studio as "Disneyland without the tram." Taking a break from a mix for the Clay Burton Band, he talked about one of his favorite techniques to make bass tracks live large.

You mentioned that you often modify the tone of a recorded track using a piece of guitar kit.

Yeah, often the notes are correct on a recording but the tone of the instrument just doesn't sit right in the mix. Today I'm using the Line 6 Bass Pod, which has nice emulation for bass—everything from a 1952 P-Bass to the latest amps. I got into how important bass tone was when I recorded Billy Sheehan about ten years back. [Check out Tom's work on Mr. Big's *Lean Into It* and *Bump Ahead* albums.] His bass rig sounded huge. Tone is so crucial to bass.

So how are you using the Bass Pod?

I'll play back the bass part from tape using a Reamp; it's a backwards direct box, allowing you to take tracks off tape (or hard disc) and run them through an amp or guitar effect, postsession. On this album I'm starting with two presets, Amp 360 and California Amp Model, and then tweaking them via the customizable parameters on the box. I can dial in just the right tone to complement the song.

How about recording bass?

You have to hear the Avalon U5 passive DI/Preamp! It's the best box out there. I won't go through the console any more for recording bass. The U5 has lots of headroom and is very clean. Take the signal out at line level and with a good compressor after it, go straight to tape. You'll really be surprised at how good your bass can sound through it.

How Much Is Enough? The Fine Line between Groove Perfection and Destruction

In today's digital audio workstation world, the ability to alter a live performance is limited only by your imagination and how much time you want to spend. It's a well-documented fact that many top artists' performances are crafted using bits and pieces of various takes inside a digital audio workstation, resulting in a believable but sometimes too-perfect performance.

Producer, engineer, and Pro Tools guru Russell Bond has been on the bleeding edge of digital audio technology for nearly 20 years. His credits include a wide range of work with artists, including Alex De Grassi, Stevan Pasero, Chris Spheeris, Michael Spiro, Bill Cutler, the Big Wu, and Michael Hedges. He has been an audio consultant to Apple Computer and spent a year as a Training Specialist for Digidesign. He continues to produce and engineer projects in the San Francisco Bay Area.

What's your point of view on perfecting a track using a digital audio workstation (DAW)?

There's no question that there are some awesome tools available today to fix and create performances, the most powerful one being the basic editing capability of the DAW itself! If I wanted a "perfect track," I could use tools such as Beat Detective to automate the process of quantizing audio with amazing speed and accuracy, but it can often result in a fairly stiff, predictable performance unless used with a certain amount of intelligence. I prefer working with live acoustic performances as opposed to loops and samples. The subtle variations in dynamics and phrasing give a recording its unique quality. I try to preserve what makes a performance uniquely human, using digital tools to enhance where needed. I've found that by first analyzing the way a particular musician interprets a rhythm, I can maintain their feel but put the track in perfect time.

Could you give us an example?

On the album *Crossing the Line* with writer/producer Bill Cutler, we had to restore a number of songs that were recorded back in 1973. The tracks were not sonically up to date, and the performances were rhythmically inconsistent. We were very nervous about completely quantizing the performances for fear of them sounding too mechanical. I spent some time looking closely at just how the musicians interpreted the grooves, and I ended up regioning out the audio to maintain the feel, while cleaning up the tempo. The results were fantastic, nearly identical to the original 30-year-old performances in terms of groove, only much tighter. It now sounds like a bunch of New York's finest session players. The process takes more time than most people are willing to spend, however. A five-minute drum track took about 13 hours of nonstop editing…and each song averaged 30–40 tracks, all of which needed to be "fixed" in order to maintain synchronization. As you know, it's easy to lose track of time in the studio!

Do you use any DAW timesaving tools?

Well, ironically, I did that project a few months before Beat Detective was part of Pro Tools, so I had to do it manually—but as a Pro Tools user, it's hard to avoid using Beat Detective and Sound Replacer to modify performances. They have a lot of features that make the process of manipulating audio very fast and flexible.

Is there a limit to how tight you should make a track using tools like Beat Detective?

Yeah, Beat Detective is especially cool, but I can see that it could be overused or abused simply because of how easy it is to use. Some great drummers instinctually play around the beat just a tiny bit, to create their unique feel. For instance on beat 2, they may hit the snare 10ms before the beat, and on beat 4, they may lay the snare hit back a few milliseconds. This gives the song its own fluid groove. Quantize that out and you lose the feel of the song.

So like any tool, you've got to use it responsibly.

Right. I like to look at keeping what makes the original performance unique, and just enhance it a bit, as necessary. Those minute changes that are played from verse to verse, even bar to bar, give breath and shape to a performance. If you let the computer make all the decisions on cleanup, you'll probably lose the spirit of the performance.

Bryan Carlstrom's Filter Farm

Producer/engineer Bryan Carlstrom has worked with high-profile artists such as the Offspring, Rob Zombie, Alice in Chains, Social Distortion, Poe, PIL, Stabbing Westward, Billy Idol, Goldfinger, and Spinal Tap. He spent a number of years collaborating with well-known producer Dave Jerden at Burbank's El Dorado Studios. An accomplished musician, Bryan found the studio to be the perfect nexus of his love for music and technology. He has built a well-equipped overdub facility in his home. Check his studio out at www.bryancarlstrom.com.

Any new toys that have found their way into your studio?

I'm always looking for ways to give a song a unique, memorable sound. Analog filters, the kind used on early synthesizers (think ARP and Oberheim), are my newest toys.

How do you use them?

I've been working lately with a new band called Level, and I find myself using the filter on quite a few instruments. The one I'm using now is called Filter Queen from Electrix [www.electrixpro.com]. For instance, if I record ambient room mics during basic tracks, when I get back home, I'll keep the original tracks (L-R) and rerecord the two channels onto two new tracks, running them through the Filter Queen. It's stereo in and out. You can do amazing sweeps and mods using the on-board low-frequency oscillators (LFOs). I especially like it on background vocals, guitars…anything that you want to tweak into an entirely new and unique sound. Electrix also makes a product called the Repeater that is the hippest new looping tool on the market. Definitely worth checking out.

How much effect do you use?

With many effects, too much of a good thing can sound bad, but with keyboard filters, the sky's the limit. I may use it subtly to add some texture to a particular track. For instance, on a "vibey"-type song, I might use it on the background vocals or drums, where there's some space in the track. Sometimes, I'll blend the dry, original signal with the filtered track, and other times I'll use the effects only. Or I may just go for it and play the filter like a musical instrument, overdubbing the effect onto the track.

How do you interface the filters?

The Filter Queen comes with stereo ¼-inch jacks that will work with either –10 or +4dB level. I've even mixed in some beats from vinyl using its RCA phono inputs. It's really flexible. Best of all, I got mine at a music store for about the cost of a decent stomp box.

Pushing the Envelope with Digital Console Technology

Aaron Reiff is a staff engineer at George Lucas's Skywalker Sound in Marin County, California. Skywalker hosts a wide range of eclectic sessions from 90-piece orchestras performing the latest soundtrack for a blockbuster movie to chamber music by the Kronos Quartet, with plenty of rock and jazz dates mixed in.

How do you use a digital console to "tweak" a mic input or tape track?

What I like to do is take a microphone and multiplex it into three channels in a digital console. [*Note:* Multiplexing refers to sending a signal to multiple locations simultaneously via a patch bay.] Then I crossover each channel, so that the first channel is low frequencies, the second channel is mid-range, and the third channel is high frequencies. So I basically EQ or filter it so I have only those bandwidths on each channel.

You can do this on any digital console, instead of EQ on a vocal channel or other critical track. If you want to get more presence or more depth, you can delay the mid-range just by a few milliseconds. This gives a totally different character to the sound.

You've used this technique primarily on vocals?

It works on everything.

Tell us about a particular session where you did this.

I just used it on a session I'm doing with a composer named Jim Barrenholt, and the project is titled *Psalms of Ra*. It's an acoustic set of neo-ancient music. So there's a lot of chanting vocals, a lot of hymn-type singing, a lot of old Egyptian text. Since it is all acoustic, it's given me some room to create interesting textures.

I was able to experiment with the vocals to get different sounds because we're trying to re-create textures you might hear chanting or singing inside a pyramid, so this is one of the tricks I used to do that.

What particular console and mic did you use?

The console was a Euphonix System 5, which I really like, and an AKG C 12 microphone. I like the System 5's high sample rates and the clarity that 24/96 offers, especially for acoustic music, room decay, and intricate sonic details. If you're tracking a rock band and close miking the instruments, you probably won't notice a big difference going to 24/96, but on a project like *Psalms of Ra*, it makes all the difference.

Taming the Digital Audio File-Format Jungle

Walk into any recording session today and you're likely to see three or four computers chugging away. One may be crunching digital audio files, another burning a CD copy, and a third, uploading an MP3 version of a rough mix to the band's Web site. When it comes to silicon sessions, computers are here to stay! Mary Ann Zahorsky discusses simple ways to harness the power of a computer to make life in the studio a bit more manageable.

Mary Ann Zahorsky is a freelance engineer who has worked on projects ranging from Wayne Wallace's Afro-Cuban jazz, Michael Bolton, MC Hammer, and Mark Twain's Grammy award–nominated spoken-word album *The Diaries of Adam & Eve*, to television post work on many popular ad campaigns.

What tools do you use to address the technical challenges created by the increasingly common use of computers and digital technology in the recording studio?

I'm not a gear hog and I love analog, but most of my clients like to work in Pro Tools and ADATs these days. A solution I've come upon is a conversion program that's really useful when people come into the studio with all kinds of different formats and unrecognizable digital audio files. It's called Barbabatch, made by Audio Ease, and it will identify and convert a digital file to any format I might need.

What do you like best about Barbabatch?

One thing that is prevalent in the recording business is that people often ship tapes that aren't well labeled. It's difficult sometimes to do something productive with the material that clients bring in. In the digital realm, many aren't sure how to label their material—they don't know what it is they're using, or what format or sampling rate, for example, and sometimes they're using a PC platform, sometimes a Mac platform. With Barbabatch, I don't even have to process the sound file. The program will at least identify it for me, then give me options for what I want to do with it.

What other equipment do you use with Barbabatch?

I'm usually bringing the material into Pro Tools to do something with it, to work with it from there. In the worst-case scenario with unidentified audio files, I just convert a file to analog, then convert it back to digital in the format I need. With Barbabatch I don't have to do all the conversion back and forth, avoiding the generation loss that would happen in the process.

How is Barbabatch different from other conversion options?

If I know that something is going to another format I can do a bounce and convert it from Pro Tools, for instance, but I have to do it one sound file at a time. Barbabatch allows me to open and grab as many files as I want, change the suffix on them, then convert them all at once—thus the "batch" in Barbabatch.

Can you think of a specific project where this tool was particularly useful?

I've done a lot of interesting music projects with it, but most recently I've done some strange stuff for Internet and Web distribution. One client came in with material they needed in a ridiculously small format (for audio quality) so it would upload fast for an interactive Web page. Since Barbabatch allows the engineer to customize formats, you have choices beyond the preset formats. You still get those preset formats, but you can customize and tweak them even further. With a lot of experimenting, I was able to compromise the bit resolution and find something that would function well for the Web page and still sound good.

For more information on the latest version of Barbabatch, go to www.audioease.com.

Laptops Make Studio Life Easier

P aul Klingberg is a Los Angeles–based producer, engineer, and 5.1 surround pioneer. His credits include work with such diverse artists as Earth, Wind & Fire, Cher, Jonathan Butler, Foreigner, Cheap Trick, El DeBarge, and Emerson, Lake & Palmer. Along with his 15 years of studio work, Paul is an accomplished musician and composer whose music has been featured in many film and multimedia projects. I originally spoke with him in 2001 when he was using an Apple PowerBook. However, the interview below updates his approach to integrating his laptop into his production and engineering work.

What computer tools do you use in the studio?

I, like so many people in the music business, have used Macintosh computers since the mid-1980s. For many years now I have traveled from studio to studio with my Apple laptop. I recently retired my PowerBook 3400. Now, I'm using a G4 iBook. It is a wonderful organizational and utility tool for my session work.

In the studio I have immediate Internet access, since all the studios I work in are Wi-Fi enabled. I no longer keep any audio software on my iBook. [Klingberg previously ran versions of Digital Performer and Pro Tools on his PowerBook.] The iBook is strictly a tool for Web and mail access, video conferencing—iChat is *great* for this!—and access to my business Web server, budgets, invoicing, and word processing.

Which audio tools or programs do you use most with your projects?

As far as audio software goes, the cool thing I do now is utilize an additional hard drive I call "Transport OS." Mac OS X let's you make an *exact*, fully bootable clone of any hard drive. I clone my main system drive on my G4 in my studio to my Transport OS FireWire drive. That way, I have an exact copy of my system and all my software, and can use it to boot up off of at any other studio with Pro Tools, Digital Performer, or Logic. All my software and configurations are there. It works great! This makes a great strategy for essential backups too.

Because pretty much all the studios I work in now have Pro Tools, all I take with me is my iBook, my Transport OS drive, and usually a data drive to record audio to. It all fits in a nice little case—although I usually have to take my speakers too. I can't work without my PMCs!

What about database software?

For my laptop in the studio, I still use the custom databases I have created using Filemaker Pro. I have used FM Pro for many years now and have gotten pretty good at some quite complex database designs that are specific to my studio work.

When starting a new project that I will be working on for some length of time, I'll create a database with all the songs that are to be recorded. I can then use that database to follow the progress in the tracking, overdubbing, and mixing. It's a good way to keep organized and manage all the details on a big project.

Can you think of specific projects where you've used this organizing system?

I have worked for the group Earth, Wind & Fire for many years, including working on quite a bit of reissue material for the band. I have built a large database catalog of all the group's albums and song titles, detailing information such as versions of songs that may have appeared on different records, awards, and sales figures. I have lists and contents of all the original tapes and even the record company bar code numbers they use for storage and archive, all of which is helpful as I remix some of their classic albums in 5.1 for DVD-Audio or SACD.

I also have designed a FM Pro cue sheet for working on a film, created another that does my own custom tape box labels, and, most importantly, a database for assembling a project budget.

Any other favorite uses for your iBook?

It's essential for e-mailing rough mixes in MP3 format. It's great for sending an update to an artist who is on the road or to a label executive in New York or Los Angeles. It's a great advance over having to make a dub and ship it across country overnight.

See the article on Paul's remix of the early Chicago albums to learn more about his preferred PMC monitors.

Bruce Swedien on the "Attack Wall"

Legendary producer/engineer Bruce Swedien is a 13-time Grammy award–winner whose credits include projects with artists such as Michael Jackson, Quincy Jones, Burt Bacharach, and Paul McCartney.

How did you find out about and acquire Acoustic Sciences Corporation's Attack Wall?

I was introduced to the Attack Wall about three or four years ago, when my old pal Arthur Noxon, the brains behind the studio tube traps that are the basis for the Attack Wall, brought one down to me and set it up in my studio. Basically, it is a group of various size traps that go around the perimeter of the recording desk. There are two sides to a tube trap—a reflective live side and an absorptive dead side. With the Attack Wall, it's the absorptive side that faces in. You put them as close as you can and all the way around the desk, and even behind your mixing environment, if you have the space.

I couldn't wait to hear what this Attack Wall would do for my listening environment, so I got out a couple of the mixes I've made over the years that I'm very familiar with. As I listened, I was absolutely amazed to hear, and in my mind's eye, to see, microphone positions in the stereo panorama that I hadn't seen in decades—I had maybe never heard these mixes as well as with the Attack Wall. I was absolutely knocked out; just floored. I ordered an Attack Wall right there, and it's been a part of my studio world ever since.

What exactly does the Attack Wall do?

In a recording or mixing situation, it provides a listening environment free of early reflections. [See Bob Skye's article, "Tips on Studio Acoustics," for more information about the importance of eliminating early reflection in your control room.] Early reflections in a music-mixing situation are definitely detrimental to stereo imaging—they blur and obscure lots of detail that might exist in the original recorded sound field. Conversely, late reflections, if they are a bit on the quiet side and very diffused, are valuable in a mixing room, because they enhance stereo imaging and the musical transparency. Here's the deal—with the Attack Wall, the sound from the speakers that escapes over the Attack Wall splashes back and forth between the bright side of the traps and the walls of the control room. What that does is, it creates kind of a very low-level, wonderful, diffused backfill that is very enjoyable. As long as you remove those early reflections from the image, the detail is astounding.

What do you like most about the Attack Wall?

I love the fact that, with the Attack Wall, the sound from the speakers is so focused and so powerful. Inside the Attack Wall with my Westlake speakers, you can discern minute degrees of left/right positioning. It gives me a feeling of security that I don't find in an ordinary mixing situation.

For more information on tube traps and the Attack Wall, check out www.tubetrap.com.

Favorite Pro "Tools"

During her career, Leann Ungar has worked with artists such as Laurie Anderson, Fishbone, Ray Charles, Leonard Cohen, Paul Winter, and Carlene Carter. She is now teaching in the Music Production and Engineering Department at Berklee College of Music in Boston.

Although I have more than 25 years of experience as an audio engineer, I'm fairly new to Pro Tools. But I have a few pet tools I use that I've really enjoyed.

The first is to duplicate the playlist. I can do several versions of a comp, maybe a solo or a vocal, each with a different playlist name. Then, it's really easy to audition the versions on the same fader with the same effects and plug-ins across it, just by calling up the different names.

I use the Waves Renaissance Compressor in an unusual way. I discovered that if you set the ratio for something lower than 1:1, for instance 0.85:1, it expands rather than compresses. This was really useful to me on a record I was mixing where I was hearing too much vocal compression on the initial recording. By automating the compression ratio, I was able to compress the quiet verses, then when the louder choruses hit, I changed to the expand mode to get some life back into the squashed moments. I was left with some overall level differences between verse and chorus, so I just brought up the verses with the fader.

Finally, automating the EQ. I had a sibilant vocal and no de-esser. But on Pro Tools, it's really easy to isolate an "s" by looking at the waveform. So I put a Focusrite in bypass across the channel. I found the sibilant frequency at 4.3k. I put the Q to the tiniest band and notched it out 10dB. Then when I found a bad "s," I turned on the EQ for just that moment with the automation. In the mix, the vocal then went to a Manley Pultec with the high end being boosted and a very wide bandwidth. This brought back just enough "s" to make it sound very natural.

Kyma Opens Up New Horizons

After working in the audio post business in San Francisco for ten years, Randy Bobo moved to Milwaukee in 1991 to open Independent Studios, which specializes in audio postproduction for television, radio, and film, original music composition and sound design. His credits include *Mystic Lands* for the Discovery Channel, the *American Portrait* series for PBS, and thousands of television and radio commercials.

I use a rather odd piece of equipment called Kyma, made by Symbolic Sound. It's a sound design tool that can be virtually anything you want, which makes it very flexible and initially challenges you with a fairly steep learning curve.

The hardware is basically a slab of DSP. You use the Kyma software and a Mac to design the sounds either from scratch or by using samples. You can do any type of synthesis you want—analog, FM, additive, subtractive. Any of the classic kinds of synthesis can be used, either separately or combined.

You can't do everything in the Kyma. At first, I thought it might be a replacement for a whole workstation, but it's really not meant to be that. But you can take any sound you can think of and have it be either the sound or a modifier to another sound. For example, you can have a sample drum loop and modulate a voice with that drum loop or you can have the drums play the voice.

We use the Kyma for specialty effects. For instance: morphing, which is pretty straightforward. Through morphing, take one sound and change it into another sound, with total control of the speed and amount that it changes. You can go from a baby crying to a siren, for example, over the course of a couple seconds. And you can stop anywhere in between. What's happening is that it's a resynthesis system, so you take the sound of a baby crying and you analyze it and turn the sound into a controller so that you're controlling a group of oscillators that make the sound, based on the waveform of the baby's cry. What you're actually hearing is not a sample of the baby's cry, but this group of 50 to 100 oscillators imitating it.

Once you've established that control, then you go through the same process with the sound you're going to morph to. You have these two sets of instructions of how to control this group of oscillators, and basically you move between the two, because it's digitally controlled. You can go anywhere in between the two sounds and come up with a sound that's half baby and half siren and use that.

Morphing is just one tiny thing it can do. We've used it mostly in spot production for a specialized effect. The theme of a client's ad campaign this year was the "techno jungle," so we made some sounds that aren't really mechanical and aren't really "jungley"—they're somewhere in between.

There's an art to the Kyma as well as a science, and I'm still learning. Right now we're using it more as a specialty device—not finishing a project in it but making sounds in it and then flying them into other workstations from there.

Part of the reason people have a hard time figuring out what this thing does is that it's so wide open. It's not like a box you buy and twiddle the knobs to get a cool sound—you really have to put some thought into it, but the possibilities really are limitless. It's a very cool piece of software.

For more information on Kyma, visit www.symbolicsound.com.

The Funky Wollensak

om Carr, senior mixer and CD mastering engineer at Digital Audio Production (formerly Music Annex Studios) in Menlo Park, California, has been in the recording industry for more than 25 years. He is best known in the Bay Area for his work on jazz and classical sessions, from solo to large ensemble. Since joining the Annex, he has been recording, mixing, and mastering for a wide range of artists and labels, including Alias Records, Warner Brothers, Windham Hill/BMG Entertainment, Miramax Films, Infinity Broadcasting, and dozens of independent labels.

A couple of things I use are oddities at best. Some time ago in a storage room of Music Annex, I found this really funky, school-library Wollensak mono cassette machine with a built-in amplifier and speaker.

By sending the signal from the tape machine and running it into the input of this Wollensak cassette machine, I get this hellacious, distorted sound on the vocal coming off the Wollensak speaker, then I mic the speaker.

To make the sound even weirder and clangier, I use a 2-foot-long aluminum piece that looks like a megaphone, though I think it used to be a lighting fixture. I put this megaphone in reverse, in front of the Wollensak speaker, and then mic up the small end of the megaphone, bringing that back as the return. It gives the track this type of distortion that makes the vocal sound so tortured. The sound is amazing.

This bizarre-looking setup has been useful when somebody has wanted a vocal that's the "internal thought" part of a song—not that filtered phone line sound, but an out-of-body voice.

The other thing I have that I use on many of my projects is one of the original Model 602 Aphex aural exciters. There are few in existence. I first noticed the Aphex appearing in credits on Linda Ronstadt's albums in the mid-1970s. Those tracks had an amazing shimmer to them. When a friend of mine told me he had one that he wasn't using, I immediately offered to buy it from him.

This old Aphex lifts individual tracks up out of the mix in a way that the newer models don't, in a way that changing the volume or the EQ does not. There's a subtle harmonic distortion and phase shift that makes the vocal seem like it's sitting out just a little ahead of the speakers. It's really cool.

Jim Dean's Studio Jambalaya

Based in the San Francisco Bay Area, Jim Dean has been producing and engineering for more than 20 years. He has worked on several gold- and platinum-selling albums and engineered 11 records that have been nominated for Grammy awards.

I've been taking some of the same projects in a high-tech and low-tech direction. That sounds a little at odds with each other, but I find the results kind of interesting.

I got hooked up to Monster Cable recently, which is high-end audio cable. What's unique to Monster is that they use different types of metals in their cable. Their philosophy is that sound travels through cable at different speeds and that they're therefore time-correcting their cables, in a sense, by having these different types of metal that react to different energy from the different frequencies.

Anyway, during a rehearsal when I had an average bass guitar going through a horrible PA, all I did to improve the sound was replace the cheapo 20-foot cable with a Monster Cable 20-foot guitar cable. The difference was unbelievable.

I switched the cable in my entire rig, which is basically a portable studio. I have a bunch of Neve, Focusrite, and API outboard preamps, and my main goal is to try to get the shortest run of cable and most direct route that I can to my preamps, compressors, and then into Pro Tools. Once I get the signal into Pro Tools, I run things back through all sorts of stuff. My favorite things to use right now are a kid's megaphone that I bought at Toys R Us, a Pro Sound Leslie simulator, and an old Sears Silvertone amplifier.

In my studio setup, I have cords that go from my patch bay out into the walls, and then at the end of those cords are a whole variety of guitar amplifiers. I've got Fender Twins, the Silvertone—which I love to death—and a variety of other amps, including old stereos. I leave microphones up in the rooms, so at almost any time I can take a signal I'm working on, patch it, turn on the amplifier, and bring up a bunch of different mics until I hear something that I like, then rerecord it back in. Or I'll try to get the cleanest signal I can through one of those amplifiers, then run it through my Toys R Us megaphone, and rerecord drums and stuff like that through it. It's really fun. My friends think it's hilarious that I'm using the Monster Cable and great microphones to get the fullest, most technically correct signal possible, but then running the sound through these really cheap toys or old stereos.

I've been using the Silvertone lately for just about anything. If you turn it up to 10, it's the greatest thing you can use on something you want to go over the top with, like a Nine Inch Nails–style vocal.

The Silvertone is all tubes and it's got tremolo, so it's killer when you use it for those real swampy guitar sounds with heavy reverb. But then you can turn the tremolo really slow and it makes a great chorus as well, a vibrato/tremolo-type effect on a vocal. If you mix a dry and a wet signal together, then you get this really ethereal effect that works great on background vocals or even steel guitar.

Chapter 6
Working with Bands

Producing a Band from A–Z

What does it take to produce a record? Los Angeles–based producer and engineer Joe Barresi will take us, from start to finish, through the process of producing a band. Barresi has produced albums for such bands as Queens of the Stone Age, Fu Manchu, L7, and Loudmouth. His engineering credits include Fastball's million-selling album *All the Pain Money Can Buy*, as well as albums for Hole, Veruca Salt, Beth Hart, the Jesus Lizard, and Anthrax.

How do you find new talent and projects to produce?

That all depends. For signed bands, sometimes it's just a matter of working on their previous record in some capacity, either engineering or mixing. You might have gotten along great in the studio, and the band may ask you to be involved on their next record as well.

I also get several tapes from my manager each week. He might know of a band looking for a producer and may think that I could be the right guy for the job, or someone at a record label might approach him because they like a record that I've done.

Many times I just hear a band that I like— a song I've heard on the radio, at a friend's house, or at a club—and approach them (or someone involved with them) about the possibility of working together in the future. On my nights off, I'm usually in a bar checking out bands—signed or unsigned—and if I like them, I go up and introduce myself. Often that leads to a friendship that could eventually turn into a working relationship. I think it's always good to get out and see bands play live because it is that kind of energy that you ultimately try to capture in the studio.

Producer/engineer Joe Barresi is pictured (seated) at LA's Sound City Recording Studios with The Nervous Return (L–R): Shane Gallagher, Greg Gordon, Jason Muller, and Anthony Crouse. Photo by Mr. Bonzai, courtesy of McDonough Management.

After you find a band you like, how do you go about striking a deal with them?

First, there are several meetings and phone conversations regarding what kind of record the band would like to make and what my role will be in achieving that goal. At that point, I would have a pretty good idea of how long and involved the recording process could be. Then I would put together a budget as appropriate. This budget would include such items as studio costs, tape costs, gear rentals, housing/airfare/per diems (if the band isn't local or if we do the record out of town), additional assistance in the form of Pro Tools editing or an additional engineer if necessary, and, of course, the engineering/mixing and production fees. Then the budget would be reviewed and modified by all parties involved—the band, the band's manager, record label A&R, my manager, and I— until we reach an agreement and everyone approves.

What happens next?

Normally, rehearsals and preproduction. Now the actual work begins!

I get the band into a rehearsal studio where we sort through their material and decide how many and which songs to record. There might be 30 or more songs or ideas to listen to, but normally we only record 12 or 13 for the album. Obviously, some material will be stronger than other material, and some songs may be perfect just the way they are. The objective here is to make every song the best it could possibly be before actually going into the recording studio.

I probably have lived with the band's demos for several weeks before preproduction, so I might have an idea about a chorus that isn't as strong as it could be or a song that may need to be shortened or rearranged. We spend a lot of time experimenting and trying out different ideas, both sonically and musically.

We also discuss how to track a song. Should the drummer play to a click? Is the tempo of the song right? Do we cut the band completely live with minimal overdubs, or will there be a lot of things to put on top? At this stage, I'm also trying to make the band feel more comfortable by telling them what to expect when the recording process begins—what kind of schedule we'll need to work with and how things can be done efficiently in the studio while still making it a fun experience.

I also start to get the band's equipment together, making sure that their drums sound great and their guitars and amps are in good working order. I might arrange to rent a few amplifiers or instruments to listen to how that might ultimately have a role in the recording process.

Ideally, you want to get as much work done in the rehearsal studio, where costs are substantially lower than in a recording studio, so that when the time comes to record, you are doing just that.

How long does all this take?

Depending on the band, preproduction is usually a two- to three-week process. Some bands are completely rehearsed and ready to go, and some need a bit more work. In some cases, I've worked with bands in Europe, and I've flown over for only a weekend of preproduction. Afterwards, we continued to send tapes back and forth and call or e-mail each other with suggestions.

Nowadays, it's a different world. With the advent of cheaper and better-quality digital recording equipment, bands can create demos at home that might actually be used in the studio as a final product. The biggest problem I see is that emphasis has been taken off of actual live performances—people playing together in a room at the same time and feeding off each other musically. Songs are put together one instrument at a time, and performances are chopped up and "visually" put in time. Proper use of new technology can be a tremendous benefit, but I think that "feel" is often overlooked.

In the end, it all comes out in the wash. Good songs usually sell. Hopefully you can be a part of taking a band to the next level and making a song into a hit—or at least getting it to a place where other people appreciate and enjoy it as much as you do!

So what usually happens once you get into the studio?

You have a certain amount of time allotted for tracking, and by this time you've probably figured out whether or not the band can play well live.

You set up and cut the basic tracks. You're mostly looking for the drum tracks. The band should play live together so they get that kind of feel, even though you might not keep anything besides the drums.

If the sound I'm looking for requires a larger, more expensive drum room, then I like to record the drums and then go to a smaller studio to do all the other tracking/overdubs and save the band some money.

Sometimes people like to record one song at a time. In that case, you need a studio with a bigger console so you can keep all the instruments set up. You would then finish all the overdubs and vocals on a song, maybe even mix it, then start on the next song. This is usually a longer, more expensive process, although each song usually comes out with its own personality because you're getting a feel for how the album is going to sound in the end. So sometimes it's a cool way to go.

What if you're working with a low budget?

Then you go in and keep as many instruments as you can. You might keep all the rhythm guitars and the bass tracks at the same time you are doing drums, maybe just touching up a few spots with a punch in or two. You might even have the singer do a vocal while you're doing that also. Sometimes a scratch vocal is magical, because the vocalist is not really concerned about having to perform. It's whatever comes out naturally. Often the scratch performance is something you go back and reference, and sometimes even keep.

What if a band doesn't play well once they get into the studio?

You can always go back and fix certain mistakes. For the most part, the way records are made today is piecemeal. You're trying to get the best performance you can from each musician. If a drummer can't play a perfect take from start to finish, then you may do dozens of takes of one song and then edit those takes together.

I like to use a razor blade and actually edit the 2-inch tape, so I might have several reels of tape with three or four takes of a song on each. I pull the best parts from the different takes and splice them together to make the ultimate performance. But nowadays, almost everyone edits with a computer—usually in Pro Tools. They dump all the drums into the computer, fix it up, and then dump it back to tape. Then you overdub each part on top of that drum take until the song is done.

How do you determine which takes are good enough for the album? Does the band help you decide?

If a take is magical, you know it instantly. Otherwise, it's up to the producer and the band to decide. After all, the producer is there to make the best possible record for the band.

Sometimes the studio makes people nervous, so a big part of production is getting everybody to feel comfortable so they're not thinking about red lights and tape rolling. I like to make the studio more like a rehearsal room, where the band is just having fun jamming.

To get this feeling, you might try not wearing headphones while tracking. You bring in little monitors or a PA so it's more like a live setup.

So it's more natural than…

It's more natural than the musicians thinking, "We're spending $1,500 a day and it's taking forever, and I gotta make this right, so if I miss this note…."

Putting everyone at ease is essential. Every situation is a little bit different, but generally you try to make everybody comfortable and to be efficient at the same time. As producer, you're in charge of the budget. If it goes over, you're the first person they scream at.

So on one hand you're trying to make everyone comfortable, and on the other hand, you also have to keep your eye on the time and money?

Exactly. I've pulled the plug in the middle of vocal sessions before. If a singer is having a throat problem, for instance, then I'll just cancel the session and have the singer come back when he or she is fresh. Or if a musician is ill or not up to speed on something, you find ways to work around it so the time you have together is not completely wasted.

You have to make a lot of judgment calls then?

Yes; you don't want the costs of the recording to be exorbitant. If you've got a $100,000 budget and you've already spent $200,000, then someone is going to be very concerned. Plus the band has to pay all this money back eventually. You try to set a feasible budget and keep within it.

If there is a problem, make sure you're in touch with the band's management and the label. Let them know where you are and how things are progressing. Unexpected things do happen. For instance, you may get a drummer who can't play, and you decide that the drums will take seven weeks to record instead of seven days. Obviously, you then have to account for the fact that you'll be several thousand dollars over your budget. You have to make the call: should you bring in a new drummer, or should you work with this drummer, which will require several weeks of editing and cost more money? That's when you balance the checkbook.

As an engineer, you show up and do your job, and no one really complains unless they hate the sounds you're getting. But as a producer, you're in charge of a lot more aspects of the process. You have to make sure that you're getting what you're looking for sonically on tape. You also have to make sure that everybody is happy and performing well and not taking too long. It could be that the studio is not working for your situation, so you need to go somewhere else. You also have time constraints. The label might say, "We need to have this record done in five weeks so we can get it out this summer."

There are many, many factors involved in producing an album. Probably the most important thing is to assess the situation before going into the studio and to work on the areas that need help before they turn into problems that cost a lot of money. Remember the budget. After it has been approved, you are responsible for maintaining it and delivering the best record you can make. Never lose sight of that goal.

What happens after you're done in the studio?

Once you're done recording all the parts, the album needs to be mixed. So you have to figure out if you're going to mix the album yourself or hire an outside mixer. Sometimes it's a good idea to bring in a fresh set of ears to mix the record. Sometimes a label will insist that a certain "name" person they've worked with in the past, or someone who's hot at the moment, mix the record. So you have to incorporate that expense into the budget.

Sometimes you go along to the mix sessions. Other times the hired mixer might not want anybody around, so you send the mixer the tapes and wait to get the final results. Hopefully, you've chosen someone who has the same vision as you do. Or you may actually mix the album yourself. It depends on a lot of factors. Every situation is unique.

Usually, I like to see the album through, even if someone else is mixing it. I like to be there to make comments or suggestions because I've lived with the songs a lot longer than they have.

Mixing a full record normally lasts anywhere from a week to three weeks, depending on the mixer, the budget, how many tracks there are, and generally how much is involved.

How involved is the band in this process?

It really varies. On most albums, the band is usually very involved in the mixing. But if they do use a big-name mixer, then many times—to keep expenses down—they'll just send the tapes and only one or two band members to wherever the album is being mixed.

On some of the records I've done, the band was really involved in the actual mixing. A lot of times, we'll do a fast, manual 24-track mix where the whole band is around the console and every person is assigned a few faders. You have the bass player doing bass rides, the singer riding the vocal, etc. This kind of mixing is a load of fun because every pass is a performance. These days, however, mixing is pretty much automated. A computer remembers the mutes and fader moves that are input, and replays them automatically.

In a typical automated mix scenario, the band doesn't have to sit around the studio all day. They usually just show up when the mix is almost done and make their final comments. Then they can head back to Melrose for some shopping!

What about playing back the mixes on various systems?

Usually you make a DAT or cassette when you're mixing. Actually, these days cassettes are a thing of the past and people are just burning CDs. Then the members of the band and I take a copy to the car or whatever stereo system is handy for a reference. In an ideal situation, you might mix one song a day, take it home for a listen on a familiar system, and then make some changes, if needed, the next day.

It's tough for me when I leave town to mix because I'm so used to the stereo in my car. That's my ultimate mix judge. When I'm in a studio that I'm not familiar with, I really have to rely on monitoring through various sets of speakers. If you can make the mix sound good on a few different pairs, then chances are it will translate into a more familiar environment later.

There's also a process of doing recalls, where a couple weeks later you might decide that a particular song isn't as good as everything else and may need to be remixed or touched up a bit. Modern consoles allow for every button and switch position to be remembered, so one can always get back to the previous mix and proceed from there.

How do you determine the order of the songs? Is it up to the producer?

I think it's collective. Many times, the label likes to get involved in that. They have an idea of what the singles are. They know what kind of record they'd like to hear and what the order of the songs should be.

Normally, you might sort through the songs and figure out what key each song is in. You probably don't want too many songs in the same key bunched together. Also, the band might have played a few of the new songs live, so they might know which ones work well together. But you can always change the song order later, once the album is mastered and sequenced.

Nowadays, you actually do the sequencing in the mastering process. In the old days, you would put all the mixes together on two big reels in a particular order, make copies for the band and for yourself, and then listen to them for continuity and "vibe." You might decide that the flow isn't great and even change the song order several more times before you actually go to mastering. These days, that work gets done during mastering, because the album is put into a computer, where the songs can be cut easily and pasted in a jiffy. You might hate the order a week later and just call the mastering engineer and say, "Switch this song with that one," or, "Put a little more space here."

Ever decide at the last minute that a song needs to be pulled?

Yes—either pulled or recut completely! You might get as far as mastering a song and decide that it's still not together, it's not happening. You might try several mixers, or even a remix, where you send a song to someone else with the intent of letting them have free reign over the entire track, usually keeping only the vocal or a few elements of the original intact. Of course, remixes are another art altogether.

If a song doesn't come together when you've mixed it several times, then it could be you've recorded it completely wrong or the performance just wasn't up to par. I've worked on records where I'm not happy with one song, even after several mixes have been done. So I've had the band recut the song completely—whatever it takes to get to the final result.

Talk a little bit about mastering a band's album. How long does it usually take?

Usually it takes a day for the actual mastering EQ, compression, and processing. You might spend a second day doing the sequencing, crossfades, timing, etc. How involved the mastering is depends on a number of things: how similar the mixes are in frequency content and level, how many edits need to be done on a song (if using parts of several different mixes), and the number of songs on the album. If it's a double record, for instance, it's probably going to take a few more days.

After the initial mastering, there might be a period of a week or two where you've lived with the product and decide that it's either great or you need to make some changes. You either phone in the changes or, if you're using a local mastering place, set up an appointment for a few hours of mastering revisions. Then you might take another CD/DAT home with you and check this new version. If you decide it's still not quite right, then obviously the whole process keeps going until it's correct.

Most mastering is pretty expensive, too—usually several hundred dollars per hour—and it comes out of the recording budget as well.

All this comes out of the same sum of money?

Yes, the recording budget entails everything—the actual recording process, the mixing, the mastering, producer, engineering, and mixer fees, preproduction rehearsals, per diems, airfares, rental cars, housing, tape, cartages to and from rehearsal and the studio, any rental gear you need, and miscellaneous things like broken strings and drum heads.

Is there ever any money left over?

Sometimes, yes, and sometimes, no. A producer's job is to try to maintain a reasonable budget so a band can make a great record and hopefully still be able to put some money in their pockets when it's all over. That doesn't always happen.

These days, it usually takes about eight weeks to set up a record once it's done. There's a period of two months, if you're lucky, where the band is either sitting around until the record is released or trying to get on a tour. Recouping money from a record is pretty difficult for a new band, so touring is a better way of making income.

What's your role in gathering information for the album credits? How involved are you?

For the most part, that's up to the label and the band. Sometimes there is no money for elaborate artwork, so credits are kept to a minimum.

If I have requested a lot of favors during the recording process, I'll say that I need to include a few "thank yous" on the record: "Joe wishes to thank so-and-so, who loaned us all this equipment…." Many times, I don't even see the artwork for the album until it comes out. You just hope that your name is spelled correctly and your credit is the way it should read, instead of in Spanish or something.

When do you get to step away from the project? Are you still involved once the CD is produced?

Once the album is mastered and everyone is perfectly happy with the mastering, then you try to let it go. You might not even think about it again until you buy it or you get an advance copy. You need a break from it for a while. Then you get really excited when you hear it again.

Normally, with most things I work on, I miss the process and the people. I don't really get away from an album even after it's all said and done. I've still got it in my car, listening to the mastering, and either digging it or wishing I'd changed a few things when it was recorded.

You don't have any part in promoting the CD?

That's really up to the label. Although a lot of times if I'm in a store and can't find the album, I'll call the A&R guy and ask, "What's going on here? You can't sell records if you can't buy 'em."

At the same time, you're spreading the word, anyway, because people want to know what you've been working on. If you're excited about something, you're playing it for friends and promoting it that way.

What about parties after the CD comes out?

Record release parties used to a big thing, but they've kind of dwindled down. Sometimes a band will just do a gig and invite whoever worked on the record, family, and friends. It's a nice way to see each other again after the record is done.

Then you start all over?

Yeah, then I'm back into another situation. I might take two or three weeks off between the tracking and the mixing just to clear my head from it and maybe do some preproduction with another band in the interim. For me, it's more like, "This production is done. Now there's an engineering gig here, then there's a mix gig here, then there's another production here." I like breaking up the production with engineering and mixing other stuff.

Would you rather be producing than engineering?

I like both. Normally when I get a gig as a producer, I'm the engineer as well, which is a difficult thing because then I'm doing the work of two people. But it's easier for me to relate what's going on in my head than to tell somebody else how I think it should sound. Producing and engineering an album is like trying to direct a movie and act in it as well.

Session Communication Tips

Fred Guarino is the founder and chief engineer of Tiki Recording in Glen Cove, New York, where he offers audio recording services to clients throughout the New York metro region. As he was putting the finishing touches on a new album for jazz drummer Chico Hamilton, Fred took some time to explain what's involved in making musicians comfortable and creative when they work in his studio.

It's important that the technology of recording not interfere with what the musicians are here to do. I try to make sure I communicate with the artists in their language, not in the technical recording jargon. If musicians have to stretch to understand what I'm talking about, it distracts them from their own performances and communication with one another. You should be musically fluent, so you can communicate with the artists in their language. It is more effective to say, "Let's start at the second chorus," than it is to say, "Let's do it again from 1 minute, 28 seconds into the take."

Similarly, the rhythm of the session, the way it moves forward in time, should be in keeping with the musical rhythm of the piece and the natural energy of the band. I try to be sensitive to the tempo of the music and the rhythmic interaction among the players, especially when we're doing multiple takes or punches. Rollbacks and new takes should fall into that rhythm and not cause disruptive delays.

One tool I use is to chart the song in musical terms as soon as possible. Often, composed music, jazz charts, and lead sheets will have letter indications to mark the natural sections of the piece. From these letters I note the corresponding locate points on my multitrack, and record these numbers on my track sheets. If there aren't letter marks on the actual score, I do the same with logical sections of the piece (intro, verse, chorus, bridge, etc.). Then, during retakes and overdubs, I can quickly go to any location in the piece in a way that makes musical sense to the artists. It's a tremendous help in making musicians comfortable and making sure that the technical work of recording doesn't disrupt the creative work of musical performance.

Learn more about Tiki Recording at www.tikirecording.com.

Studio Virgins:
Tips for Recording Young Bands

New bands appear on the scene all the time, but for many, that first session in a recording studio is a foreign experience. All too often, bands without recording experience come to the studio ill equipped for successful sessions. A little guidance can save time, reduce tension, and minimize shock at bill-paying time.

David Cuetter, an engineer from San Francisco who has played and recorded in countless bands, decided to create his own guidebook to help rookie bands prepare for their studio date. The following checklist, which you may wish to share with the "studio virgins" who appear at your door looking to make their first recording, is excerpted from his guide.

Band's Session Checklist

Preproduction

- Planning is critical. Meet the engineer ahead of time to share your music and your expectations for the sessions.
- Determine the recording format (analog, digital, 24-track, and so on).
- Book enough studio time. It always takes longer than expected.
- Hire side musicians and arrange for rental gear well in advance.
- Prepare a session schedule (transportation, song order, setup, session goals, and so on).
- Practice! There is no substitute for hours spent in the woodshed.
- Get tunes tight and arrangements down cold.
- Whether you use a simple boom box or a personal computer–based recording program, recording rehearsals can reveal flaws in arrangements, overdub options, instrumentation ideas, and so on. Do this at home rather than at studio rates.

Music

- Make multiple copies of lyrics and lead sheets for people in the studio—be sure to include one for your engineer.
- A roadmap of your songs (verse 1, chorus, verse 2, chorus, bridge, and so on) also helps engineers.

Marathon

- Rest up before the sessions. Boozing it up the night before is hardly fair. Eat well and get plenty of sleep.

Tune Up!

- Fix or replace defective equipment. Eliminate all mechanical or electrical problems—cables that buzz, microphonic tubes, rattling parts.
- Tune drums and replace worn heads.
- Set up guitars for good intonation, pickup height, and so on. Pick one reliable tuner and use it for all stringed instruments during the actual session.

Analog or Digital?

- Ask the engineer for his/her recommendation. The vast majority of today's rookies will record to digital, as the cost is much lower than analog. Analog availability, musical style, and your intended uses of the master will all affect the choice that's best for tracking and mixing.

The Big Day

Arrival

- Consult the studio about load-in and setup time.
- Arrive early.
- Leave friends and fans at home—you'll have enough to handle.

Extra! Extra!

- Bring extra strings, drum sticks, drum heads, tuning keys, cables, batteries, and anything else that's likely to break, run down, or give up.

Comfort

- Bring your Linus blanket, lava lamp, or whatever makes you feel at home.
- Dim the lights to cool things down.
- Remember your favorite snacks in case the studio isn't stocked up.

Line of Sight

- Set up in a way that's comfortable for everyone. Within the requirements for mic placement and isolation, try to set up the way you do when you practice or perform.

Testing, Testing

- A good headphone mix is a critical link between everyone in the group. One player may need a particular instrument to be louder than others. Don't settle for a marginal headphone mix. Ask for what you need.

Pump Yourself Up!

- After a few takes, ask for a playback to see if you're headed in the right direction. This will be a rough mix, but it will put everyone on the same page.

Tune!

- Tune often. Let others know you're tuning so that tape doesn't roll.
- If you think there may be a need for pitch shifting or varispeeding the tape, a tuning note recorded to tape at the head of each song can help.
- An audible count-off at the head of each tune is a tremendous help for the engineers!

Break Time

- Take breaks. Grab a soda and relax. You'll return feeling fresh, and you'll play better.

Roughs

- After each session, listen to a cassette or CD-R of rough mixes away from the studio to hear with a fresh perspective. Tell the engineer at the beginning of the session that you'll need roughs at day's end.
- Save *all* rough mixes, CD-R dailies, and so on. One just might become your final.

Mixing

Knobs and Buttons

- Give the engineer plenty of time to get started on the mix alone. (This may take several hours.)
- Once things are set up, offer suggestions and input during the mixing process.

Back Up Your Mixes

- Ask the engineer to make a backup, AKA a safety copy, of completed mixes. Some type of back-up copy is a must.

Label Everything!

- Label and date every tune, take, version, mix, master, and safety. By looking at the tape's labels, can someone figure out what is on it and where to find it? If your master were among piles of tapes, could you identify it?

Picture, Picture

- Listen to the mix as a whole. Does everything fit together? Sure, your bass sound is killer, but how does it sound with the rest of the band? Does the track capture the overall impression you intended for the tune?

Mastering

- Once the mixing is complete, it's time for mastering. In this final creative step, the mastering engineer polishes, refines, and "tightens up" your masters. Good mastering can turn a respectable mix into a great-sounding album.

Want to know more? Try The Musician's Guide to the Recording Studio *by Wayne Wadhams (Schirmer Books, New York, 1990) and magazines like* ReMix, EQ, Electronic Musician, Recording, *and* Mix.

Chapter 7
Session Tips and Techniques

Make the Most of Your Mixes with a Premix Tune-Up

Today's recording technology allows just about any musician to record music using the power of the personal computer and a host of modestly priced software and hardware options. However, when it comes to mixdown, the unused bedroom, apartment living room, garage, or attic offer less than ideal acoustic accuracy. Too often, musicians find out after the fact that problems such as too much or not enough low-frequency information or an imbalance in instrument and vocal levels plague their homemade creations. Unfortunately, few musicians have the luxury of investing in a finely tuned, accurate control room at home.

What's a recording musician to do? Enter San Francisco's innovative Paul Stubblebine Mastering (PSM for short), which now offers a "premix tune-up" service for their home and project studio clients. According to Stubblebine, who began his storied mastering career more than 30 years ago cutting vinyl for CBS Records, "It's a whole new world today when it comes to recording. Artists are able to record, overdub, and mix their entire album without ever leaving their workstation."

The workstation phenomenon provides Stubblebine and his colleagues, mastering engineer Michael Romanowski and audio and DVD authoring whiz John Greenham, the flexibility to open client recording project session files that they term "mixes in progress." Once open, the veteran ears of Stubblebine and company provide an objective assessment of the overall frequency and sonic balance of the mix.

The ears of PSM (L–R): Michael Romanowski, Paul Stubblebine, and John Greenham.

"A lot of musicians are surprised by what they hear when they listen back to their tracks in a really accurate environment," says Romanowski. "They learn what they can do to achieve a better-sounding mix, one that will translate well to a variety of systems, ultimately resulting in a better sounding album."

A recent project highlights the benefits that a mix tune-up can offer. *The Falcon* is a new CD project by members of Alkaline Trio and the Lawrence Arms, two popular indie bands. The musicians recently recorded and mixed the five-song EP (released by Red Scare and available at www.interpunk.com) in between their regular tours, using Pro Tools LE at various home and practice studio environments.

John Greenham continues, "The room(s) they were mixing in did not give them an accurate image of the low frequencies on their recording—so that was the first issue we helped them identify. Second, with the use of plug-ins come potential problems with latency issues." [*Note:* Latency is a very slight delay that may be introduced on a processed track, which can result in a "blurry" sound.]

"During their evaluation session, we were able to use the delay compensation found in Pro Tools HD 6.4 to improve the sound of the tracks by correcting the latencies caused by extensive plug-in use. They headed back to their home studio ready to mix, knowing about the low-frequency problem and with the latency situation greatly improved." In addition to Pro Tools session files, the lads at PSM have provided similar services for projects recorded using Cubase, Digital Performer, Sonar, Nuendo, Logic, and RADAR.

Premix tune-ups fall into two general categories. First, reviewing 2-channel mixes in progress mostly to check instrumental and vocal balances and overall frequency response. Alternatively, musicians may bring in their multitrack session files to be opened up and reviewed closely on the systems in the Magnolia

The Magnolia room at PSM.

and Camellia rooms. Although the second option requires more studio time, the level of sonic accuracy and detail is often very revealing as to how the sounds on an artist's album are fitting together (or not).

Paul Stubblebine pictured in the Camellia room.

Regarding the amount of time necessary for a premix tune-up, a quick Stubblebine states, "Rather than spending our time in mastering working to fix problems that the band may not have heard, after a successful premix tune-up and the resulting corrections, we receive a final mix that allows us to concentrate on polishing the album's overall sound, which results in a much more accurate sound for the artist."

Up-and-coming singer/songwriter Chris Gallagher, who mastered his first self-produced album *Will and Surrender* at PSM is a firm believer in the educational process. One of CD Baby's Top 20–selling artists, he has just finalized his second album for 2005 release by taking advantage of the premix tune-up to improve the sound of his new record. "I'm really glad I had the chance to go over my mixes with Michael [Romanowski] before we locked them in," he comments. "We were able to get our balances and our tones more dialed in…we really ended up with a much better record as a result."

When asked how much time and cost is involved in getting the sound doctors at PSE to provide a mix tune-up, Stubblebine says, "A quick check may take about an hour to open up a couple of session files and check some of the basics, for instance, relative instrument balances and tones, how the low end is translating. It's enough for the recording musicians to find out if they are on the right path. If we're going to review an entire album and help identify things to really clean up the sound, such as dealing with latency problems, then it's more likely to take a day or so."

"With respect to the costs, most premix tune-up session clients actually end up spending roughly the same amount of money overall as clients who don't use the service," according to Stubblebine. "That's because the musicians are usually able to make most of the necessary improvements to their mix back at home, once they learn what needs to be changed."

Mike Romanowski adds, "The difference is readily apparent on the final product. Regardless of the style of music, it will have more impact than many home recorded projects that didn't get a premix evaluation."

If you're one of the tens of thousands of artists working at home on your next CD release, perhaps you, too, should consider a premix tune-up before you press your CDs. "It takes an experienced mastering engineer and an accurate listening room to objectively evaluate your work," Stubblebine concludes. "At the end of the day, this results in a much improved sound, making home recording a more viable way for artists to create successful records."

Check out the PSM Web site (www.paulstubblebine.com). It's loaded with useful information about the art and science of mastering, as well as a primer on high-resolution audio formats.

For more on the artists mentioned, check out www.chrisgallagher.net and www. thefalconisbiggerthanjesus.com.

Session Talkback Tips

Barry Rudolph is a Los Angeles–based recording engineer who has worked with artists such as BBMAK, Enrique Iglesias, Najee, Byron Berline and Sundance, Lynyrd Skynyrd, Beth Hart, Rod Stewart, Pat Benatar, Eloise Laws, and the Corrs, and on the *Mission Impossible 2* soundtrack. He is a contributor to *Mix* magazine and has a wealth of gear info at www.barryrudolph.com.

We spend much of our time discussing specific mics and gear, but sometimes getting a great recording benefits from old-fashioned communications with the artist. Any tricks you use to facilitate open communication in a session?

Yes. Say you're recording a four- or five-piece rock band, everything is close-miked, and they're all playing loud. It can be very difficult when a band member wants to say something to a person in the booth, or even when the band wants to talk to each other, especially with the headphones on and with the mics turned down, because they are close to such loud sound sources compared to a speaking voice.

What I do is put up an omnidirectional microphone and run it into a mic preamp with a lot of gain. Then, I run the mic pre into a compressor and I turn the input all the way up. I turn the output down quite a bit, set a ratio of about 8:1, and set the fastest attack, which is one millisecond, and the slowest release, which is about 10 seconds. Finally, I send the output of the compressor to its own track and feed a little bit of the track into the headphones and the monitor mix in the control room.

What happens is, when nobody is playing and somebody is speaking, the compressor is fully released and the mic gain is really loud. You'll hear amps buzzing and people tapping their feet and everything. As soon as the drummer hits his drum or anybody makes any sound that is louder, the compression clamps quickly and squashes so much—I think the 1176 does 40dB of compression—the output is almost nothing. The compressor I use is the ubiquitous and very sought-after Universal Audio 1176 LN.

When the band is playing, the amount that microphone, via the compressor, is contributing is pretty minimal. It hardly factors into the rest of the sound at all—depending on how loud you monitor it, of course. Do be careful how loud you monitor the output—just enough to make sure they hear each other speaking. If it's too loud you'll hear a pretty horrible sound since it's so squashed.

It's cool, because as soon as everyone stops playing, with the slow release time, you can hear the mic come back up [*Barry imitates sh-h-h-o-o-o-p sound*], and everybody can say, "Oh, man, I messed up," or "I need to tune," or whatever, and you can hear them. Nobody has to take headphones off to hear each other, and I don't have to worry about turning a mic on and off in the control room.

For a tracking day, you can just set and forget. The bands will love it. Everyone keeps their headphones on and they don't have to scream to be heard; they just talk in a normal voice.

You can do one of these mics for each room, too, if you are tracking in separate iso booths. The drums are in their own room. But, usually you can hear the drummer talk in his overheads. Acoustic guitar, you can hear if he's in his own room. I use this technique in the room where the guitar player, bass player, and keyboard player, who is direct anyway, are playing.

What Exactly *Is* Mastering?

In the age of compact discs, digital audio workstations, and 24-bit processing, should mastering still be an essential step in the album production process? What exactly does the mastering engineer do anyway? To find out, we spoke to three talented mastering engineers: Bob Ludwig of Gateway Mastering, Masterdisk's Greg Calbi, and Gary King of the SoundLab at Discmakers.

Ludwig: Mastering is both the last creative process in the making of an album and the first step in the manufacturing process. Its purpose is to maximize the musicality inherent in the mix tape. Once that has been maximized to the artist's, the label's, and mastering engineer's satisfaction, we take off our creative hats, put on our manufacturing hats, and use our knowledge, skill, and craft to make the best transfers possible for CD, cassette, or vinyl manufacturing.

Calbi: Mastering is the last stage of mixing, where the mix is finished in terms of its sonic quality and balance. Part of that is simple assembly, leveling, and turning a group of songs into an album. Part of it is more subtle. The perspective of the mastering engineer is: "Can this mix be improved at all in terms of excitement, clarity, unity, emotion, or whatever?"

King: Mastering, AKA postproduction, should bring things together and provide the final focus for the project. It should maintain the integrity of what the artist has done. While the artist and recording engineer strive to make sure every song sounds its best, the mastering engineer tries to make the entire album sound unified. For example, track 1 may be a little brighter and have more low-end than track 2, making the second track sound weak in comparison. The mastering engineer's task is to even everything out so it flows better. So, if your master needs postproduction, it's not necessarily because there's anything wrong with the recording; it just means it's ready for the next step in the recording/manufacturing process.

What are the advantages of using professional mastering services?

King: Mastering engineers are knowledgeable about each step of the various manufacturing processes and the effects they have on the sound of a recording. A good mastering engineer optimizes the master to address these effects and the limitations of the media or formats. Just as cutting a master on a lathe for vinyl is a true craft, so mastering for digital media is a craft requiring great skill and experience.

Ludwig: It's possible to make a mix so perfect that nothing needs to be done to it. But in 99.9 percent of cases, because of a whole range of variables, there is something that can be done to improve that tape before it goes to manufacturing. Most people who have established careers in mastering have a unique gift. That gift is to hear a raw tape from a studio and imagine how it could sound, and then know what knobs to move to make it sound that way. That doesn't come easily. It may be genetic; you either have it or you don't. Of course, years of experience, listening, and accumulated craft are indispensable. You can't buy a piece of gear that will master the way one of the pros can.

Calbi: Nowadays most good recording engineers can make a clean digital transfer, but they still look to the mastering engineer for a fresh perspective or opinion of the mix. Recording engineers have such a complex job and require so much technical and musical knowledge to get the music on tape that they necessarily are deeply focused on the project they are recording. The mastering engineer has an enormous range of listening experience, a consistent, high-resolution monitoring environment, and the luxury of working without the distractions of a recording session. His or her ear training is very different from that of the recording engineer.

In my 25 years of doing this job, I've met maybe ten engineers who really felt confident enough to say, "Don't touch this mix. It is as good as it can possibly be." Ten engineers out of maybe a thousand. I always try to make a finished master sound so the engineer who recorded and mixed it feels like it really represents his or her work so he or she feels confident using it as a part of their resume, so to speak.

How can people prepare their projects to get the most from mastering?

Calbi: Simplistic as this may sound, you can't be too organized. Make sure every reel is carefully and accurately marked and labeled, that index numbers on CD-Rs or DATs correspond to index numbers on labels, and so on. The basic stages of recording are really important too. Keep every channel as quiet as possible. Don't leave unused mics open. Eliminate ground hums before you record. Keep tape noise to a minimum. The cleaner the signal is, the more the mastering engineer will be able to help.

Ludwig: This is a generalization, but for most engineers I would recommend mixing to ½-inch analog tape at 30IPS. In my experience, the effect of the analog tape actually improves the sound of most mixes. Since that is a generalization, I would recommend that one should mix to digital as well. If at all possible, digital mixes should be done through high-quality, 20-bit converters to a format that will store the information as 20-bit data. [*Note:* at the time of this interview, 20-bit gear was just becoming available. Now, 24-bit resolution is becoming the norm.] If economics are a concern and you are using a major mastering facility, save time in the mastering studio by choosing all your mixes ahead of time and assemble them on one or two timed and sequenced reels. The real point is to master from as close to the original source as possible, to assure there has been no degradation. This is a concern in digital as well as analog, since not all digital copies and transfers are clones. Talk to the mastering studio before mixing to discuss the mix process and help avoid potential problems.

King: I would echo Greg's recommendation to be sure the mixes are as free of noise as possible. Be very careful about minimizing accumulated tape hiss from bouncing and compiling tracks. Use compression on individual tracks to manage undesirable peaks. Compressing the whole mix to tame a single instrument will probably compromise the master. Also pay special attention to eliminating any unwanted distortion in the recording process. Mastering won't undistort the mix.

Finally, I would encourage artists to listen very carefully to all their recordings, and be aware of what's on the tapes before sending them off to be mastered. Many defects that cannot be remedied in mastering can be avoided through care in recording and critical listening throughout the recording process.

For more information on audio mastering, check the links to our contributor's facilities:
www.gatewaymastering.com
www.masterdisk.com
www.discmakers.com

Using the Best of Analog and Digital to Define Your Sound

J immy Douglass's recent projects include such platinum-selling acts as Missy "Misdemeanor" Elliot, Aaliyah, Ludacris, Ginuwine, Lenny Kravitz, Snoop Dogg, and Timbaland. While many of his present successes are occurring in R&B and hip-hop, Douglass spent his early years at the mixing board with rock and pop royalty, including Led Zeppelin, the Rolling Stones, Aretha Franklin, Hall & Oates (check out his work on their classic *Abandoned Luncheonette* album), and Carlos Santana, to name a few.

Have you gone entirely digital in your studio?

Oh, the old analog vs. digital debate! For me it's all a matter of how much you give up, when you give it up, and what you give up. A big part of my sound has been that I'm still pretty stuck in the analog world *because* of the sound—it just seems to be more *there* for some styles, like hip-hop. I still do all my tracking of instruments and even some vocals to a Studer tape machine. For a long time I was just using Pro Tools sparingly, as opposed to diving right into it wholeheartedly and becoming totally digital. Now I go to Pro Tools to continually bounce down vocals and keep the clarity. This way I don't experience the generation loss that I would with analog.

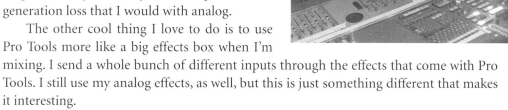

The other cool thing I love to do is to use Pro Tools more like a big effects box when I'm mixing. I send a whole bunch of different inputs through the effects that come with Pro Tools. I still use my analog effects, as well, but this is just something different that makes it interesting.

How did you discover this use for Pro Tools?

As I used Pro Tools more frequently, I got a bunch of plug-ins, and discovered some of the great ones, like guitar amps and stuff. I like AmpFarm (plug-in) for guitar amp simulation, Serato Pitch 'n Time, which is used for pitch and timing correction, and Auto-Tune for tuning instruments. With the direct recording I do, like a sequencer or a guitar through the board when I'm not using an amp, I can actually go through Pro Tools using only the effects and go right to tape. That way, I can have that analog hit again, to give it that old-time sound if I want to. I'd experiment when I was mixing and someone would say, "Hey, that sounds really cool," so I'd leave it in the Pro Tools input and go straight to tape, instead of wasting all that hard drive space.

What do you like about the Pro Tools effects?
Well, there are more of them available and they're definitely cleaner than the analog diehards.

Any other cool tools you use?
The only other thing that I still use to this day is an old TASCAM Portastudio. There's an EQ on it that I guess you would call poor. But you put stuff through it and it just sounds like, well, like it only sounds coming through there. It makes it sound kind of cheap, but it sounds like really classy cheap.

Michael Delugg: Letterman's Music Man

Mixing Music for *The Late Show*

Five nights a week, *The Late Show with David Letterman* offers up original performances by Paul Shaffer's CBS Orchestra and guest appearances by the world's most sought-after musical artists. And five nights a week, the music is mixed to CD quality and sent out over the airwaves to millions of viewers and listeners throughout the world.

Music Production Supervisor Michael Delugg is the man responsible for making all those bands sound as great on television as they do on their albums. A master recording engineer, Delugg's credits include countless television commercials and albums for artists ranging from Whitney Houston and Placido Domingo to Maynard Ferguson, Warren Zevon, Bill Evans, Barry Manilow, and the Stylistics. Now a ten-year veteran of *The Late Show*, Michael spoke to us about getting it right the first time, every day.

Tell us about your role in The Late Show.
We begin setup for each show at 11 A.M. From 2 to 4 P.M., there is a production rehearsal and finally, from 4 to 5 P.M., music setup and, if we're lucky, a full half-hour of music

run-through. At 5 P.M., the audience enters the theater, and at 5:29 we roll tape. After an hour's taping, we wrap the show, and it's on to prep work for the next day's segments.

The show has five audio mixers: sound effects, house PA, stage monitors, music mixer, and production mixer. Feeds from the sound effects mixer and my music mix, along with all dialog and audience microphones and video tape, are handled by the production mixer. Orchestrating all five to work as a unit is a challenge, but we really are a team.

How do you handle mixing different music and artists every day?

The setup for Paul Shaffer and the CBS Orchestra is pretty consistent, and most of my work there is fine-tuning the sound of the band, or covering an extra doubling or a guest soloist. The band is so talented and flexible that Paul encourages a lot of doubling on multiple instruments. The challenge is simply finding enough inputs for all the instruments.

What about guest artists?

I use a setup sheet for guest bands, with a stage floor plan and a mic plug-in chart. The band's production person and I review the physical space first. The show stage is smaller than most bands are accustomed to, and we want them to feel as comfortable and natural as possible. I take the band's stage plot and translate it into something the camera crew can shoot, something I can mix, and something that works for the band so they can hear well and feel right for the performance.

There are visual considerations for the audience and the cameras, acoustic considerations for the audience, acoustic and monitoring considerations for the performers, and audio considerations for the broadcast mix, and a half-hour to rehearse.

Obviously speed and efficiency are important. How is it done?

Planning makes all the difference. I try to study each band's recordings before I get to the theater so I know what I'm going after, the artist's approach or style. If special gear is required, I arrange for it and try it out ahead of time. It's not possible to re-create an artist's recording in our television studio, but in mixing I try to achieve the mood or effect the artist was going for and concentrate on making the song come across.

I roll the 24-track during rehearsal. Capturing all the music is important, and being able to play back a run-through makes problem solving quicker. After the rehearsal, performers frequently listen to a playback, and we can briefly discuss any changes they may want.

What do you do when the band doesn't do in the show what they did in rehearsal?

Sometimes what goes down is not what you rehearsed. But that's part of the excitement of television. Yes, there's pressure, but I like the spontaneity. Having been a musician myself, I keep in mind that the song is what's most important. You try to watch every detail, but when a performer goes off on a special moment, you make the best of the performance first and worry about the ride cymbal EQ later.

It must be frustrating to have so little time to prepare a show.

Dave Letterman sets a very high standard for this show. If we were in a recording studio instead of a television studio, and if I didn't have to worry about the PA cluster over the stage, and if we had more rehearsal time, etc., etc., etc., I could do a lot more. But we have what we have and the challenge is to make it work with what you have. That's what I enjoy.

To sample some of Mike's finest moments, pick up a copy of the 1997 Reprise album, *Live on Letterman—Music from the Late Show*, featuring 14 of the show's most notable performances, including such artists as Dave Matthews, Elvis Costello, R.E.M., Lou Reed, Lenny Kravitz, Van Morrison, and many more. It's well worth the price of admission.

Tools of Letterman's Music Man

I'm fortunate to have a well-equipped control room, with an SSL 6000 Series console and a Sony 3324 digital multitrack recorder, so I can handle a lot of situations. Microphones are a big part of my tool bag. We try to make the technology as unobtrusive as possible on the set, but I still use many standard studio microphones.

For bands, I like Shure stage mics, like the SM 57 and SM 58, and their Beta 57s, 58s, and 87s are terrific. Audix also makes some wonderful mics, like the OM6, which is a great lead vocal tool. I tend to use more EQ on it than I'm normally used to, but it has a really nice, rich sound.

The Audix D 4 is a beautiful instrument microphone. Lately, I have enjoyed using several of the Audio-Technica 4000 series microphones. I love the 4050, and I've used the smaller capsule 4033 very successfully on a number of artists recently.

Elliot Scheiner on Vocal Mics

Multiple Grammy-award winner, engineer, and producer Elliot Scheiner's list of credits reads like a Who's Who of superstars. Credits include blockbuster hits such as: the Eagles' blockbuster live album, *Hell Freezes Over*; Steely Dan's historic *Aja, Gaucho,* and *Two Against Nature* recordings, and work with Jimmy Buffett, Bruce Hornsby, Woodstock '94, Glenn Frey, Manhattan Transfer, Toto, B.B. King, George Benson, Ricki Lee Jones, Dr. John, Smokey Robinson, Big Bad Voodoo Daddy, Natalie Cole, Faith Hill, Van Morrison, and Frank Sinatra. (See also page 111 in Chapter 4, "Microphone Magic.")

What is your favorite vocal mic?

The AKG C 12 (a vintage tube microphone).

Where do you normally place the mic when you are cutting a vocal track?

I place the mic about 3 to 6 inches away from the singer, a little above mouth level…so the bottom of the mic capsule is on a line with the upper lip. I never use a windscreen, so it definitely helps if the singer knows how to work the mic.

Do you use any signal processing when recording vocals?

None at all. I cut it completely flat with no EQ or compression. Then I can work with the performance later with respect to any signal processing it may require.

Some of our readers may not have a C 12, U 67, or other vintage microphone. Any current mics that you have used with good results?

Sometimes when I go to a home or project studio, we'll use an AKG 414. It's a pretty bright mic, which is great, especially if you're recording flat like I do.

Any other suggestions for working with a vocalist to get the best possible performance on tape?

When I'm working as a producer/engineer, I always try to encourage the singer… even if it's not the perfect take. I try not to interrupt to point out small problems, unless they keep recurring in the same place each take. I want them to give me their best performance and lay down four or five passes on separate tracks. Then as we get closer and closer to the final take, I'll begin to print over the earlier takes unless they were very good. The biggest thing I've learned is to remain positive throughout and help them to put their very best onto the tape.

Neill King on Drum Miking

Producer/engineer Neill King is best known for his work on the multiplatinum 1994 CD *Dookie* for Green Day, which set the bar high for every pop and punk band in the mid-1990s. He also recorded three albums with Elvis Costello, along with recordings for Rancid, Nick Lowe, the Buzzcocks, John Hiatt, All-Star United, Primus, the Smiths, Dance Hall Crashers, Jimmy Eat World, Dada, Gob, and En Vogue. He produced three albums for British sensation Menswear. Neill runs his own indie label, Fearless Urge Records. He shared some of his drum recording techniques while at Fantasy Studios in Berkeley, California, where he was preparing to start his second album with the Northern California band, Mother Hips.

How would you characterize the sound of drums on records today?

Over the last five years, drums have taken on a more open, ambient sound and I think that's been good. The 1980s had a lot of records that featured a very tight, very controlled drum sound—a huge kick and snare with some other drums added in. Nowadays, many bands want a more natural sound.

How do you approach drum recording with a new band?

After I have reviewed the material, I try to meet the band in person at a concert or gig to get a feel for their playing style. From my point of view, the sound of the drums really comes from each individual player. Sometimes, I'll recommend we bring in a new kit for the sessions—one with new heads, a new pedal, and cymbals that haven't taken a beating on the road. I just completed an album with Age of Electric (released in May 1996 on Mercury) and we were fortunate to have a well-maintained vintage Ludwig kit in the studio. It sounded great! And the band's drum tech was a collector, so we had the luxury of choosing from a few different snares for each track.

What mics do you prefer for drums?

I like to take a pair of AKG C 12s and position them as overheads, equidistant from the center of the snare drum to minimize any phase differences. Then, before I bring up any other mics, I'll listen to the drummer with just those two. The C 12s are unique in their ability to capture the sound of the entire kit—even the kick drum. After listening a bit, I'll see what's missing and use close mics to fill out the overall drum sound as needed.

It's a bit different than starting with the kick and snare and then adding in the toms, hi-hat, and overheads. The sound is more of an entire drum kit rather than a lot of individual drums each being struck.

Besides the C 12s, what other mics do you use?

Well, a Shure SM 57 seems to work consistently well on the snare. I use the Neumann KM 84 on the hi-hat and sometimes under the snare if it needs a bit more snap. AKG 414s are great on toms with the −20dB pad—and for the kick, I'll try a Neumann FET 47, which I may augment with a Sennheiser 421 if I want a little different tone. One other very important point is to make certain you don't have any problems with phase cancellation, as that can definitely ruin your drum sound.

How big a part does the room play in the drum sound?

That depends on the sound the band is going for, but in general, live rooms are more popular today because the overall sound of the kit has a chance to breathe. The drums tend to have a bit more character, as well, rather than the same old snare drum sound or drum sample. Sometimes it helps to run a pair of smooth-sounding condenser mics, like a Neumann U 67 or M 49, off in a corner to add even more ambience to the drums. I guess capturing that character, the overall sound and energy a drummer produces—that's what's important to me when I'm recording drums.

Chris Lord-Alge on Guitars

Chris Lord-Alge started his career with an apprenticeship at H&L Studios, in Englewood Cliffs, New Jersey, at the age of 14. He is known for producing or mixing projects for Tina Turner, Eagle Eye Cherry, the Crystal Method, Goo Goo Dolls, Faith Hill, JoDee Messina, Santana, Savage Garden, Keith Richards, Warren Zevon, the Replacements, Sugar Ray, P.O.D., Cowboy Junkies, and Lindsey Buckingham's 1992 Grammy-nominated *Out of the Cradle*.

Can you share some techniques for getting the best sound from electric guitars?

You want the guitar player to get the sound he or she wants. I find smaller amps are easier to control and have a more personal sound than big racks and 4 × 12 cabinets. There's a special tone with amps that have just one speaker or with little 50-watt amps. At high volume, smaller amplifiers give a bigger sound than big amps most of the time. If you go back to Duane Allman and Eric Clapton on "Layla," they used little amplifiers like Fender Champs, and it sounds pretty damn large.

I like to pick a few amps first, then put some mics in different positions because they will become your equalizer. Usually, I'm close to the amp. I haven't found many advantages to putting the mic far back unless the guy has the amp on absolute stun. If you use a 57, 421, 414, and Telefunken 251, and put those four close to the amp in different positions and bring them up on faders, you'll find they have different EQ curves. So rather than jamming one mic in front of the amp and grabbing the EQ and going, a couple of mics will give you better tone without the EQ and all the phase problems you get when cranking up the EQ.

> At high volume, smaller amplifiers give a bigger sound than big amps most of the time. If you go back to Duane Allman and Eric Clapton on "Layla," they used little amplifiers like Fender Champs, and it sounds pretty damn large.

If you want to get even more esoteric about it, you can try different mic preamps. If you're running multiple mics, you'll want the same mic pre's instead of combining different ones, because that'll give you even more phase problems. Try different ones until you come across the perfect sound.

If I use just one mic, my first choice is a 57. And depending on how spanked or compressed you want the sound, you have an array of compressors. Usually, I start with a Fairchild for guitars, because that's best for something fat and chunky. A UREI LA 3 is my second choice.

Also, you're going to get a better sound recording electric guitars on analog than digital. If you're going digital, you may want to use a bit more compression than normal, maybe dial more low-end because digital is like a clear pane of glass. It's important to make sure the guitars have been set up well, that the intonations are in good shape, so the players are not having a tuning nightmare. A lot of guys run across a problem where they can't keep the guitar in tune and that kills the whole process. The general rule is find one good tuner and use it for all the guitars, bass, and otherwise.

What are some of the problems in recording electric bass?

With bass, people often dive in and EQ the hell out of it. I find the best thing to do is make a good signal chain, starting with a direct box, a mic pre, and a limiter. Get the chain perfect on the direct before you even start screwing around with the EQ.

A problem with bass is that the amp always seems out of phase, no matter how you flip it. That can be affected by how long the cable to the amp is, what type of mic you use, and how it's pointed. You usually want to use the same mic pre on the amp as you do on the direct. It will help your phase problem. A lot of times I'll record with a DI and amp it later because it's more controllable. But if the guy has his rig and doesn't want to do it that way, you have to experiment to get the phase right. Even at that point we'll have a DI and amp, and reamp it again later on a third track. That will fill it out if they're looking for something aggressive.

[*Note:* Reamp allows one to connect +4 level pro gear with high-impedance guitar amplifiers and stomp boxes with no loss of signal. Think of it as a reverse direct box. Its genesis is detailed at http://www.reamp.com/jc/.]

Any suggestions on working with a full band live in the studio?

It's challenging when you have more people wanting to play than the room accommodates. Say a room has two booths and you've got six guys. Then it's like 10, 15 years ago where you had to place the people very carefully because of leakage, which can either be a problem or an advantage. If you've got a drummer and singers and percussion in the same room, those drums are going into everything. You have to be creative on how you gobo [sound baffle] them and how you curtain them off. But there's also an excitement when you have a lot of people in one room with all that leakage. It becomes a big, exciting sound, but the challenge is these people nailing it because of leakage. If the drummer doesn't nail it, you have to do the whole take over. You want background singers to nail it because if you have to fix their part, the leakage goes away, and the sound changes in the middle of the song. And you have to be pretty creative to pack everyone on one 24-track tape when you have six players because you want it spread out.

It's a real challenge whenever you don't have ideal gear. You may only have a handful of decent mics, or a couple of compressors that you want. Or when you go into a place, every amp's humming, and every mic has a buzz. You have to chase down these problems quickly. You don't want to spoil the vibe because musicians won't put up with that for long. They'll lose the vibe and then what's the point?

Recording Vocals with Bob Rock

Probably best known for his spectacular multiplatinum recordings of Metallica (including 2003's best-selling album, *St. Anger*), engineer/producer Bob Rock has been helping bands make great recordings since 1976, working his magic for the likes of Aerosmith, Motley Crüe, David Bowie, Bon Jovi, Bryan Adams, and the Cult.

During a recent (and rare) lull in his hectic schedule, Bob shared some of his tips and thoughts on how he gets the best vocal performance on tape.

Do you have a philosophy of recording vocals?

Recording vocals for me has both a technical and a musical dimension, both of which must be addressed together in all recording projects.

Let's start with the technical dimension. What has 20 years of engineering taught you about recording vocals?

Most people think of getting the right drum sound or of miking the piano as the test of an engineer's skill, but I truly believe that recording vocals is the hardest skill to master in all of recording. It takes a tremendous amount of time to master. Every artist, song, vocal instrument, and environment is different for each recording. I have learned to try to get the cleanest, truest signal to tape. I use little or no EQ, recording essentially flat, and I choose the microphone very carefully.

What microphone do you like to use?

That depends entirely on the situation. I try to select the microphone for each recording that I believe will best suit the character of the singer's vocal sound and the character of the music. Recently I was working on an album with Veruca Salt, which features two female lead vocals. For Nina's voice, I chose a Shure SM 7, and for Louise, a Neumann Tube 47. Each seemed right for the singer and allowed me to create character distinctions between the two. Generally, I look for a mic that has a strong signal but won't peak easily, add a lot of sibilance, or pop too much.

What about signal processing?

Using minimal EQ and compression—watch out for overcompression and sibilance when tracking vocals—I like to record vocals digitally to get the cleanest, quietest track possible. Then, at mix time, the track is always clean and consistent. When it comes to mixing, I try to start with a present sound and go from there. These days I tend to prefer a fairly dry sound. I might add a little AMS Harmonizer to give the track some size, but not too much. I like a little reverb, especially an EMT 250 or a good plate, but again, not too much. After that, placing the vocal in the mix. Other processing is a matter of taste or the style of the band or music. Of course, overcompression, distortion, and other exaggerated processing has its place in modern recording.

Can you discuss the musical dimension of recording vocals?

These days I produce a great deal, and I often present the engineer with some technical challenges in my attempts to help the artists give their best performance. For example, in order to make a singer feel more comfortable, I might have him or her sing in the control room, listening to Auratone speakers instead of headphones. It doesn't make the engineer's life easy, but the point is to help the artist do their best possible work. With today's technology there aren't many problems for which a good engineer can't find solutions. During the tracking I'll do whatever it takes to make the artist feel confident, comfortable, and creative. During the mix I'll use whatever technology I need to make the mixed song sound right. I might use three different compressors at the same time on one track if that's what it takes—other times I won't use any.

What tips can you pass on to singers and bands that are new to the studio?

Make sure you're comfortable with the approach on the vocal and that you are not trying to do something new or unnatural. Be sure you can hear well and don't be afraid to say so if you're having difficulty. Don't be afraid of the sound of your own voice and try not to get frustrated. Most of all, remember that recording is work. Unlike a live performance, no vocalist does it in one take. Almost all good recordings are built from the best parts of many performances. Getting better is simply a matter of hard work.

Greg Goldman on Effects

Greg Goldman's credits include engineering work with the Rolling Stones, the BoDeans, Melissa Etheridge, Bruce Springsteen, Zakk Wylde, Flashlight Brown, Shawn Mullins, the Rembrandts, and three albums with roots rockers, From Good Homes (FGH). He shares his expert tips on effects use, advice on finding a good-sounding recording room, and perspective on the mix engineer's role in doing "whatever serves the song best."

How do you approach using reverb and delay in the studio?

Records are pretty dry and sort of natural sounding right now, so I try to use both reverb and delay to create a sense of space and size for the overall track and to give some separation between the instruments, rather than just putting a lot of reverb on something. As for reverb, I try to use programs with natural-sounding spaces like halls or live chambers. Sometimes I'll use a plate if there is a good one available, but I try to keep everything sounding natural so the instruments stay really present and don't get washed out in the reverb. I try to use room mics as much as possible to create a sense of natural space.

For recording, how do you select a room where you can create natural ambience and not have to add it later?

Wherever it is, whether we're recording in a barn or in somebody's house or in a studio, I try to get a live sounding room that sounds good. You can walk into a room and just sort of know if it feels good. You're looking for a place where everybody feels comfortable—a room that typically has sort of a natural warmth where everybody can hear everybody else. In a place that's real bouncy and not good acoustically, the musicians are going to have a hard time hearing each other, but if you find a place where they're comfortable playing, it's going to sound pretty good for recording. We just finished up an album recorded in a barn for FGH, and it has that great, woody sound.

Any specific examples of delay uses you can share?

Generally I like to use delays to create a sense of space, but sometimes I build a mix around a delay sound to get something creative going. On the new FGH album there is a song called "Cold Mountain" (found on 1998's *From Good Homes* album), and when I was mixing it, I put a delay on the vocal and it gave the track kind of a rolling movement, which gave it some momentum. Once I put the delay on the vocal, then the rest of the mix started coming together and the whole track started moving in a certain way that was really good, really exciting. Another mix where the vocal delay really worked was on a song called "Count On Me," on the BoDeans's (1996 release) *Blend*, where we used this old fashioned–sounding vocal slap sound that influenced the direction of the mix.

How about reverb?

In order for reverb to really make a big impact on a mix, it has to be an open sounding track—so there's room for the ambience. Because if you start putting reverb on a busy track, things get washed out and lose their impact. There's another BoDeans song called "All I Ever Wanted," which is more of a ballad, and it really lent itself to the use of reverb. We used a live chamber, which is a room in which you set up microphones and send the signal to via a pair of loudspeakers. The sound reverberates around the room and is very natural sounding. You can create a great deal of size by using a chamber or reverbs effectively on tracks that aren't too busy.

Any closing thoughts?

There's a lot of experimentation that goes into trying to create the right space in a mix. I think that's what it all boils down to—finding the appropriate space for any given song. With delays, I find it helps to get it in time with the tempo of the track. It helps even if you're using reverb. Just put the reverb predelay (or initial delay) in time with the track. Remember: do whatever serves the song and the track the best. I never want to draw attention to what I'm doing as the mixer. I want people to react by saying, "Wow, what a great song," or "What a great performance." Feel free to try anything, whether it's putting a delay on the snare drum or on the whole kit, even if it seems kind of wild. Ultimately, whatever I do has to be geared to how the song ends up feeling to the listener. There really is no right or wrong.

R&B King Michael Tarsia on Vocals

Although he's recorded it all (jazz, heavy metal, choral, classical), Michael Tarsia's true music love is R&B. The CEO and chief mixer at Philadelphia's legendary Sigma Sound Services, Tarsia is a second-generation recording engineer who built his chops as an assistant engineer during the heyday of the Philly R&B scene. (Sigma Sound was founded by his father, legendary engineer and businessman, Joe Tarsia.)

Now Tarsia has more than 15 gold and platinum records to his credit and has been the engineer of choice for such artists as Patti LaBelle, Hank Williams Jr., Dru Hill, Deniece Williams, and Teddy Pendergrass. He also was called on to engineer the historic soundtrack album that accompanied the release of the seminal documentary, *Standing in the Shadows of Motown*. Tarsia shares some of his insights in making vocal tracks soar.

Tarsia's recent recording and mixing projects have included an album for the O'Jays and a remake of the Rick James song "Fire and Desire," performed by Johnny Gil and Coco, and produced by Gerald Lavert for the soundtrack of *Booty Call*. At the time of this interview, he was working on two reggae projects and Pure Soul's sophomore album.

What tips can you offer on capturing the dynamics and emotion of a lead vocal?

Probably the most common error people make is overcompressing or overlimiting vocal tracks. Besides taking the life out of the performance by squashing its dynamics, an overcompressed track will often exhibit that unpleasant "pumping" effect that can really ruin an otherwise marvelous recording. Generally, I like to put the microphone into one channel of the console, then come out of that channel into the limiter, then out of the limiter into another channel, and then finally out of the second channel to the tape input. That way I can ride the limiter input at a console fader to take advantage of its balancing effect and still preserve the dynamics of the performance.

I never hit the limiter very hard: 3–5dB, tops. And I can monitor meter [input] levels of both the mic channel and the compressor channel at the same time. If the singer is a real artist, sings dynamically, and knows how to use the microphone, it's a shame to take all that away by overuse of a limiter.

How do you change recording techniques to accommodate for different singing styles?

Good singers always make the engineer's job easier. They know how to make technology work for them. But sometimes you encounter a singer who just has to move with the music, or even dance. That's when I consider an omni pattern microphone and carefully place the mic for the most consistent pickup of the vocal performance. Too often, we engineers get locked into a favorite method of doing a particular thing. It's wise to look at every situation and carefully select the microphone, its pickup pattern, its roll off and placement to the voice or instrument, its environment, and the sound you wish to put on tape. Be creative!

What do you do to re-create the setup for a tracking session?

Traditionally, at the end of a session someone wrote down all the settings of all the devices and how they were patched together. But [today's] electronic devices can be deviously inaccurate. Even most modern resettable consoles can't account for the common variability of electronic components inserted in the channel chain. For a vocal tracking job at Sigma, we do more than simply document knob settings. We also use a measured test tone fed through channels with limiters and other devices to document levels at various points using a standard metering setup. That way when we set up for rerecords or revisions, we can reset the exact levels at which the devices were operating, not just the placement of their knobs.

Aside from technological knowledge, what else goes into being a great vocal engineer?

I can't say enough about the importance of studio etiquette in this job. Time and again success comes down to knowing when to speak or not to speak, knowing what to say or what not to say. There are many fine engineers who are masters of the most advanced technology, but without people skills they would just be technicians. I'm not a technical wizard. I'm a knob turner who loves people and good music.

I see recording music like painting. In music, our canvas is sound. Echo and reverb give us depth of field. EQ brings color and panning gives placement. Mixing breathes life into a recording by giving color, definition, and texture to a fine song beautifully performed.

Peter Bombar's Recipe for a Great Drum Sound

Peter Bombar is Chief Engineer of Open Studios in upstate Binghamton, New York. Open Studios has handled recording projects in just about every style imaginable. The two-room facility offers a complete 5.1 surround setup including a 72-input Otari Concept 1 console and Sadie 24/96 workstation, plus a B room running Pro Tools. Peter, whose album credits include work for Atlantic, Megaforce, and Island Records, as well as jazz composer/singer/actress Jacque Tara Washington's critically acclaimed 2000 album *Jazz Passions*, has developed many tricks, not the least of which is maintaining high sonic standards in the face of shrinking budgets. Here, Peter talks about drum recording techniques.

Preproduction is mandatory. I talk with the drummer and listen to him play, really absorb his sound. Knowing ahead of time exactly what you are trying to achieve saves countless headaches come mix time. I also think economically. I learned long ago that with drums, less is more. The more mics you add, the more difficult it is to achieve a good overall sound; mixing challenges increase exponentially.

Overheads are critical. They capture the natural width and dynamics of the kit. I use an old AKG C 422 stereo mic—a personal favorite. Place a good stereo pair or a stereo mic about 6 feet over the snare, oriented to give the whole kit some good air and a nice spread. Listen carefully and invest some time in getting the placement just right.

People assume you need numerous expensive mics to record drums—Neumanns, AKG 414s, and the like. But many good drum mics are not expensive, like SM 57s— dependable snare and tom mics. I love Audio-Technica's A-T M 41 for snares, and the Shure SM 81 is terrific on hi-hat. A-T's 4051 is a good overhead choice, and Rode's NT 3 works well on drums. My favorite for toms is the Beyer M 201. On kick I use the standby AKG D 112, or a favorite modified EV RE 20, transformer bypassed. These are all great, economical mics for recording drums—some priced under $100.

Pick the best mics you have for the job. Work at the placement until you have the sound you want. I try to get the best sound I can with no EQ on the console. In fact, I rarely record the drum kit with EQ, saving that coloring for mix time. If I can't make the drums sound right without EQ, I'm doing something wrong.

Check out Open Studios at www.wskg.com/OpenStudios.htm.

Recording Bands Live with Joe Chiccarelli

I n nearly two decades of recording pop music, engineer/producer Joe Chiccarelli has
seen it all. From the Bee Gees, Oingo Boingo, and Etta James, to Beck, U2, Hole,
Elton John, Kronos Quartet, Ricky Martin, the Verve
Pipe, John Michael Montgomery, Poco, and American
Music Club, Joe's discography reads like a Billboard
chart from virtually any of the past 20 years. He caught
his first break when he was promoted from assistant to
first engineer on Frank Zappa's amazing 1979 *Sheik
Yerbouti* album.

Here, Joe discusses his approach to recording a
band—whether he prefers building a song as a studio
product, or recording a band live, as one would hear
them on stage.

How would you typify your style or approach to recording?

I don't see myself as having a particular profile or style. Every project is unique and
has its own needs or requirements. You absorb what the music is all about and adapt
yourself to that. I never really think about trying to be different. Whether you go for a real
live sound or an up-front, in-your-face sound, I believe it's about being in tune with the
music.

*How do you feel about recording a band live, as opposed to building a song from the rhythm
tracks up?*

Personally, I hate recording things piecemeal, overdubbing every instrument one at a
time. Although some great records have been made that way, most of the time I don't
believe it sounds like music. There is a magic that happens when you have a great band in
a room all playing together and inspiring each other. As an engineer or producer, you try
to capture that magic in the recording.

A big part of what I do is create an environment that makes things work for people to
perform live. It may be something really important—like a good headphone mix or simple things like turning down the lights,
putting an Oriental rug on the floor—
making the physical surroundings more
comfortable. Sometimes it means being
the gregarious person who puts everyone
at ease. Other times it means knowing
when to stay out of the way.

> Personally, I hate recording things piecemeal,
> overdubbing every instrument one at a time. Although
> some great records have been made that way, most of
> the time I don't believe it sounds like music.

What role does technology play in this process?

After doing this for almost 20 years, I've realized that all the microphones and all the technology we use are really BS. The real point is simply the music. The more you can do to make the technology invisible, the better the recording you're going to have. Over the years there have been so many brilliant records made under horrible technical conditions, like in a basement, with one microphone. It's about the performance, not what gear you use to record it.

Maybe the drummer is uncomfortable with 37 mics around, and they're getting in her way and making her self-conscious about every hit. Maybe she'd sound better with one mic on her kick drum and one condenser, compressed, over the whole kit, to give a good, general kit sound. You have to be flexible and adapt to the performers' needs to help them perform their best.

> After doing this for almost 20 years, I've realized that all the microphones and all the technology we use are really BS. The real point is simply the music.

When it comes to vocals, it's really important that the singer has a great headphone mix and likes the way he sounds. An exotic hi-fi mic might be distracting to a singer who is accustomed to hearing his voice on a stage monitor, and thinks he's singing out of tune. Then he'll start to strain, and will sing out of tune. Many times I've recorded singers using stage monitors instead of headphones, and I've even had vocalists sing in the control room while listening to studio monitor speakers. It's better to find an alternative solution than to sacrifice what might have been a great performance. Be sensitive.

How do you deal with leakage if you have no isolation booths or good separation?

If you have to isolate something that is really troublesome, be creative. I've put the bass amp in a bathtub, and even wrapped it in blankets. I've done recordings where we put the guitar amp in the kitchen and the band in the bedroom. Sometimes it's even better to use the leakage creatively. I recently did a jazz album where we couldn't avoid drum leakage in the piano mics. We moved the piano around the room and found a place where the drum leakage was mostly short, early reflections. This actually thickened up the drum sound a bit and was a pleasing effect that didn't compromise the piano track. On cuts where the pianist didn't play, I still left his mics open because it actually helped the drum sound on tape. In the end, I'd rather live with a lot of leakage and get a great performance from the whole band playing together than to have only three play live and overdub the rest later.

How do you help bands that don't have much experience with headphones in studios?

That's a tough problem. Major studios have individual headphone mixers so you can give each player what they are used to hearing. For a home or project studio, a small Mackie-type mixer can serve this purpose. I also work with individual artists, sometimes

EQ'ing to add bass to the phones or compressing to make it sound more like a floor monitor. I've even given keyboard players speakers on their racks so they can move around more comfortably while they're playing.

It's a good idea, right after recording something, to bring the band into the control room to listen to a playback on the big monitors. It will help them understand the differences between what they hear in their headphones and the music that's actually getting to tape. They will relax more when recording.

How do you approach tracking with respect to the mix process?

My philosophy of tracking bands live is that I am mixing while I track. I set up my monitor mix the way I want the record to sound in the end. I've got the finished product in mind while I record, and I print effects right on the tape. I want a sense of direction established for the project right there on the tracking date. It's also inspirational for the band to come into the control room for a playback and have it all there and in place. The closer you can come to the final product, the better they will perform in the studio. Know ahead of time what it is you want to do, and then take all the steps required to get that. It really makes life simple. Thorough preparation gives you the freedom to be spontaneous, creative, responsive, and sensitive to the artists you serve. In the end, it's all about the music.

Chapter 8
Studio Profiles

Pogo Studio: Creating Portraits of Musical Personalities

In America's heartland, midway between Chicago and St. Louis, sit the twin cities of Champaign and Urbana. Word on the street is that outside of Chicago, Champaign-Urbana, home to the University of Illinois, is the hippest place in the Land of Lincoln. Like many communities that host a major university, Champaign-Urbana boasts a wide range of art, culture, nightlife, restaurants, and, as one might expect in such a cosmopolitan atmosphere, a great recording studio.

Pogo Studio started in 1980 when founder Peter Penner pulled together a group of friends with the dream of establishing a recording studio. One of them, Mark Rubel, had a wide-ranging education and varying studio experience as a professional musician. He developed a finely tuned ear while receiving his indoctrination into the recording arts from European-trained tonmeisters and a host of others. Penner wrote a letter to legendary audio pioneer Bill Putnam, Sr., who was born in nearby Danville, Illinois, asking about any used equipment he might offer the fledgling studio. Soon Penner was the proud co-owner of a custom-built 12-channel Universal Audio tube console.

"The board had giant 3-inch Bakelite knobs for gain control," says current proprietor Mark Rubel. "He also sold us ten Universal 175 limiters…for $100 each, as well as giving us original components from the Universal Studios Chicago console he built. He spoiled us, and got us used to superior sounding equipment at a time when it was still affordable. Today this gear is nearly priceless. We still have parts of that console racked up to use, along with one remaining 175 limiter. The sound quality of Bill's designs is beautiful; it's no accident that they are classics and that he is a legend.

Mark Rubel with Pogo's vintage API/DeMedio console.

Pushing the Envelope

It's clear that Mark Rubel is an aficionado of vintage gear, and has amassed an eclectic collection of audio and musical tools to facilitate making great records. In addition to Pogo's treasure trove of unique and vintage gear, Rubel brings a no-nonsense approach to recording that's refreshing in today's "you can fix anything" recording world.

"I'm glad that my development as an audio engineer has paralleled the development of multitrack recording. We started with a 4-track tape machine, and gradually moved up to 8, 16, 24 tracks, and beyond. You learn to take a disciplined and creative approach to recording when you're forced to make the most of a limited set of tools, and it is that much more of a revelation as you acquire new abilities

A fisheye view of Pogo's control room shows the wall-to-wall vintage gear collection.

and technologies. After all, most of the major innovations in multitrack record production have come from trying to push the envelope of what was available at the time. It's a very different process from choosing among the nearly infinite options of digital recording systems."

Although Pogo's list of vintage gear is too long to list completely, its main calling card is a vintage, custom-built API/DeMedio console that was hand-built for Fantasy Records in 1971 and used to record dozens of hits. How does he keep 35-year-old gear in service? "We have very few problems," comments Rubel. "The military and broadcast specifications of the day required equipment to work day in and day out, even in the most difficult circumstances. It's funny, but our new gear is more likely to act up than the older stuff."

One piece of vintage gear that has been replaced with a newer and more reliable unit is the studio's old M79 24-track tape machine. "It sounded fabulous, but was a maintenance nightmare. We now have a 24-track Studer A80 MK IV wide-body," comments Rubel.

Having a mostly vintage-centered studio has benefits, according to Rubel. "The older gear and instruments have unique, identifiable sounds. It's a great investment too—when I keel over face-first onto the console at age 95, hopefully my wife Nancy will actually be able to sell this stuff for more than I paid for it. You can't say that with a DAW…there will never be a vintage market for 16-bit Pro Tools systems, for instance. The vintage gear also helps create the vibe that is such a draw for our studio, and allows people to hear the things that they've seen emulated in software. They soon learn that there is no substitute for the real thing. And of course, during winter, the tubes heat up the control room quite nicely—though once one of our tube compressors started shooting out sparks and smoke!"

The Petting Zoo

Not surprisingly, at this moment, Pogo Studio is advance booked for more than four months. "Pogo has been called 'a petting zoo for musicians.' For instance, we have more than 60 guitars—old Gibsons, Gretsches, Fenders, and a host of other unique and custom-built instruments. We have 20 snare drums, 40 or so vintage amps, and dozens of rare mics including Neumann U 67s, a Telefunken U 47 and a stereo SM 2 tube mic, Altec and Sony tube mics, RCA, and other ribbons. Plus, over 20 classic keyboards: a modular Moog, Wurlitzer, Clavinet, and a Mellotron 400." [*Note:* Remember the haunting flutes at the beginning of the Beatles' "Strawberry Fields Forever?" That's a Mellotron.]

Throw in Pogo's acoustic and electric sitars, timpani, grand piano, Optigan, and steel drums, adding to the total of more than 400 musical devices, and it creates what Rubel calls, "A fun place to experiment. When a musician hears a sound in their head, we most likely have the tools for them to make it real for others to hear. Since we only charge $45 an hour, musicians can afford to come here and try things out," Rubel concludes, "and oddly, the element of charging clients can contribute to the music in that they are compelled to make some choices. How many people do you know who have bought home recording equipment, started 60 songs, and never finish any of them?"

Global Client Base

The modest Rubel fails to note that his chops as an engineer and producer are also a major draw. He has worked with a diverse range of artists ranging from rockers Hum to jazz legend Henry Butler, Jay Bennett of Wilco, and up-and-coming Champaign rock band American Minor, to the late blues genius Luther Allison, for labels including Sony, Capitol, RCA, Warner/Reprise, and Jive/Zomba.

According to Rubel, "We recently made a record with a band from the UK called the Amazing Pilots (www.amazingpilots.com), *Hello My Captor* (Undertow CD-OMC-0026). They recorded here in Champaign, overdubbed in London, and mixed in France. We have also been working with a student-run record label here at the University of Illinois, Green Street Records, who annually put out a compilation of local groups of all kinds, recorded and mixed here at Pogo. The quality and strength of the music scene here is amazing!"

Pogo specializes in diversity, Rubel says, from big band jazz to bluegrass to rock of all kinds. Avant-garde composer Toby Twining has worked with Rubel for decades. "Toby composes stunningly beautiful a cappella vocal music. He incorporates fractals and intervals to create just intonation rather than traditional just temperament. This hypertonal music is on the new frontier of music; it's wonderful to be able to be part of creating something that has not been heard before." You can hear some of Rubel's recording on Twining's album *Chrysalid Requiem* by going to the Cantaloupe Records' Web site and clicking on the "Listen Now" link (www.cantaloupemusic.com/CA21007.html).

Size Matters

Another secret to Pogo's success is what Rubel describes as "our big room—not really, really big like Abbey Road, but big enough for what we do." The main studio is 32 ft. × 20 ft. with a 14-foot ceiling. It features hardwood flooring over regular joists, which Rubel claims produces beneficial coupling "you can feel through your feet," ideal for rock recording, and birch walls for added resonance.

"If you're recording rock in an overly small room, especially drums, it can get congested and boxy sounding—but you can also have a room that's too big, one of those cavernous spaces that don't add enough compression and early reflections. I think the sound of rock 'n' roll partially comes from the sound of vernacular American architecture. It's not an accident that our room size is almost identical to Sun Studios in Memphis; both are standard-sized American industrial buildings from the early twentieth century."

Blending Digital and Analog

How does Pogo integrate digital technology into its modus operandi? "Most of our recording is done on Digital Performer running on a Mac. I use it primarily as a recording and editing device and for volume automation. If you know what to do, and more importantly what *not* to do, in the digital domain, it's a wonderful resource. Rather than using it to obsessively manufacture a recording, it can provide a wonderful way to capture a compelling moment, but to still be able to correct the performance flaws that might compromise it. Digital recording does make many options available, and I like how it speeds the workflow.

"I think the difference between analog and digital recording may be less here than in other facilities, where they may need the recording medium to add a particular sound to enhance their recordings. Given so many wonderful players, instruments, and devices, the best way I have found to make a great-sounding recording has been to create the proper atmosphere, to make a great sound, and capture it well."

Rubel prefers to blend the best of both analog and digital worlds, using the vintage API/DeMedio console as a front end for Digital Performer. "I try to get sounds using careful instrument and mic selection and placement, sending the API mic pre's directly to the A/D converters, and using the rest of the console as a mixing and monitoring device.

> ...the best way I have found to make a great-sounding recording has been to create the proper atmosphere, to make a great sound, and capture it well.

"One thing I do that's a little different from other engineers is to usually use only the API mic preamps. I think it makes for a record with a more cohesive, unified sound. I like records that have an instantly identifiable sonic personality, any of the classic records—whether it's Henry Mancini, Led Zeppelin, the Kinks, or U2.

"I'm on the Grammy Producer's Committee, and we listen to tons of records each year as part of the selection process. The country records sound just like the pop records, which sound just like the rock records, all part of the homogenization of music. I was happy to vote for Tony Visconti as best producer in 2002 for David Bowie's 'Heathen,' because as soon as you hear it, you say, 'It's a Bowie record!'

"I regard music and recording as high arts that have the power to transcend space, time, language, and culture. I strive more towards the opposite of homogenization—a distillation of the essential emotional nature of a person or song. Listeners resonate emotionally to personal expression with integrity, and its lasting power to touch them creates not only better art, but ultimately better commerce, too. There's a reason people will still be listening to Ray Charles records many years from now."

Future Directions

Where does Mark Rubel see Pogo five years from now, when the studio will be celebrating its 30th anniversary? "Hopefully, doing more of the same, only better! To me, creating sonic portraits of musical personalities has to be one of the best jobs in the world. I want to continue to deepen my knowledge of the art of recording. I'm in discussions with a producer manager to help us secure projects that will be more widely heard. I also plan to keep playing in my thrash-oldies band, Captain Rat and the Blind Rivets, which is celebrating its 25th year."

Rubel has been teaching audio at the college level for 20 years now; many of his more than 1,500 students have become audio professionals in their own right. He also teaches music business classes in the Commercial Music program at Millikin University in nearby Decatur. "I regard it as a professional responsibility to try and help others to also establish happy lives doing what they love to do. I've learned so much from so many mentors, from Bill Putnam, Sr. through Les Paul, to my many friends, collaborators, and clients."

Mark Rubel is pictured here with recording pioneer Les Paul. Rubel is in the midst of doing an extensive set of interviews with the 90-year-old genius, discussing his role in the evolution of modern recording.

Between helping musicians to define their own sonic personality and mentoring the next generation of engineers and producers, the diverse talents of Mark Rubel are certain to leave a long and lasting legacy in the world of studio recording and production.

To visit Pogo online, go to http://www.pogostudio.net/.

Pogo Studio Equipment Highlights

Console: API/DeMedio 24 × 16 × 24 × 4, originally built for Fantasy Records, with Audio-Kinetics Mastermix automation

Multitrack Recorders: Studer A80 24-track MK IV wide-body; 3M M79 24-track w/dbx 216 noise reduction; Mac G5 with Digital Performer; (4) ADAT XT and (4) TASCAM DA-series digital tape machines

Mixdown Devices: Studer B67 1/2-track; Apogee Rosetta; TASCAM and Panasonic DATs; Nagra III

Monitor Speakers: Genelec 1031AP; Dunlavy SC-1 with Energy sub; Yamaha NS-10 Studio; Auratone 5C

Microphones: (2) Neumann U 67 tube; Blue/Telefunken U 47; (2) RCA DX 77, (2) Jr. Velocity, (5) BX 5, BX 1; (6) Altec 29 A tube; (2) B+O ribbons; (3) AKG 414; (2) Audio-Technica 4050, 4033, 37; (40) assorted Shure mics of all vintages

Preamps: Manley VoxBox; (9) Universal Audio 1008/1016 tube; (5) Altec 1566 tube; (4) Ampex 350 modified MX-10; (4) Quad 8; RCA tube and solid state preamps

Compressor/Limiters, Gates: Teletronix LA-2A; United Audio 175 tube; (4) UREI 1176LN blackface; (2) UREI LA-3A blackface; UREI LA-4; (3) Gates tube dynamics processors; various Valley People processors; Altec and Collins tube dynamic processors

Equalization: (2) API 550A; (15) 550; (3) API 560B; API 5554; (2) Aengus graphics; Pultec EQ-P1S; Pultec MEQ-5; (2) Lang PEQ-2; dbx 120XP Subharmonic Synthesizer

Musical Instruments: Hammond B-3 with Leslie 142; Modular Moog synthesizer (five-oscillator), Memorymoog Plus, ARP 2600, Pro Soloist, Omni, AXXE and Avatar; Big Briar Theremin; Mellotron 400; Univox string/horn machine; RMI Electra-piano and electric harpsichord; (2) Farfisa Mini-Compact; PAIA modular synth; Optigan with many discs; Lyon & Healy Troubadour Harp; Drunken Fowl, Cellini accordion, and wind machine…to name just a few of the residents of the "Petting Zoo"

Highland Studio

Why would musicians drive two hours south of San Francisco over winding one-lane roads to the top of a mountain to record tracks for their next project? To find out the answer and to get the inside word on how to get a killer acoustic guitar sound, we'll chat with ace acoustic picker, Joe Weed. A talented engineer/ producer as well as an accomplished fiddle, mandolin, and guitar player, Weed's played on hundreds of sessions and leads a number of ensembles on live and studio dates.

Joe Weed didn't start out with the extensive equipment package he operates today. Like a lot of us, he bought his first multitrack, a TASCAM 38, in the mid-1980s "because I wasn't happy with the sound that most engineers got on my acoustic instruments…so I figured I would see what I could do at home." Once bitten by the bug, the 8-track setup grew to a 30 IPS 16-track and so on. In 1990, he decided to go all the way and build his Highland Studio from the ground up.

Today, the studio is equipped with a 32-input TASCAM M2600 console with Steinberg automation. Three ADATs are synched using the Alesis BRC for 24-track digital recording. Macintosh G4s are running Pro Tools for high-resolution hard disc recording and editing. The cornucopia of outboard equipment in the spacious control room ranges from vintage tube compressors and equalizers to the latest Lexicon digital reverb and effect systems. Weed uses UREI 813B monitors with Yamaha power and NS10s for near-field listening.

But beyond the gear, what really sets Highland Studio apart is its beautifully finished tracking room. The room has variable acoustics that can be changed from absorptive to reflective by opening and closing the large two-sided diffusers that line three of the walls. The studio has an oak floor, so each instrument can be carefully placed within the acoustic space that will enhance its sound. You can hear the warmth and resonance in this room—a gorgeous woody sound perfect for recording acoustic instruments.

Unlike a lot of "bomb shelter" studio layouts that have no windows, the view to the west from the control room windows overlooks miles of virgin forest all the way to Santa Cruz and the Monterey Bay eight miles away. When you're listening to a playback, seeing the acres of redwoods and the Pacific waves crashing on the distant beach definitely helps to set the mood.

"Being out in the mountains definitely cuts down on the interruptions and puts artists in the frame of mind to really focus on their playing," he says.

Weed says that about 30 percent of his studio work is for other folks—the rest of the time is booked for his own album and soundtrack projects. He explains, "People come up here to work with me because of the sound I get on their instruments—and because sometimes it's nice to get away from the city to a more peaceful environment, to really concentrate on the music."

Weed still travels to other studios to play on session dates and when he does, he sees things a little bit differently than before he built the studio. The layout, traffic pattern, and all the details really make a difference. Weed says emphatically, "Running a successful studio takes much more than just the right equipment."

Artists often come a long way to work with Weed because of the special sound he captures on tape. So we asked him to share some of his acoustic miking secrets with us. Weed favors Neumann U 89 and KM 84 condenser microphones for acoustic recording. "The U 89s pick up the subtleties of the instrument and don't color the sound the way many other mics do," he states. "And placing the microphone in the 'sweet spot' for each particular instrument is crucial—you just have to experiment by listening to the instrument in the room and moving the mic around until you get the true sound it produces. Some people just stick a mic near the sound hole of an acoustic instrument, but they are missing a lot of the other sound that is being produced."

Weed elaborates on the mic setup for recording his vintage 1953 Martin D-28 flat top guitar. "I place one U 89 aimed toward the sound hole near the body/neck joint; this mic is the primary mic and provides the articulation for the track. The second U 89 is placed between the instrument's bridge and the lower bout, and provides the body and warmth. I record each mic on a separate track so that I have the flexibility to fine-tune the instrument's sound when tracking is completed. This setup makes the instrument much more present and easy to hear in the final mix," he comments.

Weed's Words

- The most important piece of studio equipment is your ears—trust them.

- Don't forget to work on improving your room sound. The finest microphone and digital recorder won't make up for a bad-sounding room.

- My years of experience playing helped me become a better engineer and producer. The more you know about music and instruments, the better.

- Always ask the players on your session how they like the tracks. This shows you value their opinion. Many times I've learned new recording techniques from other musicians.

- Do everything you can to foster a professional, relaxed feeling. Session vibes make or break many recording dates.

Weed's phone keeps ringing with artists who want to get the "Highland sound" on their next project, so look for many more outstanding acoustic albums to come out of the woods of Highland Studio.

Weed's fifth album is titled *The Vultures*, with special guests David Grisman, Todd Phillips, and Norton Buffalo. It features acoustic versions of ten classic instrumentals, including "Green Onions," "Sleepwalk," "Pipeline," and "Wipe Out." Check it out for some sweet acoustic sounds. He's also completed a wonderful tribute album to America's most famous composer, Stephen Foster, titled *Swanee: The Music of Stephen Foster*. The album was completed in 2001 to commemorate the composer's 175th birthday. The album's 16 tunes, performed acoustically by Joe Weed and an all-star lineup, serve as a fitting tribute to Foster.

For more information on recording acoustical instruments, be sure to check out www.highlandpublishing.com, Joe's Web site. Click on the link for Highland Studio and scroll down to the bottom to find a link to his own bluegrass recording newsletter, aptly titled Studio Insider. *It's full of detailed information on how Joe gets his world-famous acoustic sounds at Highland Studio.*

Mitch Easter's Brickhenge Fidelitorium

Producer/engineer Mitch Easter has helped define today's alternative rock sound. His work with artists R.E.M., Suzanne Vega, Game Theory, Velvet Crush, Marshall Crenshaw, and Motocaster is innovative in its straightforward approach—letting the artists' strengths shine through on each album.

Mitch was interviewed at his own studio, Brickhenge Fidelitorium, in North Carolina just prior to his jaunt to Europe to produce a new record. He talked about his studio setup and offered a few tips and observations on making records.

What's the layout of your studio?

The control room is downstairs. I have a few old keyboards in the downstairs hallway we use for overdubbing. We do basic tracks in four upstairs rooms. They're like iso rooms that open up onto a large central hallway. Each musician can set up in their own room, although on the Velvet Crush sessions we're doing now, everybody is in one room so we can avoid using headphones. We can move downstairs for overdubbing when the musicians prefer to play in the control room.

The upstairs rooms have high ceilings and are pretty much square. I bought some tube traps and added some absorptive fiberglass panels to take care of the flutter problem, but the rooms are still slightly live. The hallway is very live, so it can be a pretty effective reverberant space. I can crack the door of a room and pick up the indirect sound of an instrument with another mic to add some space to that track.

You're known for using experimental recording techniques. Could you share some examples?

Well, I have a sort of irreverent attitude, so I've been inclined to do things that were supposed to be wrong. I recently did a record with a band called Motocaster. When I listened to their demo, the drums were amazingly punchy, right in your face. It turned out they had stuck an SM 58 over the drum kit and then run it through a BOSS compressor—one of these stomp boxes guitarists use! So I shamelessly copied their technique and added that to the usual hi-fi multimic setup. That added a fabulous rock 'n' roll smash to the drums. But I've always liked using cheap or ancient, wheezing gear along with the usual pro gear, because I really think the "action" sound comes from musically effective distortion. Sometimes this oddball gear makes a bold sonic statement you just can't get any other way.

Any other favorite "deviant methods" you'd be willing to share?

The Mu-Tron Bi-Phase pedal. For my money, it still sounds better than almost any digital device on the market. I've used a fuzz box on the snare for effect. I like tape delays, for instance a Space Echo, especially if the tape has a little crease in it. It's cool because it has a certain randomness to it that digital delays don't have. I love stuff like that.

Could you pass along any mic tips to our readers?

I love the Shure SM 7 on electric guitar. It's a lot flatter than a 57 with a solid middle. Plus, for tone control, I'll use a second, different mic on the speaker box and experiment with its placement. Also, the Coles 4038, which sounds great on guitar and everything else. Another mic that I love is the EV RE 2000. It's a US-built solid-state condenser mic that sounds great on just about everything. It has a very smooth response with a built-in heater to repel humidity; keeping the humidity constant assures consistent frequency response.

> I've always liked using cheap or ancient, wheezing gear along with the usual pro gear, because I really think the "action" sound comes from musically effective distortion.

Any closing thoughts?

Spend time listening to records. It sounds obvious, but I always hear new things in old and new records that amaze me. The other night I was listening to "Penny Lane" by the Beatles. There are a couple of random snare hits that occur that sound totally different from the rest of the track. It's a wonderful, unique randomness. Another record that impressed me is the first Johnny Winter album on Columbia. It has this big, shameless, thuddy sound. Today, you'd probably filter all that thuddiness out. But the record is still clear; it still grabs you. I'm fascinated by what made that record sound the way it does. All they had to work with was mic technique, a little compression, EQ, and tape delay. Yet that record is awesome. I think about those questions and try to apply some of what I hear to my own recordings.

I aspire to the greatness that those guys got in the 1970s! Records are so much drier (less reverb and echo) now. So I look at what I can do with compression and distortion. You know, four different compressors all have a switch marked 4:1, but each one of those compressors will have a completely different result on an instrument in the 4:1 setting. You have to really know what each tool will do, in order to make the best use of it in a session. Sometimes you actually can use a pumping sound (from a compressor/limiter) to make a track work better.

Brickhenge Fidelitorium Equipment Highlights

Console: 1978 Neve Broadcast console (40 × 16 × 16)

Tape Machines: Lyrec TR532; 3M M-79, M-56, M-64, M-23; MCI JH-110C; (3) ADATs

Outboard Gear: Pultec EQs and MEQs; Neve 2254e and 33314a compressors; UREI 1178; Universal Audio 175; Allison Gain Brains; Gates Sta-Level; dbx 162 and 166 compressors

Effects: EMT plate; Eventide H3000; Lexicon 200; Jam Man; Prime Time; Dynacord DRP 15; DeltaLab Effectron; various tape delays; Ecoplate II

For a virtual tour of the studio, please visit www.fidelitorium.com.

Red Dot Rising in California's Central Valley

In an industrial park about an hour east of San Francisco, a local DJ is spinning wax on a pair of turntables, while engineer Anthony Cole is recording the live mix into Pro Tools. The session will result in a new demo CD for the DJ, once Cole transfers the performance onto a CD-R master. It's another busy day at Red Dot Recording, located in Tracy, California. Once a sleepy farm community in California's Central Valley, Tracy is now a rapidly growing city of more than 70,000, a distant suburb of the San Francisco Bay Area. With the influx of new residents, business has steadily grown for Red Dot owner Chris Holmes. Rising regional artists who frequent the studio include the Megan Slankard Band, Thirst, Sensory Lullaby, and Sol Rebelz.

At the tender age of 15, the recording bug infected Holmes. Through a mutual acquaintance, his band was able to secure a deal on a two-day session at Sausalito's legendary Plant Recording Studios. They worked with an up-and-coming studio assistant named Rob Beaton. (Now based at Los Angeles's RKS Mastering, Beaton's credits include work with the Low Millions, Adam Cohen, Sammy Hagar, Huey Lewis and the News, Todd Rundgren, Buckethead, Heathen, and others.)

Red Dot's Anthony Cole pictured between sessions.

"Rob really taught and inspired me to follow my passion. As I learned from him, I decided to buy my own 8-track and started experimenting with home recording," Holmes states. "Rob next started working for an indie label called 911 Entertainment, which had an in-house studio, so he was engineering and producing all their albums. He brought me in to assist him at the 911 studio. That's where I learned Pro Tools, the API console, vintage mic preamps—the big stuff. When 911 went out of business, there was no way I could go back to my 8-track, so I had no choice but to jump into building a real studio."

Holmes started Red Dot—yes, as in the "Record" button—in the heart of Tracy's downtown four years ago, but about 18 months ago, city plans to redevelop the downtown area led him to the conclusion that Red Dot needed a more musician-friendly location. Holmes consulted with acousticians Scott and Denise Lawton for the new design, which opened just over a year ago. The studio features a spacious 23 ft. × 15 ft. control room, twin iso booths, a main studio with an 11-foot ceiling, plus a studio lounge and office. The heart of the studio is a Macintosh G4 running a loaded version of Pro Tools 5.1. In addition to the excellent acoustics at Red Dot, the studio has a great street reputation with local bands in part because of Holmes's hand-picked mic collection. Starting with a pristine Neumann M 149 tube vocal mic and including an array of AKG, Earthworks, Studio Projects, and Shure mics, Red Dot provides a level of quality that most home studios can't approach.

Helping bands to achieve killer guitar tones is another Red Dot strong suit. Holmes, himself a guitar player, says, "The best tones I've ever gotten are a combination of Amp Farm (the Pro Tools plug-in) and miking a good-sounding amp. Some people just use Amp Farm, doubling the part to beef it up, but to my ear, that sounds kinda muddy and a little synthetic. So I start with the Amp Farm sound, laying the part down twice. Next, I have the part played through an amp live two more times, and with a stereo spread created from the four tracks, I'll be able to put a really full, in-your-face guitar sound together that fills up the track nicely."

What about a cleaner guitar tone? "Once the player has a nice sound, I just use a good mic and run it into Pro Tools. If you record a delay through an amp or pedal, it doesn't hit the stereo field right. And if you're doubling the delayed part, it gets messy quickly. I'll have the guitarist lay down the clean track, double it, then play with it later using the effects in Pro Tools."

Another secret to the Red Dot sound is using Class A preamps to record on the way in to Pro Tools. Holmes cites the dozen or so channels of discrete preamps as being "crucial" to getting a warm, realistic rock sound. In addition to Avalon, dbx, and ART preamps, Red Dot has invested in a Trident S100 8-channel sidecar mixer, with Class A preamps and EQ designed by John Oram. It provides a tight, present drum sound, with a powerful bottom end on the kick. "It's made a huge difference in everything we've done, because it provides a very natural sounding warmth to whatever we record through it," says Cole. Holmes adds, "We'll use it on drums for basic tracking, but then I find myself going to it for bass, guitar, and vocal overdubs because it just sounds so good."

> ...taking the time to isolate each drum and eliminate the sympathetic tones from the various drums makes a radical difference in what the final drum sound and overall mix will sound like.

Just as important as the mic pre's used for basic tracks and overdubs, is working with musicians to help them create the best sound possible *before* the record button is ever engaged. "Another one of my mentors, Ramey Salyer, taught me that when it comes to drum sounds, taking the time to isolate each drum and eliminate the sympathetic tones from the various drums makes a radical difference in what the final drum sound and overall mix will sound like," relates Holmes.

"I used to just mic up the drum set and try to get the best tone that I could, given that time is usually a concern, especially for young bands. Ramey brought in a drummer and we started out just hitting one tom, and we heard sympathetic tones being created from another tom, so we worked to find the offending drum. By a little fine-tuning or dampening, we tweaked until each drum had its own sound and no other drum, including the snare, was exciting any other drum. This cleans up an overall drum sound dramatically, so when I'm hearing problems with a drum kit, I'll take the time to first eliminate those tones, and the overall sound of the project will really benefit. It's night and day," concludes Holmes.

Red Dot's Tips for Helping New Bands Succeed in the Studio

* Encourage the band to get new strings and drum heads, and have spares at the ready. Eliminate buzzes on guitars, basses, and amps before coming to the session, to save time.

* Good timing is critical. Ask the band to practice the songs using an electronic metronome or click track before the session. If timing issues come up during recording, have the band play live to a click track.

* Take the time to live with your mixes for a day or two. "Sometimes making tiny changes can bring a song to life," says Holmes. "I recently brought the guitars up 0.5dB and reduced the strings by 0.5dB and the mix that resulted was a totally different animal."

* Emphasize the importance of knowing your arrangements inside and out, with and without vocals.

To reinforce the point that the craft of recording is a never-ending evolutionary path for all engineers, Holmes mentions a recent epiphany regarding the nuances of drum levels in the final mix. "I was finding that after my client's albums had been mastered, the drums were beefed up a bit. So I've learned to pull back the kick and snare some as I mix, which has made a big difference in my overall sound on the finished record. Listen to a good drummer and engineer collaborate, such as Kenny Aranoff and Brenden O'Brien. The drums are still distinguishable and well separated but not demanding your attention. Instead they support the groove as a bed for the song to sit on top of. Tweaking my levels has made a big difference in how polished the final CDs sound."

Cole adjusting drum mics before a session.

Holmes and Cole agree on their prime mission: Keeping Red Dot on the tip of area musicians' tongues. Although positive buzz among area bands is the number-one source of new clients, they also regularly scout for new talent at area clubs, and take fliers and postcards to area music stores. "I mostly look for new talent in the hip-hop, electronica, or drum and bass genres," Cole states. Holmes admits, "I'm more of a rock guy," so this diversity helps to broaden their appeal to different sets of musicians.

"It's really all about the performance, and as engineers, our job is to make good music sound even better," concludes Cole. With a new studio, a growing list of regional clients, and a real dedication to providing a lot of "bang for the buck," Red Dot is on its way to becoming one of the more successful studios in California's Central Valley.

Paradise Studios

Like virtually all studio owners/producers, Craig Long and Kirt Shearer of Paradise Studios began with their own love of music. Singer/songwriters themselves, they started recording music together in high school. According to Kirt, "Before there were such things as Portastudios, we had TEAC 4-track, reel-to-reel decks and we were ping-ponging things back and forth." Adds Craig, "We thought if we put those two 4-tracks in the same room, we could control the universe."

Well, not quite the universe. But after five years of recording their own work and charging others by the hour for sessions in Craig's home, in 1986 the duo took over a studio built in a former Circle-K just south of downtown Sacramento, California. They called it Paradise.

As Craig puts it, "Sitting at the controls for 20 years, you become very familiar with how to obtain what people want, as long as they're able to describe it. Musical direction is an extremely important part of what we do, and that applies to song structure, performance, and even something as basic as selecting the right sound."

"The key for me," says Kirt, "was sitting back and watching people who did not know how to accomplish their goals and having my own ideas about how to help them."

Besides handling the mixing board, Craig estimates the two play instruments on "70 percent of the work that comes through the door." Says Kirt, "Clients look at us as the guys who can fix stuff. We'll even help write or arrange their songs."

All of which goes a long way toward explaining why Paradise Studios has grown from selling time by the hour to a respected production house with gold and platinum albums to their credit.

Paradise got its first big break mixing the Tesla *Five-Man Acoustic Jam* album that went platinum in 1990. That album was recorded live in Philadelphia but "needed some fixing and cleaning up," most of which was done at Paradise, according to Craig. Soon after came the Tony! Toni! Toné! *Sons of Soul* album, plus a song with the group for the soundtrack of the Janet Jackson film *Poetic Justice*. Another recent client was R&B star Bobby Brown. Other notable Paradise Studio clients include New Edition, Art 'N Soul, Karen White, Jessica Williams, Cake, Mark Farner, and Hillary Stagg.

They had the musical chops and they acquired the studio. But what's their business secret for evolving from selling studio time to working with the major labels, especially

Paradise proprietors Kirt Shearer (foreground) and Craig Long.

in out-of-the-way Sacramento? "Really, it's word-of-mouth," says Kirt. "We started by making informal suggestions, and once people learned to trust us, they decided they could hire us to help out with production. We began acquiring a reputation for creative know-how."

Long and Shearer, however, aren't leaving their roots behind. "We still get everything from local people who have songs and don't know how to produce them, to major label projects and radio jingles for ad agencies. We haven't abandoned by-the-hour recording either," Craig emphasizes. "We still give clients who book a few hours someone behind the board who knows music and can help out if needed. A lot of people have their own recording equipment now, and a lot of new studios are competing with low introductory rates. But there will always be a demand for studios that have the people, equipment, and know-how to put it all together the right way. That's why we've been successful."

Success does have its rewards. Not only is Paradise constantly busy, but Kirt and Craig have hired another engineer who is also, in Craig's words, "a very good musician." That means that after 20 years of working seven days a week, the two are going to be able to take some time off.

So what about their own music? "I want to pursue a project of my own right now," says Kirt, "but I'm getting a multiple personality about it. I'm considering either new age or alternative rock, even though my natural keyboard style is jazz."

But really, what genre of music do they most prefer playing and recording? "To tell the truth," replies Craig, "anything that sounds good," which is definitely the word-of-mouth on Paradise Studios.

For a quick tour of Paradise, visit www.paradisestudios.net.

Paradise Studios Equipment Highlights

Console: Trident 80B (30 × 24 × 24) with 40-channel automation

Tape Machines: (2) MCI JH-24 24-track with AL-II & III; (2) Fostex B-16 multitracks; Fostex E-2 2-channel analog master recorder; Ampex ATR-102 ½-inch 2-track; Panasonic SV-4100; (2) Sony DAT digital master recorders; (2) JVC TD-V66 cassette decks; TASCAM 3440 4-track

Outboard Gear: All the "usual" toys, including a 2-channel Neve 1272 Class "A" mic preamp; Lexicon 480L dual stereo digital reverb; Lexicon PCM-70 & LXP-1 w/remote; Yamaha SPX-900, (2) SPX-90 digital effects and harmonizers; Yamaha REV-5; Drawmer noise gates (two channels); (3) UREI 1176 LN compressors; Aphex "Dominator II" peak output levelers (two channels); UREI 813A main studio monitors

Instruments: Baldwin grand piano; Hammond B-3 organ; Roland S-770 sampler; Korg T3, Korg M1 synthesizers; Yamaha DX-7 & TX 816 synthesizers; Memorymoog "Plus" synthesizer; Gretsch six-piece drum kit with power toms and Zildjian cymbals; 1962 Fender Jazz bass

The Track Factory

The Track Factory, the recording studio built in the mid-1990s by veteran engineer Yianni Papadopoulos, is among the more successful in New York. Top artists including Salt 'n Pepa, Was (Not Was), Johnny Gill, Wailing Souls, and Traci Lords have all sought Yianni's expertise in this unusual location: a quiet residential neighborhood in Long Island City, New York, across the East River from Manhattan. The peaceful surroundings may be one of the Track Factory's key assets. The one-room studio was booked even before the equipment was unpacked and has remained booked solid ever since. With business booming, Yianni has completed the transition from a freelance engineer to a busy but content studio owner.

Why did you build the Track Factory?

Today's synth and MIDI setups can be very elaborate, and in a commercial studio they don't have the luxury of leaving your project set up. So a lot of time is lost in doing setups, in tracking down lost patches, in training an assistant in your project and your methods.

The Track Factory was built specifically to address the way pop music is recorded these days: to allow a client to walk in the door with a disc, a keyboard, a MIDI controller, or a whole rack, and to be working ten or fifteen minutes after arrival.

What brought you to Long Island City?

This community is my home. But also, this place is free from the distractions of a midtown studio. It takes clients no longer to get here than to most major New York studios, but once they're here, they feel like they've shed the distractions and chaos of the city and can focus in a relaxed, creative way.

How do you market yourself and your studio?

Most of my business comes to me by word of mouth. The best marketing tool you have is the quality of your work. I have always tried to be the very best at every job I do. In this business you work long hours: 14-, 16-hour sessions, day after day. After that many hours, the client knows if you're good or not. If you are, they'll call you again. The Track Factory also has a Web site (http://www.gmx1.com/trackfactory) linked with a lot of record labels and music-oriented businesses. Because the links are good, a lot of the right people see the site. That also helps.

You're very efficiency oriented. Where does that come from, and how do you prevent it from intruding on the vibe and creative atmosphere?

I learned recording the traditional way in New York studios: working as a floor sweeper, setup boy, dub guy, assistant engineer, staff engineer, and finally independent.

As trainees, we were taught to literally run from task to task. I pride myself on being very fast and efficient in all my work, and that comes from good training. Clients come to me because I save them time and money, and I'm a good engineer. And I do it without intruding on the creative process. I try to take the hassle of the technical details away from the producer and distractions and nuisances away from the artists. That makes them more creative and productive. Whether you're dealing with a garage band or Salt 'n Pepa, you're dealing with artists, and there's a psychology to engineering that goes far beyond the technical requirements of your job. Being sensitive to the artist's and producer's environments, anticipating their needs, and delivering before they have to ask: that's important.

The Track Factory control room.

What kinds of projects have you been working on lately?

R&B is certainly the core of my business, but I also do a lot of music for New York Latin labels, especially radio remixes, compilations, and club versions of music recorded in Puerto Rico and the Dominican Republic. I've done work for Johnny Gill, Diana King, Maxi Priest, Big Mountain, and so on. But I really record all kinds of music.

Are you at all involved in Greek music?

I am currently working on several recording projects for Greek musicians to be distributed in Greece. Some of the finest Greek musicians in the world, both pop and ethnic, are right here in this community, but they are almost unknown in the rest of the world. I'm working with labels in Greece to create new outlets for these artists in their homeland. Living and working in New York exposes you to every kind of culture and music you can imagine. I've recorded almost every musical style and learned something new from each experience. Every engineer should seek out opportunities to hear, study, and record as many different kinds of music as possible. The studio business gets very competitive, but the music makes it all worthwhile. There is nothing more exciting than the feeling you get, after an all-night session, printing the mix and hearing all the music unfold so perfectly!

The Track Factory Equipment Highlights

Console and Tape Machines: Soundtracs Topaz 32-channel in-line console with automation; Mackie CR1604 16-channel mixer; TASCAM ATR80 2-inch 24-track tape recorder; Panasonic SV3700 DAT; Sony DTC700 DAT (2)

Outboard Gear: Altec 1567A tube mic preamp; Summit Audio TLA-200A tube limiter; Ensoniq DP/4; Yamaha SPX900 and SPX90; Sony MU-R201 reverb

Computers and MIDI: Emagic LogicAudio 2.5.2; Emagic SoundDriver 1.57 (Universal Sound Editor/ Librarian); Digidesign AudioMedia II; MOTU MIDI Time Piece II; Akai S100HD; Roland JD990, JV880, D50, D550, Juno 106, MKS-30

Microphones: Neumann U 87A; AKG 414, D 112, and D 321; Sennheiser 421 and 441; Shure SM 57, SM 58; EV N/D 257 and N/D 357

Pachyderm's Formula for Success: Word-of-Mouth Attracts Rock Stars

Why would a megastar rock band like Nirvana go all the way to a rural Minnesota studio to record 1993's multiplatinum-selling album, *In Utero*? For the same reason that other top rock acts, such as Soul Asylum, Son Volt, P.J. Harvey, and many others seek out Pachyderm Recording Studio: the chance to make records in a world-class studio in a beautiful country setting only 35 minutes from an international airport and urban center.

The word is out on Pachyderm: state-of-the-art facilities, quality product, and a bucolic residential complex without the isolation of more remote "retreat" studios. Those were the qualities that led producer Steve Albini, who had worked on another project at Pachyderm, to convince Nirvana to bring the project that would become *In Utero* to the studio in Cannon Falls, just southeast of Minneapolis.

Without an aggressive sales plan and well-removed from the great entertainment centers, Pachyderm has relied on word-of-mouth to build its reputation over the 16 years of its existence. It's an enviable success story and one that came about, according to founder/owner Jim Nickel, "against the odds."

The odds to which Nickel refers are not really a question of location. Other rural studios offering creative retreats have succeeded. The real odds, according to Nickel, were that the musician/composers who founded Pachyderm in 1989 "had no real business experience." What Pachyderm's founders did have, however, was a clear eye to the opportunity developing at that time in their own front yard. In the late 1980s, the number of Minneapolis-area bands signing with major labels surged. Pachyderm was built in the first place to service that burgeoning local market. The Minneapolis music scene was the foundation for Pachyderm's initial success.

But it's a long way from being a hot local recording studio to being the destination for major music acts from all over the world. Today, in fact, 80 percent of Pachyderm's business is from well outside the Minneapolis area. Other big-name artists who've made Pachyderm a studio of choice include Luna, Kelly Willis, Gwen Mars, Kelley Deal, Live, and the Last Hard Men.

Pachyderm's spacious control room features a vintage Neve 8068.

Getting a reputation that brings in that kind of talent, of course, takes more than local success and a lovely country setting—especially absent an aggressive sales effort. The next building block in Pachyderm's success was to create a world-class facility that would turn out world-class product.

And what a studio they built. The Pachyderm complex includes a 1,500-square-foot live room for recording (with an awesome drum sound, according to those who have heard it) and a state-of-the-art control room built around a carefully maintained vintage Neve 8068 console. Add to that Studer multitrack recorders, a Bosendorfer grand piano, and a collection of vintage microphones, and you have a studio that can hold its own with any in the world. [See equipment list.]

What finally puts Pachyderm over the top in distinctiveness is its exceptional country setting and great accommodations. There are other country retreats but this one is a huge garden. The studio is built into a hillside on a 40-acre, wooded private park with a trout stream, miles of hiking trails, and wild turkeys. The lodgelike residence has cathedral ceilings, an indoor swimming pool, and a screened-in, treetop gazebo. And, in case a performer needs an urban changeup, Minneapolis and its international airport are close by.

"It's a great place for bands who live in a fishbowl on the road," says Nickel. "It's beautiful and people love to work here. Who could imagine that in 35 minutes, you can be at the airport?" Even though Jim and his partners claim little real business experience and don't aggressively market the studio, they still have a keen eye for new business opportunities. "Live at Pachyderm," initially a program produced at the studio for a Minneapolis FM station, will make its debut later this year as a biweekly program for Internet broadcast over Web radio. The show is produced in association with Ambient Creek, which delivers extremely high-fidelity stereo over a phone/modem line. Recent shows have included appearances by Luna, Wilco, They Might Be Giants, Frank Black, and Hum.

While Internet radio is the studio's next big project, Nickel and company are already brainstorming an even bigger one. "The larger objective is to be operating our own label by next summer," says Nickel. "The goal is for Pachyderm to record music for its own label, showcasing Pachyderm artists."

If successful, that will make the Pachyderm name known to music lovers well beyond the coteries of musicians and bands who already appreciate the studio, and continue to build on the solid achievements of Jim Nickel and his partners.

For a virtual tour of Pachyderm, go to www.pachydermstudio.com.

Pachyderm Recording Equipment Highlights

- Neve 8068 Console (32 input) w/Uptown 990 Moving Fader Automation
- Studer A820 & A827 24-track tape machines
- Studer A80 ½-inch 2-track tape machine w/Dolby SR
- Genelec 1031A studio monitors
- Focusrite 8-pack (6 ISA 110 Eqs & 2 ISA 180 compressors)
- GML stereo parametric EQ
- (2) TubeTech compressors
- Joe Meek stereo compressor and Joe Meek Tube Channel VC2
- (4) John Hardy M-1 mic preamplifiers
- TubeTech stereo mic preamplifiers
- (2) dbx 160X compressors
- Drawmer 241 compressor
- Quantec Room Simulator XLC
- AMS RMX 16
- (2) Klark Teknik DN780s
- (2) TC Electronics 2290
- Eventide H3000
- Microphones: AKG C 12, AKG C 24 (Stereo), AKG C 28 (Figure 8), AKG 414, Philips C 12A, 2 B&K 4004 Omnis, 2 Neumann CMU 563 Omni (East German), Neumann M 249, Neumann SM 2 (Stereo)
- Bosendorfer grand piano
- Hammond BV organ
- Slingerland drum kit
- Vox AC30 guitar amp
- Bluesland Combo guitar amp
- Benedict Groove Master guitar
- Benedict Groove Master bass
- Gibson Melody Maker guitar

Chapter 9

Making Money with Your Studio

Eleven Questions to Ask—and Answer—Before Building or Remodeling Your Recording Studio

By Dave Malekpour

While the main focus of this article is on commercial studios, concepts for apportioning budgets and getting optimum performance from the studio as a whole apply as well to project and home studios that aren't necessarily operating as for-profit businesses.

Introduction

Succeeding in the recording studio business today is like hitting a moving target. Technological advances that are actually shrinking the professional market (in favor of project and home studios), fierce competition, and steep business cycles, make owning a commercial studio a challenging task. Success depends on building the right kind of studio for the market in which you are competing. While questions about gear and technology are often foremost in a studio operator's mind, the fact is that answers about gear follow—or should follow—from the business decisions you've made. Your studio should be the embodiment of your business plan. The "right studio" follows from the right business plan.

This article is intended to give the studio owner/operator a solid overview of decisions that need to be made *before* embarking on building or remodeling a commercial recording studio. These are the questions every studio owner should answer to determine the right solutions for their facilities. Experience has shown that having a studio building or remodeling project go smoothly—not to mention ultimately succeeding as a business—depends on answering these questions correctly.

1. What do I need to know about my market?

I could have begun by saying the first three steps in building or remodeling a commercial studio are: research, research, research. Building or remodeling a studio means positioning it to succeed. The first questions are therefore business ones. I emphasize this, as basic as it sounds, because, in my experience, many studio people come into the business for the reason that they, like me, were musicians and are in love with making music. In practice, they have a tendency to forget the business basics as they concentrate on achieving beautiful sounds.

Who are your actual (or targeted) customers and who are your competitors for their business—that is, who is currently serving your target customers and at what price and level of service?

You have to know that you can at least match the level of service, at the price being offered by your competition. But the studio business is far too risky to settle for matching the other guys. Ultimately, you are asking how your facility will distinguish itself from this competition. You have to figure out the competitive advantage or unserved niche that will give you a steady core clientele.

If, for example, your marketplace doesn't have an SSL or Pro Tools system, having either is a great way to stand out—as long as

> Experience has shown that having a studio building or remodeling project go smoothly—not to mention ultimately succeeding as a business—depends on answering these questions correctly.

there are customers who will support them. By the same token, if every studio on the block has these tools, not having them would be a disadvantage. If you can't afford an SSL, you might find a niche offering a less powerful console at a significantly lower price, or by finding another competitive advantage altogether.

In a major market with a mature studio industry, it may not be possible or even particularly desirable to attain an advantage in gear. The quality of your engineers and other staff is something you cannot ignore in any case, and always offers the possibility of a competitive advantage. The kind of amenities you can offer may also allow you to stand out. Don't forget that, as with any business, having repeat customers in the studio business depends on forming personal relationships.

When entering a market, it's generally better to be more focused and less broad in your services. That doesn't mean you turn away other business, or don't pursue secondary markets. But it does mean that you know whether your core market is A-list recording acts or up-and-coming artists, rock bands or classical orchestras, or whether your clients are local or will be coming from distant locales, and so on. Understanding your core clientele affects virtually every subsequent decision you make, from the size of your live rooms to the console you install, to the amenities you offer.

> Understanding your core clientele affects virtually every subsequent decision you make.

2. What do I need to keep in mind about the competition?

That it's essentially local. Even if you're a world-class studio in New York, London, or Los Angeles whose core clientele are superstars, your competition is still essentially local in the sense that you are in competition with other New York, London, or Los Angeles studios for those very acts. The question remains: why choose you and not the other guy down the block?

It's a goal of most studios to build up a core of artists and producers who want to return again and again to a certain studio because they have bonded with the environment or the people. But you can't forget that acts and producers can come and go with the trends, and that even the most durable acts, however much they like a certain studio, will likely want to go elsewhere at some point for a new sound or vibe, or simply for a creative jolt.

That means you can't rest on your laurels. You have to keep selling your studio to your core market and the new faces in it. It also means you have to be careful to keep your competitive edge, even as your competition is likely trying to wipe it out. So you have to keep your market research current. Remember that every client that comes into your studio offers you a chance to do informal but in-depth research on their needs and attitudes in relation to studios. Find out why they booked your studio. Was it the staff, amenities, location, gear, killer microphones, etc.? More importantly, ask what turned them off about your competition. Knowing *exactly* what keeps clients coming back for more is one of the key ingredients for any studio's success.

3. How do I create a capital budget for building or remodeling my studio?

Calculate your return. Calculating the realistic return on your facility, based on your research into services and prices in your market, goes a long way toward determining your capital budget for construction and gear. Even if you're paying cash out of pocket, rather than borrowing, it pays to calculate the cost of your investment in relation to return.

> Knowing *exactly* what keeps clients coming back for more is one of the key ingredients for any studio's success.

Your research should tell you the going day or hour rate in your market for the kind of facility you envision. At Professional Audio Design, we recommend that brand-new studios calculate income on the basis of 15 rented days per month. That's a solid, conservative figure for entering a market. An established studio will have more history to go on and may use another figure. So, if the day rate is $1,200, your monthly income on 15 rented days is $18,000/month. Out of this you have to cover rent, salaries, utilities, and other operating costs. What remains must carry your capital investment in your plant, as well as meet the profit goals that have been set.

Day rate		$1,200
Number of days booked	×	15
Monthly Studio Income		$18,000

Next, figure that the typical equipment lease runs for 60 months. Although the exact number varies, a ballpark figure is that you're going to pay $2,500 a month for every $100,000 borrowed. With studio gear, the goal is to pay off the equipment (or amortize it) over five years—just about the time to upgrade. Computer-based equipment shortens that term, since the effective lifespan of computer gear is shorter—about three years. So, if you purchase a $35,000 digital workstation, then $12,000 a year represents the cost of operating the equipment (and not profit) for the three-year term it would take to pay it off.

Mixing Board

Monthly lease payment	$2,500
Term of lease (for $100,000 board)	60 months

Computer Workstation

Monthly lease payment	$1,150
Term of lease (for $35,000 workstation)	36 months

These calculations set the parameters for how much you should spend on outfitting your facility, in relation to the return you can expect. If the equations between capital investment, operating expenses, and return don't balance, it's time to reexamine your business plan. Don't forget to add in your regular operating costs. If this is your first business venture, be sure to consult with an accountant who can get you up to speed on the various operating expenses you'll need to plan for in your overall budget.

Once a budget for equipment and facilities has been set, the problem remains of apportioning the money, with the goal of achieving the best possible studio package. The biggest mistake people make in studio building is dramatically underestimating the cost of installation and wiring—all the infrastructure that is out of sight and out of mind—at least until it malfunctions. Figure that up to 20 percent of the total equipment budget will go to installation and wiring. The percentage may drop when installing expensive pieces of gear, such as a $300,000 console. But a typical SSL room will still cost a healthy $15,000–30,000—up to 10 percent—for wiring and ancillary interfacing. Interconnections for a digital work environment cost less than for an analog environment, but the savings are generally cancelled out by the costs of routers, patch bays, and sample rate converters.

Remember that gear comes and goes, and can be fixed, upgraded, and enhanced—but fixing the wiring once the walls and floors have been sealed up comes at a high price. It simply does not pay in the long run to skimp on installation and infrastructure—especially if it means a lost session, lost business, and a reputation for things not working right.

> The biggest mistake people make in studio building is dramatically underestimating the cost of installation and wiring.

4. Is it better to build from the ground up or remodel an existing space?

Everyone's fantasy is building a studio from the ground up. But you are unlikely to do so, especially in a major market where land is at a premium. Besides, there are advantages to remodeling or building out a preexisting structure. Basic infrastructure like plumbing and power will likely be in place and zoning issues are typically easier to navigate than with new buildings. You will probably still have to wire the place, but old factories and warehouses often have heavy electrical wiring in place, which can be a huge savings.

When considering an existing building, be sure to hire your acoustician or studio designer before you sign a lease so he can evaluate proposed sites. An experienced designer can see nuances in the structure and infrastructure that can have a tremendous impact on the cost and ultimate success of your facility. When choosing a designer, never go by reputation alone. Each designer has different qualities to offer. Visit rooms actually designed by the people you are considering, and pick the one whose taste as well as acoustic expertise matches your needs and budget.

Be sure to include in your lease agreement up-front provisions for studio operations such as noise levels, 24-hour operation, parking access, and so on.

5. Is it better to lease or buy equipment?

The great advantages of leasing big-ticket gear are that it requires a smaller outlay of money up front, is typically secured by the equipment itself, and pays for the equipment as it's being used. Equipment leases are also far easier to qualify for than traditional money loans. For loans, banks will want to see business plans, tax returns, and require additional security. Most leasing companies, by contrast, never see your business plans or tax returns, and are comfortable securing the lease with the equipment itself until it is paid off.

Leasing also makes upgrading easier and has tax advantages, since lease payments are typically 100 percent deductible. It is also a good way for a new business to establish credit. Even my most successful customers prefer leasing because it allows for the asset to be paid for as it's being used.

It makes sense to pay outright for some assets—usually smaller ticket items such as vintage microphones or outboard gear, both of which tend to appreciate over time and whose value lies in part in the fact that they won't ever be upgraded.

6. How do I put together a successful "studio package?"

A typical pitfall in building or remodeling a studio comes when people fixate on particular pieces of prized gear. There's nothing wrong with trying to design a studio package that incorporates these pieces of equipment. But the goal is achieving optimum performance from the studio as a whole and that, depending on budget, probably requires compromise. If buying one coveted master reverb means not being able to afford good outboard limiters and delays, the result won't be an effective mixing environment. In that case, it would be better to buy a step or two down on the master reverb and have better outboard gear.

Again, your research into your core market will go a long way toward determining what gear you acquire and how it all fits together. Your ultimate goal is to achieve the "sound" your clients want in an atmosphere they feel comfortable working in.

> Your ultimate goal is to achieve the "sound" your clients want in an atmosphere they feel comfortable working in.

7. How do I choose the right console for my studio?

For most professional studios doing music recording with multiple microphones, an analog console remains best for recording and/or mixing. For project or home studios, where the console is less of a marketing factor, a small-format digital console is usually more cost effective. Professional postproduction environments for film and broadcast are going to want all-digital environments. But for large tracking rooms and environments with acoustic space, an analog input structure is best.

An analog console can work terrifically in combination with Pro Tools or other digital systems. Some of our clients with large tracking rooms are recording to Pro Tools or another digital workstation but still want the multiple mic inputs and faders that an analog console provides.

One reason is that people are concerned about the amount of resampling in digital consoles. Every time you move a fader in some of these consoles, it's resampling thousands of times, which can change the depth of field and truncate the sound. Even if you're going through A/D-D/A converters three or four times with an analog console, there will be less resampling than making mixing changes in the digital domain. Another factor is that people in music recording continue to prefer the more natural sound of analog. A comfortable and tactile working surface that can accommodate three or four people is another issue in a larger studio.

If your business is oriented toward tracking music, an analog console is your best choice. Which one to choose depends on your market analysis, in terms of what your targeted customers expect, want, and feel comfortable with. The console is the centerpiece of your setup and you have to think about the marquee value of your choice.

8. How important is monitoring?

It's not too much to say that good monitoring is key to a successful recording or mixing room. In a very real sense, your room's sound is the tangible product you are selling. Every decision you make about a recording—and every judgment a client forms about your work—is derived from your monitors. Having a great-sounding monitoring environment is one of the best competitive features a studio can offer.

Unfortunately, some engineers have gotten comfortable with the idea that as long as you have a good set of near fields, the rest takes care of itself, with the big speakers being there for loudness. While an engineer is concentrating on the near fields, however, the client is likely listening to how impressive he sounds—or doesn't sound—on the main system. Also, if you can't hear all the nuances of the tracks in your monitoring chain, you're not going to make the best decisions about recording.

> Your room's sound is the tangible product you are selling.

9. What do I do about storage and archiving?

Digital technology both helps and complicates the issue of storage. In the digital domain, you're going to need both working media and backup media, and a cost-effective way to keep track of it. And you must provide a portable medium to the customer—something he can take away and use in other environments. The problem is that there are currently about six competing storage formats, and digital standards are always evolving.

Laying everything off to analog tape is one obvious solution, but it can be costly and brings with it issues of correct storage environments. More and more studios are working with 9 and 18GB removable hard drives that they can just give to the customer. As hard drives become cheaper, that becomes a better and better solution. When a roll of 2-inch tape with 15 minutes of storage costs $150, paying $300 for a hard drive with 30 minutes of storage is no problem.

We find more of our clients centralizing hard-drive storage via Storage Area Networks (SANs), which offer studios increased flexibility in configuring project architecture and work flow, and expand the potentials for remote and workgroup collaborations. SANs also improve security and control, and easily accommodate removable hard drives brought by the client.

SANs and removable media together are the future of storage and archiving in professional recording studios. Right now, the more store-and-take formats a studio can offer its clients, the better.

10. What's the one sure advantage commercial studios can have over home and project studios?

The room itself. A great-sounding room is an indispensable competitive point. With so much professional-grade gear and software available for home and project studios, the excellent acoustics provided by a well-designed commercial studio are a vital draw. Of course, it requires a great-sounding microphone package to capture a great room's sound. And don't forget the amenities—the lounges, edit suite comforts, recreation, and so on—that can distinguish the professional studio from nonprofessional sites.

11. What do I do about 5.1?

Get with the program. Be prepared. In today's market, you absolutely have to build or remodel with the idea that your studio will one day be used for multichannel monitoring, even if not right away. At the very least, make sure there are troughs to bring wiring to free-standing speaker positions for multichannel monitoring so you won't have to lay cabling on the floor when the occasion arises. With a bit of planning, it certainly is possible to lay out a room and provide treatments that will allow it to be equally suitable for stereo monitoring today and 5.1 monitoring tomorrow.

Dave Malekpour, the owner and president of Professional Audio Design, has been in the business of providing professional consultation, technical services, and equipment to the studio market since 1986. He can be reached at DaveM@proaudiodesign.com.

Bill Cuomo: From Player to Producer

You've taken the plunge and invested in your own studio. You sell some time to a few bands, record some of your own tunes, and keep up with the latest gear. Are there other ways to make your investment pay off? Can you parlay your engineering skills and love of music into a more lucrative career as an arranger or a producer?

We headed to Nashville to ask top arranger/producer Bill Cuomo these questions. Cuomo owns and operates his home studio facility, Manzanita Recording, in the suburbs of Nashville. There, he recorded, mixed, and coproduced (along with Robert White Johnson) *Beyond All the Limits* and *Unbelievable Love* for Parnell Harris. Both albums were Grammy-award nominees, and *Unbelievable Love* earned Cuomo a Dove award. Cuomo and Johnson have collaborated on four songs for Kathy Troccoli, two of which have made it to No. 1 on the Christian charts.

Cuomo is best known for the multiplatinum smash "Bette Davis Eyes" (his arrangement earned a 1981 Record of the Year for Kim Carnes) and for the Steve Perry hit "Oh Sherrie," which Cuomo co-wrote. He has arranged or produced tracks for a tremendous range of artists, including Don Henley, Barbra Streisand, Whitesnake, Herb Alpert, and REO Speedwagon. He also arranged the title track for the James Bond flick *Never Say Never Again*.

Any tips for someone with a home or project studio on getting started as a producer?

It's difficult when labels basically say, "Experienced help wanted." Where do you start? Well, you have a powerful tool to get artists to work with you: your studio. Go around and check out the local talent. Introduce yourself to someone whose music you really like, and invite them to record some sides in your facility. You'll get a good feel as to how you get along in the studio and whether or not you complement each other. The most important thing for an aspiring producer is "saddle time," getting as much time behind the board as you can. Work creatively with the artist; don't just hit the record button. For me, the studio is one of my main creative tools. Engineering comes about naturally, since it helps you arrange and produce. It would be a lot harder to achieve what I want to hear without a working knowledge of the studio. I hear parts and sounds blending with the track in my head, even before I start recording.

Is it essential to be a musician?

Being a player helps, as does having a musical background. You can sit down with a guitar or a keyboard and run over a tune with an artist, try different things on the verse or the chorus. The gifted producers I know are all very musical, whether they play or not. They can explain exactly what they want to musicians in a session. If you can't get your point across musically, it's like speaking English in a foreign country.

How hard do you work to perfect your demos?

Very hard. Of course, having my own studio allows me to work until I'm happy with a song I write, no matter how long it takes. Cutting the best demo you can is crucial in selling a song, since today's demos are so good. As your combined skills improve, you'll eventually stumble onto something on one of your demos that just can't be beat. It could be a hit song or your first arranging, playing, or producing break. That happened to me more than once. When I did the Streisand duet with Carnes, "Make No Mistake He's Mine," Barbra loved the demo and the string/synth parts so much that she wanted the exact feel on the master, only with a real orchestra.

Sometimes, however, beating the demo isn't all that easy. I hear that some artists, like Tom Petty, don't believe in demos, since trying to recreate the parts and the relaxed atmosphere of a demo on a master can sound too thought-out. The rule of thumb is, treat each track as a master and try to make each recording your absolute best.

How do you know when a tune has the potential to be a hit?

When you're involved with a really good song, no one, even the musicians, can get enough of it. Everyone wants to hear it again and again, even after days of working on it. Sometimes the song is not an obvious "formula record" either, like "Bette Davis Eyes," but it really sticks and you don't tire of it. These are good signs that the song may be a winner.

Any other tips?

If you begin working with an artist, arranging, etc., you've taken the first step to producing. If you work well together and want to get more serious, set goals in the form of a legal agreement. You'll be investing a lot of studio and personal time, effort, and talent in their career, so it's best to be clear at the outset. Also, remember that the technology is always secondary to the song. That's what it's all about as a producer— allowing the artist and the song to shine.

Manzanita Recording Equipment Highlights

Recorders and Console: Trident 80B console with Optifile Automation; Trident "Flexmix" 8-input sideboard; Otari RADAR 24-track digital workstation with ADAT link; Otari MTR-12h recorder with Dolby SR; TEAC DA-P20 portable DAT recorder; Otari DTR-8 DAT recorder; Akai 4-track Dr-4d hard disk recorder

Microphones: AKG "The Tube," AKG 460 (2), AKG 451, AKG D 112; Telefunken 582; Microtech Geffel 300 pencil mic; Milab DC 96; EV RE 20; EV 408 "Ball" mic (4); Sennheiser 421; Shure SM 57 (5)

Miscellaneous: Tannoy SGM-15 large monitor speakers; Tannoy 6.5 and Kef 101-3 small monitors; Carver amplifiers

Growing Up with Tommy Uzzo

How does a Long Island suburbanite with a 4-track garage studio rise to prominence in the New York hip-hop scene? Ask Tommy Uzzo. From a modest home studio, engineer/mixer Uzzo created Mirror Image Recorders, a two-facility operation that churns out hits for clients such as Coolio, K7, Redman, TKA, and Shaquille O'Neal.

Growing up on Long Island, Uzzo caught the recording bug, like many engineers, while playing in high school rock 'n' roll bands. "I had a Shure mic mixer and a TEAC 3340 tape recorder, and I recorded every group I was involved with," he recalls. While working as a professional musician, Tommy turned the family garage into a home studio.

With a TAC Scorpion console and an old 24-track analog machine, he recorded demos to promote his own songs. Eventually, people started to notice the quality of the demos and he became known for his abilities as an engineer.

By the time Uzzo recorded George Lamond's chart-topping "Bad of the Heart" for Columbia, he was getting calls to work as an independent engineer in studios all over New York and Long Island, including Soundtracks, Unique, Right Track, and the Hit Factory.

Eventually the frustrations of working as an independent in so many different studios convinced Uzzo to reconsider his work. The result was a complete rebuilding of the old garage studio of his youth. The newly remodeled and reequipped studio became his new home base and favorite place to work. Fitted with an SSL 4048 E/G console with Total Recall, Sony digital and analog tape recorders, and a generous array of MIDI and outboard gear, Mirror Image Recorders quickly became popular with a wide range of record labels, music producers, and ad agencies.

It wasn't long before Uzzo was turning down sessions for lack of time. "At first," Uzzo recalls, "I considered building a larger studio on Long Island, with a good room for recording piano and tracking a band. Eventually, the economics of the Long Island market led me to look at Manhattan, and everyone—except my wife and my mom—said I was crazy, that there were too many studios in New York already."

Although he reconsidered the tracking room concept, Uzzo opted for a different direction to accommodate the mixing that is the core of his work. He leased space in the Film Center Building in New York's theater district in fall 1996 and created a facility that mirrored the technical installation at the Long Island studio: SSL 4048G+ with Total Recall, Studer A827 24-track recorders, JBL4330 monitors, multiple DAT recorders, identical MIDI rig and outboard complement, Creamware TripleDAT and TDAT-16 digital audio workstations.

The Manhattan studio, Mirror Image West, opened in February 1997. It's spacious, with generous control room and recording room, multiple iso booths, and comfortable lounge areas. Now, with two facilities in operation, clients may choose which to use, based on personal preference, expediency, artist vibe, need to get away, and so on.

But technical considerations are unnecessary. Whatever Uzzo can do in one studio, he can do in the other. "Often jobs move from one room to the other due to scheduling, convenience, or choice," he notes. "Producers really seem to like having the choice of location for their artists."

With multiple rooms to book, Uzzo realizes that he can no longer engineer all sessions himself. The studios therefore must appeal to independent engineers as well. "A well-maintained, well-equipped studio is very important," Uzzo says. "The fact that both studios are technically identical makes the independent engineer's job easier. Engineers like Greg Mann, Joe Quimba, and Eric Lake are regulars here, and I try to make sure the studio works as well for them as it does for me."

When asked if managing a busy, multiroom studio business has changed his role, Uzzo says, "I definitely see expanding the business in the not-too-distant future. But above all, I love to engineer. When I was younger I wanted to be a producer. Now I see clearly that I'm most interested in the sound, in getting a good mix."

He adds, "Most of my success in the business has been the result of working hard to give my clients exactly what they want. I try not to forget that. It's not the rooms that bring the business; it's our continuing efforts to do the best job possible."

Studio Marketing 101

What does it take to get your studio humming with bookings? "Studio Marketing 101" is a primer to guide you through the basics of making your studio the destination of choice for local artists and bands, and getting your studio investment working to earn you a profit.

Mission Statement

In one or two sentences, sum up what you want to be known for—the best grunge recordings in NYC, or killer demos at rock-bottom prices. Your mission statement describes why people would want to part with some of their hard-earned cash to book time with you. Write it down and keep it visible. Adapt it as new opportunities arise. Your marketing actions should spotlight your mission statement.

Target Marketing

A new studio will often run an ad announcing they're open for business, and then they'll wait for the phone to ring. This simply doesn't work. Before you spend any money on ads in your local paper or music magazine, take the time to figure out who your customers will be. By learning what segments of the market would be interested in your services, you'll be able to tailor your marketing message directly for that segment. This is called "target marketing." To find out precisely who may want to buy time from you, follow these steps:

- First, make an educated guess as to who is your best potential client. If you produce great hip-hop tracks, start with local hip-hop acts; if you write soaring instrumental music, look for student and documentary filmmakers.

- Next, talk to several people in your target market group. Ask them what they need in a studio or a sound track. If they already use a studio, find out what they like and don't like. Listen carefully to what they tell you and take notes.

    Pretty soon, you'll have first-hand knowledge of what prospective customers look for in a studio. Put that knowledge to work.

Getting the Word Out

One of the best ways to start marketing your studio is with a flier. Take the time to make your flier look professional and communicate what your research has told you is *most* important to your prospective customers. Start by using these five tried and tested tips on flier development:

- Just like a pop song, every flier has to have a hook that gets people to remember it. Write two or three hooks ("huge tracking room"…"all digital recording"…"best rates in West LA") and use the strongest one.

- If your studio looks impressive, use a photo. Pictures sell.

- If you upgrade your studio, update your flier right away ("New sampler," "Now 48 tracks").

- If you need help with the design, go to your local college's art or graphics department, and find a student familiar with desktop graphics programs that will work for a small fee or in exchange for some studio time.

- Experiment and have fun—fliers are an inexpensive way to learn what works in marketing. Try a year-end special, a demo deal ("tape, dubs, and setup time included"), or host a listening party for a new CD you've just finished. Each of these can be promoted by a well-designed flier.

Next, enlist the aid of friends and post the fliers (with permission) at music stores, clubs, music schools, rehearsal halls, and anywhere else your target market may see them. After you've tackled one target market, you'll probably have identified a few others to investigate. Keep creating fliers and pitches for each new market. Remember: if you identify your target markets, find out what they look for in a studio, and get the word out that you can deliver, you're going to see an upturn in business.

David vs. Goliath

Compete and win against any studio in your market—no matter what its size. How? The answer is easy, but requires hard work and a commitment on your part to build a quality studio mailing list and then focus your marketing toward those qualified prospects. Here's how it's done.

Uncover Hidden Treasure

One of the most overlooked marketing assets is your "house list." A house list is a database of clients who have already worked at your studio, plus all the prospects that have called and requested information or rates. Your house list can be up to three times as effective to market to than an outside list. If you haven't been recording the name, address, and telephone number of every single client or prospect, you're missing an opportunity to uncover hidden treasure. Today, database programs like Filemaker Pro and Microsoft Works or MS Access make it very easy to store, sort, and keep track of every single person who comes to your studio or requests rates.

These people are much easier to sell to than someone who has no idea who you are or why your studio might be a good choice for their recording project, because they have already heard of you and expressed interest. To a savvy database marketer, a house list is money in the bank. Now with a few ideas on your part, and a small investment in postage and postcards, you can harvest the cash crop.

Building Your List

Build your list by advertising your studio in local magazines and the Yellow Pages and continuously adding the names of any and all prospective clients to your database. You can also boost your list by adding names from published directories of local bands, local songwriter's associations, and other music organizations. Offer to exchange names with such organizations and agree to offer a special discount to their members. Consider offering a prize promotion exclusively for their members, such as a drawing to "Win 10 hours of studio time from Savvy Studios."

You can send a two-panel postcard, including a coupon to be returned by mail or dropped into a hat at an open mic event that you help sponsor. Promo ideas such as these help get musicians talking about and calling up your studio. You'll also build up your house list much more quickly if you invest in such tactics.

Remember, as your list grows, you increase the number of people seeing and responding to your postcards and letters. The cost difference between designing, printing and mailing 200 and 2,000 postcards is fairly small. And of course, the more qualified prospects and clients you mail to, the better the response. The number of qualified names on your house list is a good barometer for measuring your business health. Are you adding 2 or 200 names to your list each month? Set a monthly goal.

What about E-mail Lists?

It's essential that you also use e-mail as a means to stay in contact with clients and prospects. But don't make the mistake of relying only on e-mail. The best marketers today combine traditional mailing of postcards or fliers with regular e-mail "news" of what's happening at your studio. Don't overuse any single medium, but use e-mail instead for special "e-mail-only" offers and announcements. Be sure to respect e-mail privacy and don't sell or trade your client e-mail addresses. Doing so may destroy your clients' confidence in you and your studio.

The Offer

Each time you upgrade or add key gear, let everyone on your house list know with a postcard or e-mail—and include a strong offer. For example, when your studio upgrades from 8- to 24-track, take the opportunity to offer a "preferred customer" coupon to record on 24-track for the price of an 8-track session. Package deals have historically been the best performing offers for studios.

For example:

- **Rising Stars CD:** For a reasonable flat rate, offer to record one song each from 15 of your area's best new bands, then press 1,000 CDs. Provide each band with 50 and keep the few extras to show off what you can do. Be sure to drop off a copy at your local college and FM radio stations, local music stores, and the local newspaper, too.

- **Block Booking:** Bands normally need more time than they think to finish a project, so offer them a special rate on prepaid block bookings like "20 percent off our regular studio rate on bookings of 25 or more hours."
- **CD Package:** Put together a package deal to record and mix five songs and manufacture CDs for the band.

Call to Action

Another important point is to end your postcard or letter with what's known as a "call to action." Even the strongest offers and hippest postcards need this to overcome inertia and get the person to pick up the phone or stop by.

A good call to action reminds readers of the offer and its benefit and inspires immediate response ("Call by August 15th to take advantage of 24-track recording at 8-track prices!"). Any act that's been thinking about recording a demo will be motivated to get organized and save money while your special offer is available. Be sure to print your phone number in bold letters next to your call to action.

When should you send out postcards? As often as your budget allows. If you're on a tight budget, take a look at your previous years' booking schedules to determine when your bookings are usually down. For many studios, the down periods correspond to the middle of summer (vacations) and the Thanksgiving to New Year's season. Send out your postcard about four to six weeks before you normally hit one of these down periods and make your offer specifically cover those times.

Studio Test Drives Build Business

Anyone who bought a used car without driving it would probably be considered a bit off. Why not allow bands to "test drive" your studio by inviting them in to see and hear just what your studio is capable of doing?

Attracting musicians to your studio to see the gear and meet you can instantly enlarge your pool of potential clients—and it isn't all that difficult to do. One easy, low-cost way is to offer free informational clinics.

Sell Yourself

If you own and operate a studio, you not only have to convince people that you have the right room and equipment to record their music—you also have to sell them on your chops as an engineer. Nearly as important is getting potential customers to feel comfortable with you. Even casual rapport provides a powerful inducement for musicians to bring their work to you rather than to a complete stranger.

Musicians are always trying to meet people they can work with and learn from about the recording process and the newest equipment. The perfect way to meet your clients' goals: Host a free clinic. Spotlight your strengths: drum miking, MIDI sequencing, or getting the ultimate guitar crunch. Introduce and promote new or especially high-tech gear—or perhaps you have a special technique with older equipment that can make for an exciting clinic. Hook up with a local music store to cosponsor the clinic. That way, you can target clientele and the store can do some advertising. A free clinic can be promoted at no cost, especially in local alternative and free publications, and perhaps even in a public service announcement on a local radio station.

Make the Clinic Worthwhile

Successful clinics usually run about 60 to 90 minutes, which includes time for questions and discussion. Rehearse your presentation so you can run through it without a hitch. Keep the tone as informal and personable as possible. Include hands-on demonstrations and playbacks in your studio and control room. Without the hardware, the clinic is likely to seem sketchy. Communicate your excitement about the topic, and about recording and music in general. Enthusiasm for your work will breed enthusiasm to work with you. A significant side benefit of the clinics is that they are a very cost-effective way to gain insight into the changing needs and concerns of your customers.

Remember that to draw attendees to your clinic, the topic must interest your prospective clients. If, for example, drum miking is your forté, present it with a snappy title that would interest bands, such as "Studio Drum Miking Techniques That Work." Don't forget to think target market for your clinics. If there are a lot of metal bands in your area, try a clinic on shred guitar sounds in the studio or something else that will attract your target customers.

At the conclusion of the presentation, bring out some refreshments to encourage people to mingle and talk. Be sure everybody has signed a guest list, which includes a column for their e-mail addresses and snail mail. Everyone should leave with a studio brochure and/or your business card. You might also want to offer a clinic special offer, say, "buy three hours, get one free," or some other deal.

Remember: people are much more likely to call back the person they've already met. After the success of your first studio clinic, pick another topic of interest

Studio Clinic Organizing Tips

- For maximum attendance, schedule it for a weekday evening or weekend day.

- Design an eye-catching, clearly written flier and post it everywhere musicians will see it.

- If attendance space is limited, be sure to say so on the flier, but always take the names and addresses of others interested for future clinics and promotions.

- If a local music store is cosponsoring your clinic, include the music store's name and logo on the flier, and keep their counter stacked with fliers. Also, offer to cover the cost of mailing the flier to the store's house list as well as your own.

- Enlist a few helpers to hand out cards and fliers on the day of the clinic, make sure guests have signed in, and assist with seating and refreshments.

and begin planning your next one! (That is, after you've added all your new prospects to your house list.)

For the cost of a few phone calls, fliers, a mailing, and a bit of time and effort on your part, you can expand your pool of likely clients—and establish a growing reputation as a resource where musicians find a knowledgeable, helpful professional.

Niche Marketing: What Is It and Why Does It Work?

Before developing a viable marketing plan for your studio, you must precisely define the scope of the product or service you offer and identify the market you wish to serve. Although this may sound like an elementary task, the constant changes in the studio business make it an ongoing necessity.

One agent of change is growth. As your business grows, new services are added, so new markets need to be served. You may have started alone with a mixer, ADAT, and garage, and developed over time into a full-service recording studio. At this point, distinguishing your studio from all the others in your region is critical for your continued success.

On a regular basis reexamine exactly what your business does best and who it can do it for. In other words, get a handle on niche marketing. Only by identifying your niche—the services and markets your studio can best serve—can you focus your marketing strategy.

> On a regular basis reexamine exactly what your business does best and who it can do it for.

Answer these six questions to see how you can shape your business into a successful niche player:

- What are you best known for?

- What are your greatest strengths?

- Have you done a good job getting the word out to bands about those strengths?

- Is there something unique that you can offer or add that your competitors lack?

- Do you offer a new or cutting-edge service?

- Better yet, is there something special that bands have called you for that you don't already offer?

Once you have answered these questions, you should be ready to form an action plan to position yourself as the leading provider of a particular service in your region.

Let's say your studio is better at building MIDI tracks than your competition. Or, local bands have an interest in the sound that only vintage tube guitar amps produce, and you have a nice collection of Marshalls, Vibrolux Reverbs, and Ampegs. Or, perhaps you happen to own a few classic Ludwig or Gretsch wood drum sets that would be perfect for hip-hop artists looking to get away from canned drum samples.

These situations are good examples of niche marketing opportunities. Use the tactics previously presented (fliers, clinics, promotions, mailing list management) to play up your best assets.

Conversely, if ten studios in town specialize in automated mixdown, that's probably not the area likely to become your niche. Be sure you've done your homework and that someone else isn't already filling the market need for a particular recording service.

However, if you already face tough competition, find a way to corner the market. Find out what unique or specialized services your target market is looking for (try sending a survey to your mailing list), or offer affordable package deals. At all times, stay one step ahead of the competition by catering to your market.

Niche marketing is one of the best ways to maintain your edge as technology becomes increasingly affordable and accessible. In the studio business, niche markets are often short-lived and change quickly as a result of shifts in technology, fashion, and taste. Nimble niche marketers can get in on the front edge of a new studio technology and milk it for added profits, while the non-niche competition is stuck selling yesterday's services.

As a musician, engineer, or studio owner, you must constantly monitor your marketplace, looking for niches to fill. Talk often with musicians to learn their recording wants and needs. They may not know exactly how to verbalize it (that's where your expertise comes in), but chances are they know exactly the sound they're looking for.

If you regularly reassess your assets, taking stock of your talents, unique abilities, unusual instruments or equipment, ideal location, and so on, and if you continually study your market for new needs, missing elements, and changes in fashion, style, and trend, you will find one or more niches that you can and should address. Niche markets require well-planned but swift action. If you don't fill a particular niche, someone else will. And if a fashion-driven niche isn't filled quickly, the potential for profit will be lost just as quickly as fashion changes. To succeed as a niche marketer, follow these tips:

- Keep an ear to the street to stay abreast of niche opportunities.

- Talk to musicians to verify interest.

- Assess the cost of adding more gear and determine how to price services accordingly. Do the math to see what the likelihood is that your investment will make a profit.

- Then and only then, if the dollars and cents make sense, don't delay. Get plugged in and get the word out about your new service.

By following these tips and using effective marketing strategies, you can carve out your niche and stay current—two of the most important elements of viability and success.

Chapter 10
New Horizons

What Is Podcasting?

Podcasting, according to the online encyclopedia *Wikipedia*, is a way of publishing sound files to the Internet, allowing users to subscribe to a feed and receive new audio files automatically. Although the term podcasting derives from Apple's iPod digital music player, any digital audio player, mobile phone, PDA, or computer using appropriate software can download and play podcasts.

Podcasting works like any computer desktop aggregator. You subscribe to a set of feeds, which you view on your desktop as text, graphics, animation, and so on. If you subscribe to AOL or Yahoo, they choose the information and feeds you see on their home screen when you log on to their service. Podcasting lets you hear the feeds rather than view them. You can program your computer to automatically check for and download your favorite podcasts (think TIVO for audio) or you can surf the archives of thousands of hours of podcasts looking for what interests you. Either way, it's free and about as far from commercial radio as one can get.

A quick check of www.podcast.net, one directory to programming, shows an amazing array of audio programs in dozens of languages. Under music, there are currently 12 categories ranging from rap to opera. Shift over to www.ipodder.org, hosted by former MTV-VJ Adam Curry (who some call the "podfather"), and again, the first thing that strikes you is the incredible range of programming that people are creating! Curry's site ranges from podcasts that discuss tattoos/body piercing to drama to trucking, along with 14 categories of music.

Listening to a podcast simply requires a quick download of podcast playback software. To create your own podcast, download free software such as iPodder, Doppler (Windows), or iPodderX (Mac) and begin to create your own programming. Podcasts function using RSS (Really Simple Syndication) files, which are delivered as an XML file to your podcast software and your MP3 player.

I spent a little time checking out a few examples of podcasts and, as one might expect, anything goes. Here's a few that I found interesting that you might want to explore.

Indie label Razor and Tie Records has a section on their site with podcasts that include songs by artists including Sam Champion, the Chemistry, Danko Jones, and the Giraffes, as well as a quirky Danko Jones tour diary (http://www.razorandtie.com/label/podcasting/).

To download the podcasts, once you've gotten some free podcasting software, simply select and copy the link for a particular band's podcast and paste it into your "Add a Feed" window in your podcasting software and then hit "Check All" under the Tools menu. These instructions are for iPodder other podcasting applications work in similar fashion.

Jumping across the ocean, a new voice in podcasting based in Birmingham, England, is Phil Coyne, whose weekly show, "Bitjobs for the Masses," features new and unsigned music, primarily from the UK, but also includes requests from fans around the world (http://www.bitjobs.net/). Phil mixes engaging commentary with some interesting tracks and a bit of evangelizing for the podcasting phenomenon. He's also an advocate for the voluntary shareware program, Podshare, that's being touted as helping to support the fledgling business of podcasting.

There is a freshness and vibrancy to podcasting that is infectious. In the wake of the downloading debate, record companies suing consumers, consolidation of the record and radio industry, it's high time that musicians and music lovers have a new platform to discover and share new music. Welcome to the future—welcome to podcasting!

More Podcasting Links

www.podcast.net

www.ipodder.org

www.podcastingnews.com

http://podcrawl.typepad.com

www.podcastalley.com

Toward a Higher Resolution Future

D VD-Audio and Super Audio CD (SACD) have been touted as the next wave of music delivery technology that consumer electronics manufacturers and record companies are betting on. In Part 1 of this story, we take a look at each format. Part 2 will explain what recording musicians and studios need to begin doing to accommodate the new formats in their everyday work, and Part 3 will introduce you to some of the favorite DVD-A and SACD releases as picked by audio pros familiar with the new formats.

Part 1: New Formats to Succeed the Venerable Compact Disc

Time waits for no one and no technology. The relatively young compact disc, launched in the early 1980s, is facing competition from two newer consumer music delivery formats, the DVD-Audio (DVD-A) disc and the Super Audio CD (SACD). If these new formats are successful, will they render every piece of studio gear you currently use to the junk pile? Hardly, but the changes heralded by these two new formats are important enough that every engineer and studio owner needs to begin assessing how the rapidly evolving music delivery world affects what they do.

A bit of skepticism with respect to new consumer music delivery formats (does anyone remember Digital Compact Cassette and MiniDisc?) may be in order. And don't count out the new contenders to dethrone the mighty CD completely as players for both new formats offer backward compatibility for CD.

What's in a Name? DVD-Audio

DVD-Audio is one of three related formats all based on the Digital Versatile Disc. DVD-Video has been the fastest growing new technology in history. According to the DVD Entertainment Group (DEG), Consumer Electronics Association (CEA) 2004 data shows that more than 70 million US households had a DVD player. Since DVDs were first introduced in 1997, more than 127 million DVD players have been sold. In 2004, Americans spent more than $21.2 billion on DVD purchases and rentals, with purchases accounting for nearly three-quarters of that, at $15.5 billion—including a significant amount of music video purchases. Consumers have grown accustomed to the excellent picture quality, 5.1 channel sound, plus all the bonus materials and hidden content (known as "Easter eggs") that can be unlocked by finding hidden buttons within a DVD's menu structure. DVD-ROM, the second of the sister formats, has become the de facto standard drive in most desktop and notebook computers. The primary backers of the third of the sister formats, DVD-Audio, include Toshiba, Matsushita, JVC, Mitsubishi, Hitachi, and Warner Music Group and its affiliates.

A single-sided, single layer DVD-Audio disc presents the recording artist, producer, engineer, and record label with a whopping 4.7GB of space—roughly eight times the space available on a CD. The format's architects, Working Group 4 (WG-4) of the DVD Forum, envisioned the format as the next step in the evolution of high-quality audio. Where the CD offers consumers 16-bit, 44.1k digital audio, DVD-A creators can choose any sampling rate and bit resolution up to 192k and 24-bit.

DVD-Audio also brings the same multichannel listening experience popularized first by Laser Disc, then by DVD-Video. For the first time, the "you are there" level of quality and clarity of sound reproduction once only available in the studio can now be delivered to consumers.

However, this same "master quality" caused an 18-month delay in the launch of DVD-Audio. Why? Because of the major labels' fear of piracy. DVD uses a Content Scrambling System (CSS) algorithm to scramble the data found on any DVD to prevent illegal copying. However, in 2001, a young computer whiz in Scandinavia used open-source Linux to write de-CSS software, and then posted it on the Web, allowing any DVD owner to burn a copy of their DVDs as easily as one can burn a copy of a CD. In response, the DVD Forum decided that a more robust encryption scheme was needed and spent the next year and a half coming up with one.

Chicken or Egg?

Are consumers ready to rush out and replace their CD players with a new DVD-Audio player? (How many CDs do you own?) Will there be enough software that takes advantage of the new medium to excite consumers? So far, the main interest in DVD-A and SACD formats has come from the audiophile market, but with the price of DVD-A compatible players dropping to the sub-$100 range, many consumers will end up purchasing a DVD player capable of playing both audio and video discs. Further, to ensure compatibility with the millions of players (video and ROM) already sold, most DVD-Audio producers are including a Dolby Digital version of their multichannel mix on each DVD-Audio disc. That way, a consumer who has yet to invest in a DVD-Audio compatible player can enjoy the music now, and when they decide to upgrade or add a second unit that is DVD-A capable, the disc can be played back on the DVD-A player, unlocking the high-resolution content.

DVD-Audio discs have been coming out at a slow but steady pace, most notably from the 5.1 Entertainment Group and Warner Music and its affiliates. The rate of releases has been steadily increasing as the mastering tools have become more available and the process of making a DVD-Audio disc including the mastering, menu construction, and overall authoring process (called *muxing*) become more standardized. At press time there were close to 5,000 DVD-V music video titles and almost 1,000 DVD-Audio titles on the market.

Whither SACD?

Sony developed Super Audio CD in cooperation with Philips, who brought you the CD. It's no coincidence, then, that the new format is viewed as an extension of the CD format. Originally designed as a high-resolution, 2-channel music delivery system, the technology is based on Sony's highly regarded 1-bit Direct Stream Digital (DSD) system, which uses a sampling rate of 2.8224MHz to achieve a frequency response of 100kHz and a dynamic range of more than 120dB. To clarify, SACD is a release format like CD, LP, or cassette, and DSD is a recording technology like PCM or analog.

SACD has been available on the market in Japan for a number of years and has been well received by the country's audiophile market. Producers and engineers listening to recordings made using Sony's proprietary DSD system remark on the openness, clarity, and realism. Many also comment that DSD/SACD has an "almost analog" warmth that is missing from most 16-bit PCM digital recordings. One key difference between the two formats is that SACD is a "pure music" delivery format, while DVD-A, true to its "versatile" namesake, offers producers a much broader multimedia palette.

Sony and its affiliates have by far led the way with a good number of SACD releases. The entire Rolling Stones catalog, much of Bob Dylan's catalog on Columbia, and Pink Floyd's classic *Dark Side of the Moon* have been reissued on hybrid SACD. One layer is a traditional Red Book 44.1k, 16-bit CD program and the second layer holds the high-resolution SACD version. With more than 3,500 SACD titles available in mid-2005, the format has been embraced not only by Sony and its affiliates, but by a wide range of indie labels, some of which have a long history of trailblazing high-resolution recording.

At its inception, SACD's lack of multichannel capabilities was viewed as a potential liability, and a format war developed between DVD-A and SACD proponents. However, in fall 2000, Sony and Philips announced that multichannel SACD was not only possible, but that a player would be shipping in 2001 to accommodate multichannel SACD. This first player, the Philips SACD 1000 multichannel SACD and DVD-Video player, debuted at a price of $1,999.

The rush toward true convergence took on a new look in 2003 when a host of consumer electronics manufacturers debuted true universal players capable of playing stereo and multichannel SACD, DVD-Video, and Audio, as well as MP3, WMA, and Video CD. Prices quickly came down for such universal players, and at the time of this writing, you can purchase a Pioneer DV-578A-S universal player for a street price of about $100. It plays a vast array of digital media including all the new high-resolution formats and offers 24-bit, 192k D/A converters. In just six short years, truly affordable high-resolution, multiformat music delivery is a reality.

Part 2: New Music Delivery Formats Mean Changes for Studios

Repeat after Me: "Format Wars Never Favor Record Labels"

You thought the only audio delivery format war going on today was between Apple's wildly successful iTunes and the rest of the downloading community? Wrong! History is littered with format wars when it comes to consumer delivery media. (Remember 33 vs. 45 RPM, or Betamax vs. VHS?) History proves that consumers always have the final say in format wars, because they vote with their ATM card, not any predetermined, business-driven criteria.

With the replacement market for CD players estimated at $25 billion by the Consumer Electronics Association, don't expect either side of the DVD vs. SACD format struggle to just walk away from the table. Sony's move into the content business (remember its acquisition of CBS Records and Columbia Pictures in the early 1990s?) is paying dividends, as Sony-affiliated labels such as Telarc, DMP, Delos, and Virgin all committed to help Sony build the catalog of titles for the SACD format as quickly as possible during the early years of the 21st century.

Meanwhile, Warner Music Group, including Warner Brothers, Rhino, Atlantic, Elektra, Nonesuch, Teldec, and others, was not to be outdone; they created DVD-Audio titles at an ever-increasing pace during the same time frame. Los Angeles–based indie label 5.1 Entertainment Group also became a strong player in the multichannel record business, reissuing titles by many US and UK superstars, as well.

Enter DualDisc

In late 2004, due to less than stellar sales of the DVD-Audio albums, Warner executives took a page out of the Sony playbook and introduced the DualDisc. DualDisc is similar to the hybrid SACD in that each record provides playback on either a current CD player or a high-resolution DVD-Audio player. One side of the DualDisc offers the full-length 16-bit/44.1k CD, and the other side offers a smorgasbord of DVD options (remember that "versatile" is in DVD's name). As an example, the March 2005 release by Jennifer Lopez, *Rebirth*, sold more than 600,000 units, one third of which were DualDisc copies, during its first week of release. Many fans were excited and willing to pay to get the DualDisc version, since it offered unique features such as an exclusive behind-the-scenes documentary of the making of *Rebirth* and the video "Hold You Down" with Fat Joe. The DualDisc is also the only place fans can get the special remix of "Get Right," featuring rapper Fabulous. A current list of DualDisc releases can be found at www.dualdisc.com. So it appears now the DVD-Audio-only format may likely be another relic of the past, joining DCC and MD as "pretenders" to the fixed-media delivery throne.

One interesting footnote to the format debate is that in mid-2005, the major labels—Warner, Sony/BMG, Universal, and EMI/Capitol—are all planning to release product in the DualDisc format. That is a promising sign for music consumers who don't give a hoot about format wars when it comes to getting their favorite artist's latest release.

It's going to be interesting keeping tabs on the evolution of whatever format does replace the CD. For the latest information on the battle, follow the mags that cover the audiophile market such as *Sound & Vision* (www.soundandvisionmag.com) and *Stereophile* (www.stereophile.com). A more independent viewpoint that praises SACD as a music-only format and challenges the wisdom of the DualDisc may be found at Audiophile Audition (http://www.audaud.com/article.php?ArticleID=162).

Don't worry that the CD is going away tomorrow. Remember when the demise of the trusty audio cassette was predicted as CDs roared into prominence in the mid-1980s? Cassette players are still popular and selling in cars, boom boxes, and walk-along units. In fact, outside of the most highly industrialized nations, cassettes still account for a steady and significant portion of prerecorded music sales.

CDs will not be passé tomorrow. Compact disc is today's fixed media king, racking up more than 90 percent of all prerecorded units shipped in 2004, according to the RIAA year-end stats. It will remain king for the near future. The majority of the world is still 2-channel when it comes to music, but the changes being brought about by the high-resolution and multichannel formats discussed herein can't be ignored. The key point is that the world's largest and most influential music and electronics companies are committed to establishing a viable, high-resolution fixed media alternative to the CD and the ubiquitous downloadable music track.

Musicians and studios, take note and plan for your future success in the new higher resolution, multichannel future. The amazing success of the DVD-Video may be the point of entry for the music industry. With so much of the US market already enjoying DVD-Video daily, perhaps the DualDisc, which is 100 percent DVD-V player friendly while maintaining backward compatibility with the massive installed base of CD players, will be the beginning of the end for the venerable CD.

> The key point is that the world's largest and most influential music and electronics companies are committed to establishing a viable, high-resolution fixed media alternative to the CD and the ubiquitous downloadable music track.

What Does This Evolution Mean to You?

Whether you are working in a modest home studio with a Mackie and an ADAT or you have a million-dollar studio at your disposal, there are three main things to consider in your everyday session flow.

1. Digital Audio Resolution

Take a few hours to map out your signal flow from microphone to cable to console to recorder to processors, back to console, and out to mixdown formats. Look carefully at each step in the chain and consider what you can do to improve the quality. If you've been recording at 16-bit, start thinking about upgrading to 24-bit. Look at your various D/A and A/D converters and consider upgrading them. (Be sure to review Richard Elen's excellent article "Why Use External Digital Converters?" and the interview with Mogami cable guru Phil Tennison, "How to Get the Most Out of Your Studio Cabling.") Consider your mixdown format. If you've been using 16-bit DAT or CD-R, one of the best upgrades would be to consider a higher resolution mixdown system such as the TASCAM DV-RA 1000 master recorder. Utilizing DVD+RW media, it allows recording at up to 192k/24-bit so you can take advantage of the high-resolution capabilities of DualDisc and also allows you to mix down to DSD file format to make the most of SACD. Another choice is the Alesis Masterlink, which allows recording of up to 24-bit/96k audio as AIFF files using CD-R media.

If you are running a high-resolution DAW, you can also mixdown within your system, saving your mix as a high-resolution file. If you want to mix in high resolution, multi-channel, then consider checking out the highly rated and easy to use discWelder family of products from Minnetonka Audio Software. The latest version, discWelder Bronze, is available for Mac and PC and is very affordable, retailing at this writing for $99.

More importantly, encourage your studio clients to go beyond 16-bit. Share this article with them. Invest in a higher resolution mixdown system, such as those referenced above. Then, play your clients a demo in your studio, showing how good a well-made high-resolution recording can sound. It won't happen overnight, but you'll be pleasantly surprised that most artists will warm to the idea of providing a final product to their fans that is much closer to the original recording than was previously available on a 16-bit, 44.1k CD.

2. Surround Sound

Go outside today and close your eyes. With your ears now acting as your primary input device, you'll be amazed at what a 360-degree experience our ears provide. Since the advent of stereo in the 1960s, recording engineers and artists have been working to create the perception of spatial depth from two point source speakers—and what a job they've done! Listening to my own favorite CDs by Steely Dan, Pink Floyd, or Prince, I'm amazed at the depth and subtlety that comes back from two channels.

But it is time to start thinking about recording and mixing for more than two channels. It may not be right for every project, but there will be music that you work on that will benefit. A few years back, I was fortunate to hear a multichannel demo of a recording done by Herbie Hancock called *Dis Is Da Drum*, which was released in stereo in 1993. Herbie said that the original music he conceived was so dense that it couldn't be reproduced by two channels. In the surround sound version, each instrument stands out clearly, yet intermingles with the others, bringing Hancock's musical vision to life. And with five speakers rather than two, your clients will be pleasantly surprised by the creative possibilities offered by a center channel and two surround channels.

Find an audiophile retail store in your area and ask for a demo of multichannel, high-resolution audio to get some ideas on how other mixers, artists, and producers are using the higher resolution and extra channels creatively. Take those ideas and bring them back to your studio. It's like having a wider canvas and more colors with which to sonically paint. Set up a low-priced DVD surround system in your studio's lounge to show off surround even if you're not quite ready to invest in the extra speakers for your mix room. (Complete home-theater-in-a-box systems are available for $250–$400.)

3. Think Archive

Many music albums end up recorded on a hard disc, mixed to CD-R, DVD+RW, or AIFF file, mastered, and pressed to CD. Unfortunately, as new formats come out, artists often want to reissue older material and are unable to locate or, worse yet, play back earlier recordings. Start now to investigate what systems you can put in place to create survivable backups of your clients' recordings for this purpose. This will create an additional revenue source for your studio, and more importantly, will bring peace of mind to both the artist and the record label. At this writing, it appears that analog tape (remember that?) is finding new popularity as an archiving format, since its format compatibility and tape longevity, when properly stored, are well known to the music industry.

Part 3: DVD-Audio and SACD Top Album Picks

Now that we've surveyed the two rivals to replace the compact disc as the next generation of optical media—Super Audio CD and DVD-Audio—we've asked two music industry veterans, Brent Butterworth and David Glasser, to share their picks for noteworthy releases in each format. So get out your credit card and pick up a copy of these ten albums to find out for yourself whether or not these new high-resolution, multichannel formats are worthy of the hype, or are more likely to end up as another "also ran" in the history of audio format evolution.

Brent Butterworth, editor of *Home Entertainment* magazine.

Brent Butterworth: DVD-Audio Gems

When it comes to surround sound, the name Dolby is synonymous with quality. Brent Butterworth, who is now editor of *Home Entertainment* magazine, was Dolby's Director of Consumer Technology Marketing. In that capacity, he was responsible for informing and educating manufacturers, consumers, dealers, and press about Dolby technologies—especially those relating to surround. Pre-Dolby, he served as editor-in-chief of etown.com and editorial director of *Home Theater* magazine. He is an avid audiophile and musician who has been seen tracking to a set of ADATs at his home studio on more than one occasion.

The Corrs, *In Blue* (Atlantic DVD.A 83352-9)

The Celtic-influenced, folky tunes that dominate this release sound nice in 5.1, but what captivated me is the 5.1 mix on the pop hit "Breathless." It combines in-your-face, multichannel swirling effects in the intro with a huge, enveloping, yet natural band sound on the verse and chorus. Even if you've heard this song a thousand times before in stereo (and you probably have), those background vocals at the end of the verses going "doot, doot" from the surround speakers are a guaranteed goose bump generator.

Deep Purple, *Machine Head* (Rhino R9 76664)

This 5.1 remix of one of rock's most influential albums teaches you more about the band than you could learn from reading a hundred interviews. With Ritchie Blackmore's guitar isolated in the left front and Jon Lord's organ moved over to the right side, you can—for the first time—hear how the tunes were structured and exactly who is playing what. The entire disc sounds even more kick-ass than it did on my car 8-track deck 25 years ago. You can't resist turning this one up. The interactive extras include excellent concert footage, lengthy and fascinating essays on the band and the making of *Machine Head*, and even the looseleaf sheet on which Roger Glover scrawled the lyrics to "Smoke on the Water."

Aaron Neville, *Devotion* (Silverline 80128-9)

Most engineers stick with a single mixing concept for a DVD-Audio disc—i.e., band in front with ambience in rear, listener in the middle of the band, etc. *Devotion* is one of the few that changes the 5.1 mixing technique from cut to cut. My favorite is "Mary Don't You Weep," on which Neville sounds out from the front, while a gospel choir backs him up in the surrounds. It's like being in a Mississippi Baptist church on Sunday morning. The other cuts also sound great, no matter whether engineer Gary Lux pans Neville's voice straight to the center or spreads it out across the front soundstage.

Bucky Pizzarelli, *Swing Live* **(Chesky CHDVD222)**

Audiophiles who insist that multichannel audio can't sound natural might stop their whining once they hear this masterful mix. *Swing Live* carries the lush ambience for which Chesky is known into full surround sound. I have never before heard a live jazz recording sound so realistic. The music was recorded with a Calrec Soundfield mic, then laid down on disc in Chesky's "2/4/6" scheme, with stereo, 4.0, and 6.0 versions all on the same disc. It defaults to the 4.0 mix, which is the one you want; the 6.0 mix sounds nice, but requires a highly unusual speaker setup, which you're probably not going to bother assembling. Bucky really cooks on this date, too.

Inside the Music—New Age **(Silverline 72434-92356-9-4)**

The category may have you holding your nose, but the sound of the 5.1 mixes on this disc will definitely perk up your ears. I have used this disc for every DVD-Audio demonstration I've ever done. Lots of great mixes here, but the standout—and maybe my all-time-favorite 5.1 music mix—is Cusco's "Montezuma," which sets a swirling pan flute to the powerful beat of drums surrounding the listener. The extended dynamic range you get with 5.1 speakers and amps versus stereo's two really pays off here. Not only could no stereo system recreate the spatial effects on this cut, but few could produce sufficient dynamics to keep those drums from distorting.

SACD's Finest Five: David Glasser

Mastering engineer David Glasser has been on the forefront of SACD and DSD technology since it was first released. He is founder and co-owner of Airshow Mastering, a mastering studio with facilities in Boulder, Colorado, and Springfield, Virginia. Glasser himself has recorded and mastered dozens of SACD projects, making him one of the most experienced in the new format. We asked him to select five of his favorite SACD releases to share with our readers. [*Note:* Glasser mastered the three titles marked with an asterisk.]

Guano Apes, *Don't Give Me Names*
(Super Sonic Records 051, Distributed by BMG)

I heard this recording at the Surround 2000 conference in Los Angeles and it blew me away. Mixed by premier rock engineer Ronald Prent and mastered by Bob Ludwig, the music literally jumps out of the speakers and envelops you. Honestly, this is the best surround mix I've heard. Anyone who says that hard-rock music can't benefit from high-res formats like SACD hasn't heard this album.

Jimmie Lee Robinson, *All My Life** (Analogue Productions Original APO 2011SA)

Chicagoan Jimmie Lee Robinson plays acoustic Delta Blues (with spurs on!). This direct-to-stereo session was recorded at Chad Kassem's Blue Heaven studio in Salina, Kansas, by Katsuhiko Naito, and it really captures the nuances of a couple musicians sitting around and playing. The material is raw blues by Willie Dixon, Howlin' Wolf, Muddy Waters, and Jimmie Lee, and the emotion really shines through.

David Johansen & The Harry Smiths, *David Johansen & The Harry Smiths* (Chesky Records SACD225)

Chesky Records is known for its purist approach to recording, and David Johansen is known for his over-the-top, chameleonlike musical incarnations. The combination works perfectly, with Johansen mining the vaults of country blues and other roots music. I was skeptical at first, having worked on the reissue of the legendary *Harry Smith Anthology*, from which the band takes its name, but Johansen nails it, with respect, intensity, and humor. This is a great 3D recording.

Jim Ferguson, *Deep Summer Music** (Challenge Records SA AL 75060)

Jim Ferguson is an acoustic bass player and singer of standards in the cabaret tradition. This record always gives me goose bumps—the bass is so real and detailed, and the performances of songs by Sammy Kahn, Henry Mancini, Loonis McGlohan, Yip Harburg, Ferguson, and others is first rate, especially the closer "In the Wee Small Hours of the Morning," produced by Jim Ferguson, recorded to 24-track analog, and mixed to DSD by Brendan Harkin.

Mike Oldfield, *Tubular Bells** (Virgin SACDV2001)

I remember the original release of this groundbreaking recording in 1973. The layering of instruments, and sound for sound's sake, really laid the groundwork for both the new age and psychedelia that followed. For Virgin Records' first multichannel SACD release, engineer Simon Heyworth traveled from London to Airshow Mastering with the original ½-inch quad masters mixed in 1973. Oldfield's 4.0 channel mixes were compelling and suited the music perfectly.

Mixing Classic Albums in Surround,
Chicago II and *V* Go Multichannel

Interest in mining record label vaults for classic recordings that merit reissue in a new high-resolution format such as DVD-Audio or SACD continues to grow rapidly. Two such albums are *Chicago II*, the 1970 follow-up album to the band's seminal debut, 1969's eponymous *Chicago Transit Authority,* and 1972's *Chicago V*. The seven-piece band Chicago embarked on a whole new approach to music that combined rock, blues, jazz, avant-garde, and classical influences into something entirely new and exciting. Quite simply, on their first five records, they made rock music that no other band had attempted.

Paul Klingberg at work in Red Note Studio control room.

Veteran engineer Paul Klingberg was asked to first remix *Chicago II* in advanced resolution, 5.1-channel DVD-A by Rhino Entertainment. The 2003 reissue is available as Rhino catalog #73841. He teamed with his longtime friend, reissue producer John Kellogg on both the *Chicago II* and *Chicago V* (catalog # 73842, mixed a few months after *Chicago II*) surround-sound reissue projects. Together, they've collaborated on a variety of classic rock surround music reissues, including Deep Purple's *Machine Head*, *Foreigner* and *Foreigner 4*, ELP's *Brain Salad Surgery*, and a remix of *Chicago X*.

The first concern with any reissue project is the condition of the original master tapes. In this case, *Chicago II* was mostly recorded to 2-inch, 16-track analog on 3M stock. The date of the recordings confirmed for Paul that the tapes should be in playable shape, as it predated the tape formulation change in the early 1970s that has resulted in sticky-shed syndrome for many masters from that era. *Chicago II* played perfectly as it was transferred into Pro Tools, Klingberg's digital workstation of choice. He used the Apogee A/D 8000 converters because to his ears, "there's nothing else that compares to their quality." The files were recorded at 24-bit resolution, 48k sampling in his Mac G4 computer running Pro Tools HD3 at Red Note Studio, Paul's private, custom surround-sound mixing suite in Santa Monica, California.

Next, Klingberg takes care of basic housekeeping, including naming tracks, songs, confirming run times, and listening to individual tracks and performances. In many cases, original take sheets stored with the masters reveal secrets such as unused solos, alternate endings, and the like. "At this stage, it's very helpful to be in communication with a member of the band and/or the original producer, to ensure that the path the remixer takes is one that is true to the original artistic intent," states Klingberg. For both Chicago projects, he communicated regularly with founding member, trumpeter, and vocalist Lee Loughnane, who also approved the surround remixes prior to their release.

Although Klingberg came of age as an "analog guy," he now appreciates having the tracks in front of him displayed in the Pro Tools GUI. "Having a visual, seeing exactly where all the parts line up, gives you another form of help in understanding the overall structure of the music." It was particularly helpful in working with *Chicago II*'s magnum opus, "Ballet for a Girl in Buchannon," the ambitious 30-minute centerpiece of the original four-LP set. Interestingly, that entire piece exists on a 1-inch, 8-channel multitrack master, so he decided to split it out onto 24 "virtual tracks" using Pro Tools to isolate various parts, thereby giving him much greater control and flexibility in assigning sounds throughout the 5.1 channel sound field. Klingberg also striped the final stereo mix that was issued as a reference for instrument balances and overall sound into Pro Tools, in rough sync with the multitrack files. "This allows real-time switching between the 5.1 mix I'm building and the original stereo master. It also allows me to see a number of things quickly. First, if any edits were made on the multitrack or 2-track master, and second, it keeps me on task with what I see as job No. 1 for any reissue mixer, that is to maintain the feel and the emotion of the original, while hopefully enhancing that feel with the tools that DVD-Audio brings to the table—namely advanced 24-bit resolution and the 5.1-channel sound field," according to Klingberg.

Klingberg's biggest challenge in bringing these two Chicago albums to the new DVD-Audio format was "the lack of space around the original instruments. The tracks were cut very dry, as was the norm at that time, so that the impression to the listener is that the band is playing together in a fairly dead-sounding studio." To put the performance into the 5.1 sound field, "requires attention to detail and subtleties that provide the listener with aural cues that they are hearing the music in a three-dimensional space, but don't compromise the direct, punchy impact of the original recordings."

Klingberg utilizes the center channel to place whatever the original mixer had in the "phantom" center, the image created by bussing a track equally to left and right speakers in a stereo mix. For the Chicago reissues, Klingberg placed bass and vocals in the center, as well as in the L-R channels. "Nothing is ever placed exclusively in the center channel, instead a track like bass or lead vocal can be mixed to the L-C-R and really anchor the mix with a strong frontal perspective," Klingberg states. "Using the center channel gives a big boost in imaging accuracy. I also use very little effects on any track that is added to the center channel, as it tends to blur that instrument's sound."

To widen the listener's perspective, Klingberg takes a track mixed to the right channel, for instance, a keyboard part, and moves it further right by adding some of that track to the right surround (RS) channel. "I try to create an ambience, a fullness for that instrument that lets the listener know the source is coming from a bit further to the right than any stereo mix can provide. I also like to use subtle, short delays on particular parts and return those delays to both the L-R front channels as well as the surround channels. It's important that you do this tastefully, as too much can quickly distract the listener and sound gimmicky. Done properly, within a few seconds, listeners know that they are hearing a mix that is somehow bigger sounding, but very true to the original."

With regard to the subwoofer or "boom" channel (the "dot-1" in 5.1), Klingberg again proves the adage that a little bit can go a long way. "Ninety-nine percent of what I feed to the boom channel is bass guitar. And I process it via a relic of the disco era, a dbx 120A subharmonic synthesizer. It's a unit that produces a subharmonic in the 30–40Hz range, which again, creates this sense of added depth to the original bass track. I band-filter the unit's output so that no information above 60Hz goes to the sub channel. I test it in the mix by taking the sub in and out. Again, when it's on, you should get a subtle enhancement to the overall low end of the song, not a thunderous effect. No part of the bass content of the mix is dependent on the LFE channel since some listeners may not have a subwoofer. Instead, it's simply another enhancement.

"Likewise, I never put any drums in the sub for the same reason." What about a song where there is no bass guitar? "On the final track on *Chicago V*, 'Alma Mater,' there's no bass guitar, so I put a shade of the piano into the dbx 120 to give the tune a little more depth," he states. He also eschews bass management schemes while mixing. According to Klingberg, "For mixing pop music, I find full-range speakers are best because you get an accurate image on the low-end range, 80–120Hz, which is critical on pop records." He does, however, use a bass-managed consumer home theater reference system in the studio lounge to check reference mixes. "There is also a wonderful resource available online that offers a solid nuts-and-bolts explanation of multichannel music production. It's a white paper on the Dolby Labs Web site that details everything from recommended speaker placement to what level to use for your reference tones for your multichannel master." [*Note:* Check out http://www.dolby.com/assets/pdf/tech_library/4_Multichannel_Music_Mixing.pdf to access the paper.]

For his monitors, Klingberg favors PMC AML-1s. He says, "I use a number of systems, but my current setup includes five full-range PMC AML-1s. They sound great here in my control room and translate well to many other systems." The UK-made two-way PMCs are biamped and boast a usable frequency range of 35Hz–25kHz, more than covering that 80–120Hz range mentioned earlier (www.pmcloudspeaker.com). For his subwoofer, he relies on an M&K 5000-series powered unit (www.mkprofessional.com).

Speaking of mastering, Klingberg believes it's crucial to develop a relationship with a knowledgeable mastering engineer, especially when mixing for 5.1-channel release. "With the range of digital processing and plug-ins, it's easy to think, 'Why not master my own project?'…but I think you are missing the point of what a good mastering engineer brings to the project. It's so much more than the equipment. It's their ears and years of experience, too. A good mastering house is evaluating mixes by dozens of top engineers each week, and their input as far as how your album stacks up is vital to producing a mix that will be competitive in the marketplace."

Klingberg will sometimes send a "work in progress" check-disc over to Future Disc's Steve Hall as he's mixing an album. That way, he can get feedback as to how the 5.1 mixes are translating and incorporate any suggestions that the mastering engineer may offer. He uses Minnetonka's convenient discWelder software to rip reference DVD-A discs as he progresses.

For *Chicago II*, Klingberg transferred the original multitracks into Pro Tools but mixed through an analog desk, a Euphonix 2000. By the time he was called on for the 5.1 reissue of *Chicago V*, he recalls, "Pro Tools had jumped a level in speed, power, and flexibility, and I decided to do the whole project, including 5.1 mixing, using Pro Tools HD3. Before I upgraded to the HD3 system, there simply wasn't enough horsepower to do everything required to do a competitive 5.1 mix inside the computer. Now, with dramatically more processing power available, 5.1 dynamics and EQ work very nicely. I can work for a few hours on one tune, switch tunes for a while, and get right back to where I was at on the earlier tune, without having to reset the console or specific outboard gear. The sonic quality is there and now also the speed."

After the mixes were completed, it was time for the entire team to rendezvous at the mastering studio. "Chicago's Lee Loughnane and Jeff Magid, the band's technical liaison for the reissues, arrived at Future Disc and previewed the mixes," according to Klingberg. "When an artist hears their music in surround sound and compares it to the stereo master, if you've done your job right, they don't want to hear the stereo again." The end-result of the team's work is two new advanced-resolution, surround-sound reissues that showcase one of rock's truly innovative bands at the peak of its creative prowess.

For more information on Paul Klingberg and a complete discography, visit www. paulklingberg.com.

All about Recordable CD

By Paul Elliott, Discmakers Mastering Engineer

When CD-R was introduced in 1988, engineers welcomed the new format as a great studio tool. Unfortunately, only a few studios were able initially to use the format, because the first CD audio recorder from Yamaha carried a $35,000 price tag and blank discs cost $100 each! Discs were recorded in real-time and were often hit-or-miss propositions. Since that time, recordable CD technology has developed at warp speed and now offers studios a wide assortment of better, cheaper, and faster options with regard to the various types of recorders and blank discs. Let's take a look at the choices.

CD-R Media

A manufactured CD gets pressed from a mold and stores its data by using "pits" and "lands" pressed in its plastic layer, which is then coated with a thin layer of aluminum. When being optically read, those pits and lands reflect the laser's light back in various ways. These various reflections are then converted to the series of 1's and 0's corresponding to the digital audio bit stream encoded on the disc.

CD-Rs have a thin layer of dye that is slightly altered by the recorder's laser to change its reflectivity. This allows data to be stored on the CD-R disc. These marks or bubbles in the disc's dye layer have relatively the same reflective properties of a pressed disc, so that CD-Rs are compatible with almost every CD player. The storage capacity for both the pressed and recordable discs is identical. For most discs, about 74 minutes of audio or 650MB of data is the maximum. It is possible to go over 74 minutes or 650MB of data, but it's not necessarily recommended, and different, more expensive, media needs to be used.

There are many brands of blank CD-R media on the market. How are we to know which ones to choose? After all, after spending a lot of time and money on recording and mixing, the last thing an engineer wants is to worry about the reliability of the media. Even though there are many brands to choose from, basically there are only a few different formulations of CD-R media.

You've probably noticed that CD-Rs have different coloring from brand to brand. Some are silver on the top with green or blue on the bottom. Others are gold and green, and so forth. That's because there are a small number dye combinations and reflective layers that are used to make virtually every CD-R. All reflective layers are either gold or silver. The dye materials come in five different flavors: Cyanine, Phthalocyanine, Metallized Azo, Advanced Phthalocyanine, and Formazan. Since a small group of companies holds the patents on the different combinations of dye and reflective layers, each brand licenses one of the various combinations, or buys the discs from a large supplier and patent holder such as Taiyo Yuden.

For a comprehensive look into the different formulations, how the different brands performed when tested, and just about anything else you could possibly want to know on the CD-R technology, check out some of the excellent CD-R FAQ sites on the Web. The best place to find out which is the best CD-R to use in your recorder is to ask the manufacturer. Find out which discs were used to test your model and which speed performed the best if your unit is a multispeed recorder.

> One thing to keep in mind is that a CD-R is more delicate than a commercially pressed CD. It's very easy to damage a CD-R by scratching the surface.

Since CD-Rs are made differently than pressed CDs, problems can occur. One thing to keep in mind is that a CD-R is more delicate than a commercially pressed CD. It's very easy to damage a CD-R by scratching the surface. Here are a few tips on how to avoid damaging your CD-R.

- Do not write on the top of the disc with a ballpoint pen. If you want to write on the disc, use a felt-tipped pen. The top layer of the disc is very easy to scratch and you may even scratch off the reflective part of the disc.

- Be careful when applying a label to your CD-R. Don't leave any bubbles and make sure that the label is centered. Either of these problems can cause read errors. If the label is off-center, it may cause the disc to wobble when played. Do not attempt to remove a label after it has been applied to a disc as the adhesive may rip off the reflective layer.

Another thing to keep in mind is that, although the media and recorders are designed to work reliably in a variety of situations, problems sometimes occur. For instance, occasionally a CD-R may not play back on all CD players. This happens most often when you're dealing with older players or recorders. It doesn't mean you did something wrong; it's just that in the world of CD-R, nothing is 100 percent foolproof.

CD-RW Media

The differences between CD-RW and CD-R are slight. CD-RW (Re-Write) means that you can erase and rewrite data on the same disc, which can be extremely useful. First, CD-RW uses a mixed metal alloy instead of a dye layer, as does CD-R. Second, CD-RW employs phase-change technology to record your data, altering the reflectivity of the dye layer by changing the phase of the alloy, rather than creating a mark or a bubble, as regular CD-R systems do.

CD-RW discs cannot be recorded in a regular CD-R drive. However, a CD-R blank will work fine in your CD-RW drive. Other than these differences, they are basically the same as a CD-R with respect to handling and use.

Let's delve into the hardware that makes easy-to-use CD duplication practical for any studio today.

CD Burners

At the bottom of the food chain are CD burners, the small units that fit into a drive bay of your PC or Mac. They are well suited for small runs of a few discs at a time. One drawback is that they tie up your PC while you are making copies.

CD burners take image, data, audio, or video files from a computer or external hard disk and burn the image onto a blank CD-R. They come in two classes: CD-R (Recordable) and CD-RW (Re-Writable). CD-R is a write-once format and CD-RW allows you to make multiple passes on the same disc. Deciding your needs and your system requirements will go a long way in determining which burners you choose and which software you use to burn. Do your homework by figuring out what speeds you need, whether you want CD-RW or not, what formats you want to record (ROM, CD-Plus, MP3, Red Book, and so on), which burners are compatible with your system software, and whether you have a SCSI or USB port.

After you answer those questions, you'll have a better handle on what unit will best meet your needs. The recording speed of the burners ranges from single speed (1x) to 12x or higher. Many of the most popular burners come bundled with a software package that will help you burn your discs. For example, Plextor and Yamaha burners bundle in Adaptec Easy CD Creator, which is a good, general-purpose software program that is easy to get up and running.

CD Replicators

If you have clients who need more than one or two discs at a time, then a CD copier, tower, or autoloader may be better suited to your needs. As CD-R has become more popular, many different brands of CD replicators have come on the market. Once again, start by making a list of what kind of speed, quantity, and printing will work best for you and your clients. If you want to make many copies, then you may be looking for a CD autoloader that can automate hundreds of discs at speeds as high as 16x. Or you just may want to make up one copy of your music to send to radio stations or A&R guys. In that case, a single disc copier will work just fine. There are three classes of CD-R replicator on the market.

Copiers are the cheapest and simplest replicators to use. These were the first type of CD replicator developed and usually consist of a reader and a recorder. Most incorporate a hard disk to store the master or source disc's data so you don't have to upload the master every time you want to record another copy. Front panel controls are typically very easy to navigate. Most record one disc at a time, so to make multiple copies, blank media needs to be manually reloaded each time a burn is finished.

An entry-level, stand-alone CD copier.

A stand-alone CD tower.

Towers are similar to copiers, except that they have multiple slave devices vertically mounted in one enclosure. Blank discs are hand-loaded but you can make multiple copies at the same time. Some tower units require a host PC and others are stand-alone devices. They produce as many copies per run as the number of slave bays the unit employs, so a four-bay model makes four CD copies each pass.

Autoloaders are the most diverse group of CD replicators. The largest of the three types, they incorporate robotics in order to load and unload the media into the recorders. Some are as simple as a single-disc duplicator and others are very complex, including such features on-board disc printing and diagnostics. Autoloaders are often used by larger studios and even CD manufacturers for short CD orders that are too small in quantity to duplicate profitably on their high-volume LBRs (Laser Beam Recorders). Most autoloaders have an integrated printer built in or provide a way to incorporate a printer on the back end of the system. The cost of such units is considerably greater than copiers or towers due to the higher volume of discs that they can turn out.

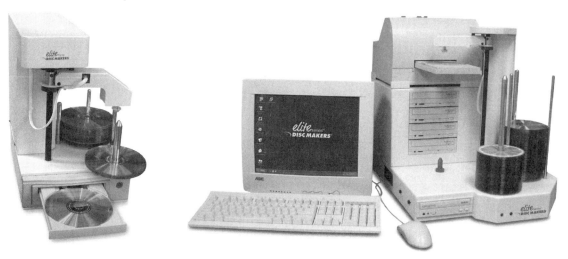

An entry-level, single-disc replicator with autoloader.

A multidisc unit with autoloader and integrated printer.

Printers

Once you begin providing your customers with CD-Rs, they'll soon be asking you to print information on the disc itself. There are three types of on-disc printing available for use with these systems. They include thermal inkjet, thermal wax transfer, and photo-quality inkjet. Some of the processes are monochrome (one color) and others offer very realistic full-color. Automation is an option. Print quality ranges anywhere from 300dpi to 1440dpi. Most printers require use of a computer to lay out and host the file that will be printed on each disc. Most companies making replication devices offer templates for CD artwork on their Web sites. Some units also offer silkscreen printing that gives a more professional-looking CD, but will also cost more.

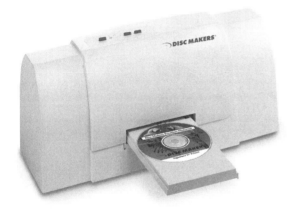

An entry-level CD printer.

A high-end thermal printer.

Now that you know more about CD-R media and recording devices, jump in and start burning your own discs at whatever level makes sense for you. It's easy, convenient, and one more service you can offer to your studio clients to keep them coming back to you again and again.

Paul Elliott has mastered more than 1,000 albums during his nine years at Disc-makers' Soundlab. He's played music his entire life and cites his father, a music teacher, with raising him on "jazz and Elvis." His latest band, 7Star, has released an independent album featuring Paul on guitar and keyboards.

An informative summary of how recordable CD technology was invented is available online at http://www.roxio.com/en/support/cdr/historycdr.html.

Surround Sound in the Music Studio

Producer/Engineer Paul Klingberg Talks about Speaker Placement for 5.1 Surround Monitoring

Surround-sound mixing and monitoring is old news in the film business—at least if you're counting in "tech years," which go by a lot faster than calendar years. Multichannel surround sound for theaters has been around since the late 1980s, and for DVD-Video since the mid-1990s. Now, with new releases in DVD-Audio and mutlichannel SACD coming along at a small flood—mostly remixed classics to begin with—discrete 6-channel sound is beginning to invade the music studio in a big way.

For producers and engineers, however, creating 5.1 surround music mixes is not as simple as adopting what was learned in the film post studio. For one thing, according to producer/engineer Paul Klingberg, the distribution of sound over six channels—three front, two surrounds, and an LFE (low-frequency effects) subwoofer (the .1, or "boom" channel)—is determined in film by the visual field and the goal of placing the viewer in the middle of the action. But in music, the mix becomes a much more impressionistic endeavor. The monitoring environment also differs, says Klingberg.

As one of the music business' pioneers in 5.1 mixing, Klingberg should know. He's known for working with such musical stars as Earth, Wind & Fire, Cher, Jonathan Butler, James Ingram, Cheap Trick, El DeBarge, and Emerson, Lake & Palmer. He's also consulted with Dolby Laboratories on the development of the Dolby Digital 5.1 format, and has remixed 5.1 tracks for multichannel release for Earth, Wind & Fire, Foreigner, Deep Purple, Chicago, and Emerson, Lake & Palmer (including classic tracks, "Lucky Man" and "Brain Salad Surgery"). Plus, he's designed two studios specifically for 5.1 music mixing, including the one at Maurice White of Earth, Wind & Fire's Magnet Vision studios in Santa Monica, where he currently does much of his work.

"The book on 5.1 music mixing hasn't been completely written yet," concedes Klingberg. "People are trying to take what they know about stereo mixing and extrapolate that into this whole new dimension of sound."

Speaker placement is crucial, says Klingberg, and is first determined by the type of speakers chosen, a choice that corresponds to the differences between theatrical and near-field music monitoring. "In theatrical-style monitoring, the surround speakers are not full-range speakers and don't have a lot of directionality. They're made for bigger rooms and are placed around the room, creating more of a wash of sound than a focused sound. I prefer a focused, near-field setup, which I feel is more appropriate to music and more like the home-theater setting where the music will be heard.

"In theater-style mixing, the room is part of the mix. In near field, you're taking the room out of the mix and focusing on the sweet spot. Traditional music mixers are most comfortable with this style of (near-field) monitoring."

Klingberg next insists on five identical full-range speakers. "Use a good-sounding, full-range speaker you like," he says, "It can be any five, as long as they're identical. I put them in an exact square, left-center-right in front, and the two surrounds, left and right, in the rear. This creates a very accurate listening position."

The subwoofer can end up anywhere in the room, but at Magnet Vision studio, he has two subwoofers lined up on his square in front. "Traditionally, the subwoofer goes against a load-bearing wall," he says. "After extensive listening and measuring, we decided to put them in front, but every single room is different." Why two subwoofers? "For more head-room and a clean powerful sound down in that register, so nothing is overdriven. Not powerful as in how loud it can be, but having the ability to capture transients without distorting or clipping, which is very important."

In many ways, the subwoofer is the most mysterious part of the speaker configuration for 5.1 surround. "I certainly never used one in music mixing until I started doing multichannel mixes," notes Klingberg. "It's not as clear as it is in theatrical film mixes what you use that speaker for. It's not the bass channel, as many people think, though if you want a little more oomph and bass headroom, you can put it there."

"Most home theater playback systems will be of the THX type, which calls for a subwoofer. I feel most confident doing my 6-channel music mixing with this type of system, versus a more traditional system that would not have a subwoofer. If the consumer has the ability to produce 40 cycles in their home theater system, I need to be able to monitor that 40Hz when I'm mixing. Traditional monitoring systems don't allow this."

In many studios, the speakers are soffit-mounted into the walls, creating a large sound field in the room. Consistent with his squared-off, near-field configuration, Klingberg has his speakers standing on stands at equal ear height. "That's the way I hear it best," he says.

"Monitoring in general is much more demanding and critical in a surround environment," continues Klingberg. "If you're working in stereo, and one speaker sounds consistently louder, it's obvious. Now that we have five speakers and a subwoofer, it's much harder to judge the relative balance between them. You have to 'tune' your room by using pink noise and an SPL meter."

Despite that caution, Klingberg allows that in the end the engineer has to rely on his best tool—his ears. "The designer of the speakers came here with his computer and calibration microphone and spent six hours aligning and tweaking the speakers. He did a great job, but afterwards I found I needed to fine-tune things. One way that I verified the accuracy of my room was to listen to my mixes in other studios. Just because the computer's acoustical analysis of your room says it's absolutely perfect doesn't mean it is. At the end of the day, you have to rely on your ears."

Resources

Books

All You Need Is Ears, by Sir George Martin and Jeremy Hornsby (St. Martin's Press, 1995)

Audio Recording for Profit, by Chris Stone, edited by David Goggin (Focal Press, 2000)

Behind the Glass, by Howard Massey (Backbeat Books, 2000)

Inside the Hits, by Wayne Wadhams (Berklee Press, 2001)

Inside Tracks, by Richard Buskin (Avon Books, 1999)

Make Mine Music, by Bruce Swedien (Hal Leonard, 2003)

Modern Recording Techniques, 6th Edition, by David Miles Huber and Robert Runstein (Focal Press, 2005)

Practical Recording Techniques, 3rd Edition, by Bruce and Jenny Bartlett (Focal Press, 2002)

Pro Tools Surround Sound Mixing, by Rich Tozzoli (Backbeat Books, 2005)

Recording Guitar and Bass, by Huw Price (Backbeat Books, 2000)

The Art of Recording, by William Moylan (Focal Press, 2004)

The Microphone Book, 2nd Edition, by John Eargle (Focal Press, 2004)

Magazines

Most have online archives available.

Electronic Musician
EQ
Mix
Pro Sound News
Recording
Sound on Sound
Tape Op

Online

www.aes.org (Audio Engineering Society)

www.dolby.com/assets/pdf/tech_library/4_Multichannel_Music_Mixing.pdf
(Dolby white paper on multichannel music mixing)

www.grammy.com (The Recording Academy)

www.musicplayernetwork.com

www.prosoundweb.com

www.spars.com (Society of Professional Audio Recording Services)

About the Author

Photo by Therese Kuebel

Arriving in California as a teenager in the summer of 1965, Keith Hatschek used his birthday money to make a down payment on a red Orpheus electric guitar (with whammy bar) and 4 watt Kay amplifier. His passion for music and technology has continued unabated for more than 30 years. After 14 formative years of musical performing, recording, and songwriting, he built his own commercial recording studio, Bayshore Studios. Four years later, he joined one of the leading recording studios in the US, Music Annex, Inc.

During his 12-year stint with Music Annex, Hatschek worked as recording engineer, producer, project manager, Director of Client Services, and Vice President of Sales and Marketing. He also produced albums, soundtracks for film and television, and the soundtrack for Apple Computer's first CD-ROM. He led Music Annex's diversification efforts from traditional recording services into duplication and digital audio postproduction. During this same time, Music Annex grew from 10 to 75 employees and into multimillion dollar annual revenues.

From 1995 to 2001, he headed Keith Hatschek & Associates, a San Francisco Bay Area–based marketing and public relations firm serving the entertainment and media technology industries. Agency clientele included firms in the broadcast, postproduction, music, recording, and consumer electronics industries.

Hatschek accepted a full-time appointment in 2001 as Chairman of the Music Management program at University of the Pacific in Stockton, California. He lectures frequently around the country on music industry careers and consults with a number of music industry companies. He is the author of the book *How to Get a Job in the Music and Recording Industry,* published by Berklee Press. He also facilitates online classes at Berkleemusic.com in music industry public relations and career development, and contributes frequent essays on the music industry to various print and online publications.

Hatschek is a voting member and past chapter Vice President of the Recording Academy, an Associate Member of the Audio Engineering Society, and an NAMM-Affiliated Music Business Institution (NAMBI) and Music and Entertainment Industry Educator's Association (MEIEA) faculty advisor. Hatschek holds a Bachelor of Arts degree from the University of California, Berkeley, and a Graduate Certificate in Marketing, awarded with Distinction, from the same institution.

Acknowledgments

I t's been a labor of love to compile these interviews and articles into a book that I hope will find its way into the hands of many of the world's up-and-coming musicians, recording professionals, and studio enthusiasts.

I owe many thanks to a number of helpful and supportive individuals. To start, I want to acknowledge Morris Ballen and Tony VanVeen of Discmakers, who had the vision to create a quarterly newsletter, *Pro Studio Edition,* full of useful recording tips. They immediately saw the value of bringing knowledge directly from top engineers to a broader base of recordists. They truly understand that by providing knowledge and resources to musicians and recording studios, they are helping to foster a recording community that will continue to grow and prosper.

When I first ventured out in 1995 to gather these interviews, I wrote and edited these pieces alone, in a tiny one-room office at Second and Market Streets in San Francisco. The next six years of research, writing, and editing the columns were undertaken in association with my staff at Keith Hatschek & Associates, including my colleagues Robert Anbian, Whitney Pinion, Merrie Harper, and Bruce Merley. Our associates, Therese Kuebel, Michelle Jouan, Tina Walters, Paul Schiefen, Matt Pivetti, Pat Ahern, Kim Williams, and Natalie Stocker, ably supported us. When I joined the academic world full-time in 2002, I was back on my own again, doing these interviews with new appreciation for just how much work my staff had invested in bringing some of these stories to life. Additionally, a number of my students assisted with various research and preliminary editing tasks—especially Melanie Sanguinet and Will Crew.

For some pieces, the experts proved not only knowledgeable on their particular subject, but also ready, willing, and able to pen their own article! My heartiest thanks go out to colleagues John Eargle, Steve Davis, Richard Elen, Bob Skye, Nick Colleran, John La Grou, Paul de Benedictis, Klaus Heyne, Jimmy Robinson, David Cuetter, Paul Elliot, Dave Malekpour, Bruce Merley, Robert Stevens, and Karl Winkler.

Scott McCormick of Discmakers deserves special mention as the stalwart editor of *Pro Studio Edition.* He has been an excellent sounding board and has kept me on task with our mission of providing easy-to-understand columns for all levels of recording folk. He and his designers dug many of the photos, graphics, and text files out of their archives to ensure the completeness of this book. A high-five to each of you!

To Steve Anderson, David Chase, Carolyn Eads, Silvea Rodriguez, David Duggan, and the rest of the University of the Pacific Conservatory's faculty, students, and staff: thanks for supporting my writing, research, teaching, and passion for recording and music technology. It's an honor to be a part of such a dedicated institution.

To my wife Laura and daughters Elyse and Megan, you are a wellspring of support, enthusiasm, and love. Muchas gracias!

No one becomes a recording engineer on their own, so my appreciation must be extended to the many contributors to my career success, including (but not limited to): Carson C. Taylor, Jim Treulich, John Palladino, Leo DeGar Kulka, Roger Wiersema, Kent Bancroft, Rainer Gembalczyk, Jap Ji Singh Khalsa, Ann Fry, David Porter, Russell Bond, Tom Carr, Jim Dean, Don Harriss, Fred Catero, Tom Size, Don Puluse, Will Moylan, Shirley P. Kaye, Marc Greenberg, Paul Stubblebine, Leslie Ann Jones, John Kellogg, Jim Mack, Joe Ryan, Roy Pritts, Theresa Leonard, and the many other friends, colleagues, musicians, and engineers with whom I had the good fortune to work.

For more than 20 years, my friends at the Society of Professional Audio Recording Services (SPARS) have continually inspired me to better understand and refine the craft of recording and the business of providing audio services for profit. Additionally, the many friends and colleagues among the members and staff of the Recording Academy have also been a valued resource. For kindly agreeing to review portions of the book and offering words of support, my sincere thanks to my friends John Altmann, Jeff Greenberg, and Frank Wells. For anyone I missed, please accept my apology and thanks, as the omission is simply a matter of not enough RAM remaining in the cranial CPU!

To my friend Al Schmitt, thanks for sharing not only a number of great tips in both the foreword and your extended interview, but also with emphasizing the "intangibles" that so many young engineers and musicians don't learn. Your emphasis on punctuality, an easy-going manner, and flexibility need to be a part of every aspiring engineer's skill set. May your chip shots always land within a fader's length of the cup!

Special thanks are due to the folks at Backbeat Books, including Richard Johnston, Amy Miller, Susan Gedutis Lindsay, Kevin Becketti, Nina Lesowitz, and Steve Moore. Thanks also to the Happenstance crew, including Maureen Forys, Andrea Fox, Jack Lewis, and Laurie Stewart. I appreciate your care, thoroughness, and attention to detail, which has greatly improved the book. And finally, thank you to Clive Young for steering me in their direction.

Index